Gillian Broome was a primary teacher in London before she married Bill and moved to La Rochelle where she taught at the university. Her experiences in France have created new opportunities and interests. She now writes feature articles and is a guide to a local château. She has two children and two grandchildren in Spain.

Gillian Broome

Chasing Our Dream in La Rochelle

For Chris & Sian,

I know you love France, so I guess you'll love this account of our efforts to find the 'French' way of life.

Gillian Broome

AUSTIN MACAULEY PUBLISHERS™
LONDON • CAMBRIDGE • NEW YORK • SHARJAH

Copyright © Gillian Broome (2017)

The right of Gillian Broome to be identified as author of this work has been asserted by her in accordance with section 77 and 78 of the Copyright, Designs and Patents Act 1988.
All rights reserved. No part of this publication may be reproduced, stored in a retrieval system, or transmitted in any form or by any means, electronic, mechanical, photocopying, recording, or otherwise, without the prior permission of the publishers.

Any person who commits any unauthorized act in relation to this publication may be liable to criminal prosecution and civil claims for damages.

A CIP catalogue record for this title is available from the British Library.

ISBN 9781786930156 (Paperback)
ISBN 9781786930163 (Hardback)
ISBN 9781786930170 (E-Book)

www.austinmacauley.com

First Published (2017)
Austin Macauley Publishers Ltd.
25 Canada Square
Canary Wharf
London
E14 5LQ

To my patient husband

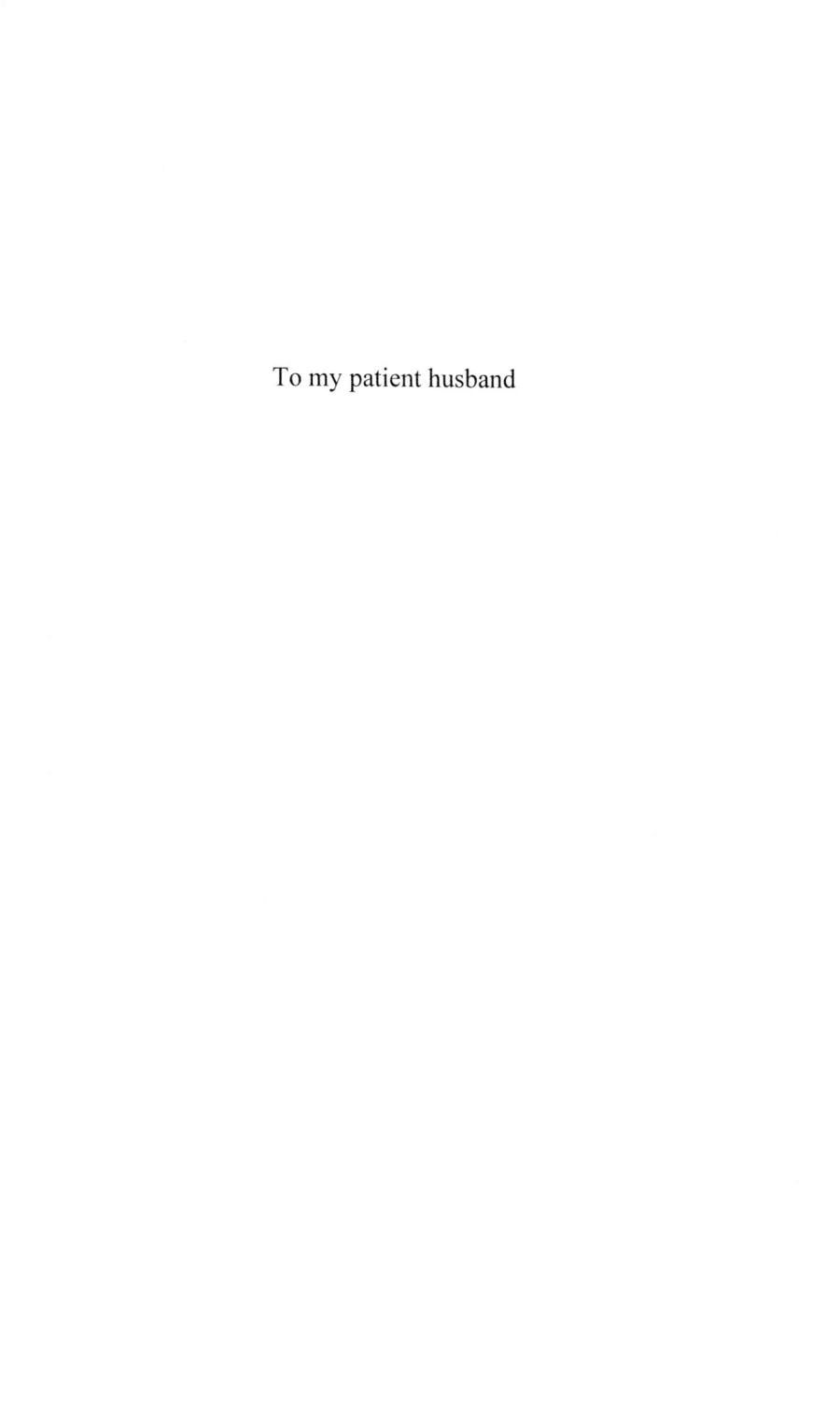

ACKNOWLEDGEMENTS

To my son for technical and literary advice. To Bernard Keller for his illustrations. To my colleagues and our neighbours without whom there would have been no book.

PREFACE

The worst part of setting out on a big adventure is saying goodbye to those you are leaving behind. In our case, our respective mothers and sons.

After that, the excitement of novelty takes over.

First Year

CHAPTER 1

Job Hunting in La Rochelle

Twin towers with flags fluttering stood proud at the entrance to the harbour at La Rochelle. A tide of tourists was wandering along looking at boats bobbing at their moorings, the stalls, or enjoying the early evening sun at one of the many cafés along the surrounding boulevard. We were tempted to join them, but shouldn't we be disciplining ourselves to job-hunt? I needed to find work. It was now the first week of June and we had till the end of the month before schools closed for the summer holidays. It was also two weeks before I had to accept or decline an offer I'd been made at a school in Normandy. 'Our security', we called it, but ideally we both wanted somewhere further south. La Rochelle was the first language school on my 'list of possibles'.

"Right," Bill said, "It's too late to go to the school now, so -"

"We can join the tourist throng!"

An evening of music and laughter. And so much to see. Fairy lights decorated the avenue of trees alongside the harbour. Restaurants, with tables spread right across the boulevard, were busy, with waiters weaving their way carrying huge dishes of *fruits de mer* crowned with an acrobatic *langoustine*, pinchers bending backwards to pierce its abdomen. A variety of buskers were performing under the trees, jugglers, a Peruvian pipe band, performing dogs jumping through hoops, dancers and artists. Crowds had collected round these: one was a straight artist, the other a cartoon artist eliciting knowing smiles and comments at the quickly sketched bulbous nose or protruding ears. We watched fascinated.

"Your wife, Monsieur ... I can see her ..." the cartoon artist waved his charcoal theatrically at Bill.

"Perhaps he wants a beautiful portrait for a beautiful lady," cut in the other.

I blushed.

"My wife needs no portrait – it's engraved here, in my heart." Bill gestured dramatically whilst hugging me to him.

We wandered from one to another, as we had plenty of time to stand and absorb what was going on. At the end of the boulevard was a convenient restaurant overlooking the harbour. We sat sipping our wine and tackling a mound of brown shrimps, apparently a local delicacy. We didn't need to talk, just the occasional 'delicious'... 'lovely'... We were assimilating our experiences, listening to the music of the nearby French conversations.

Eventually we left and wandered to the quayside, away from the noise and bustle, where we stood arms round each other. The haunting melodies of the Peruvian band we'd seen earlier in the evening floated across. Ahead of us was still water with white masts and cordage reflected in triangles. Some of the moored yachts showed signs of habitation. On one, washing hung from a line strung between masts, on another a family of cats played hide and seek on deck, and further on, a couple lounged in canvas chairs, drinks in hand. Beyond were the large luxury schooners, white and gleaming, chrome wheels catching the light of the rising moon. The plop of a fish disturbed the perfect reflections and the white lines wriggled like a child's skipping rope. A yacht with a light at the masthead glided in silently between the two towers at the entrance.

At that moment we fell in love with La Rochelle.

But would I get a job here?

The following morning, I set off for the school which overlooked an old dock pool, quiet after the animation of the harbour area. I went in to try to arrange an interview. I felt fairly confident, after all I had years of general teaching experience, although admittedly I was a novice in language teaching, but I had good marks from my course, an English as a foreign language teaching course I had taken the previous year, and I had already been offered a language school job in Normandy. This was on hold while we considered whether I should accept it. Too far north, was what we had thought. Half an hour later I emerged, feeling a little dazed.

Bill greeted me with, "So when's the interview?"

"No interview… I've been offered a job. Just like that."

He grinned. "What? Just like that? Good for you. Now let's go to one of those bars and enjoy the sun while you can fill me in with the details."

A row of pavement bars and restaurants bordered the harbour, where boats edged in through the towers bustling busily to their moorings. We chose a café and settled to watch a fascinating world go by: tourists with cameras slung over shoulders, elegant perfumed ladies in high heels, backpackers and New Age trendies. A complete mixture. We sat sipping our coffees, absorbed.

Bill, always astute where money was concerned, suddenly turned and uttered the key word, "Salary?"

"Don't know. We didn't discuss that." He made one of his funny faces that meant he'd got a dreamer for a wife. "But she said to ring her tomorrow with any questions. Anyway, there's no rush. Barbara said to take a couple of weeks to think about it."

"Barbara? Who's Barbara?"

"The boss. She's American."

"What's she like? Do you like her?"

"Yes, I do. Difficult to describe, actually. She's a bit like quicksilver, but she's got a quirky sense of humour. I think we'll get on well, and with it being such a small establishment, I hope we'll become friends."

We talked it through. The job seemed exactly what I wanted, part-time, two thirds of the week, classes at the school rather than out in companies, which was something I had disliked about the Normandy job, a freedom of teaching style, with some translating work as it arose. The school was modern, well set out with a language laboratory and a library.

"There don't seem to be any snags," I said confidently.

Bill gave me a considered look. "Sure? Sounds too perfect to me… perhaps we just haven't thought of all the right questions. But let's put it on the back burner for the moment and go and explore a bit more of the town."

Yesterday we had seen La Rochelle as tourists, today we belonged: this was going to be our town now. Our first impressions were of colonnaded streets leading to the market square. Half-timbered houses, except that when we looked more closely we realized the 'timbers' were covered with a facing of small, rectangular slates nailed into place. Glimpses of paved courtyards planted with small box hedges. A tall tower near the harbour entrance with an oriel window to the seaward side, presumably the original lighthouse. The jewel was the town hall, standing in a square like a fairytale castle, surrounded by a wall with crenellations.

Yes, it was a beautiful town, full of history I was sure. We returned to the campervan to relax and discuss our immediate plans. We had from now to the end of August to explore. We would head south.

Before I went to sleep I said to myself, 'No more governors breathing down my neck, no more interminable administration forms, no more school finances. What bliss…'

CHAPTER 2

A Whirlwind Year

I'd met Bill at a dance on a Greek island, where I was the only other Brit attempting the steps of the stately regional dances. What had started as a holiday romance fired up as we fell in love. Living on the opposite sides of England, we met at weekends and survived by phone calls.

My daughter watched as one evening I put the phone down looking puzzled. "What's up, Mum?"

"I don't know… but I think Bill's asked me to marry him."

"How d'you mean 'you don't know?' How can you not know something like that?"

"It's his Scottish accent. It's stronger on the phone."

We stared at each other. Rachel walked to the window. Then turned. "Mum, he's nice, Bill, I like him. He seems sincere, he's fun and he's obviously madly in love with you, but… Well, I'm leaving for Kenya in two weeks, for two years. Promise me one thing," she faltered. "You won't rush into things."

"Don't jump in with two big feet and regret later, you mean."

"You said it. But yes. You can be… impulsive." She came and sat by me on the sofa and gave me a hug. "I love you, Mum, and I don't want you to get hurt."

"Especially when you're not there to pick up the pieces," I laughed. "Anyway, you're going to have to put all your energies into your first teaching job and seeing what Kenya is like."

It seems she had much the same conversation with Bill. He was most amused but respected her for her care for her mum. He felt close to Rachel, he said, perhaps because having worked in Kenya for twenty-five years he had become interested in her volunteer work, or perhaps because he liked feeling useful by giving her practical advice.

When she left, I was glad Bill was there as I felt a bit bereft. Last child leaving home. My son, Gareth, had left two years earlier and was working as an editor in central London.

One evening, sometime in October, I was moaning to Bill about officialdom spoiling the aspects of my job that I loved. "The role of being a head-teacher has completely changed. A head is not a head-teacher any more, but a manager. Do you know, the Chief Education Officer actually ticked me off today for being in a classroom?"

"Chuck it. Resign."

"I've applied for an inspector's post."

"No, chuck it completely. Inspectors are still part of the teaching profession and are still subject to the officialdom you are complaining about. Try something totally different."

"Don't be daft, Bill. I'm on the promotional ladder, on the up."

He gave me a funny look and changed the subject.

Within six months, I'd resigned. I had no idea what a relief this would be. I felt instantly as though a huge load had been taken off my shoulders. I was uncertain of the future, but I felt I'd done the right thing. I wanted my new life with Bill to be without something that could drag our relationship down.

One day, after a lovely walk along the Seven Sisters cliffs, we were lounging on the grass, watching the gulls gliding on the air currents. Bill took my hand and caressed it. "You know I want to marry you…" I nodded. "But – well, first I'm Scottish, not English and second I've spent virtually all my working life abroad and don't want to spend the rest of it in England."

"No problem. We can live in France."

"France!" He sat up and stared at me. "Well, I was thinking perhaps, Spain. Why France?"

I turned to face him. My reply had been impulsive. Now I took a deep breath. "First, very practical, I speak French, I don't speak Spanish and if I'm to work – I know you're taking early retirement, but I'll still be working – I'll need to be able to speak the language."

Bill nodded, "Makes sense. And yes, I'm almost certain to get early retirement as the centre is changing from an environmental study centre to an outward bound centre unit. They won't need a manager in a collar and tie. They'll be looking for a trendy young man in a tracksuit."

We'd discussed this before and I was anxious to give my other reasons, so I squeezed his hand to gain his attention. "And second, when I was a teenager I stayed with families in Paris and loved the French way of life. I've always dreamed of living in France one day. And lastly, my grandparents were French, from Alsace. They were proud of having taken British nationality, but a lot remained French in their way of living. So from very early on, I've felt an affinity for everything French."

Bill stared at me. "After all that, what can I say? France it is, my darling."

The following weekend he arrived with details of a course for teaching English as a foreign language.

"You say you love teaching; this could be the answer."

We bought a small, left-hand drive camping car. In France campervans are called camping cars, which pleased me because 'campervan' seemed too lowly a name for the lovely vehicle we had bought. I decided to christen her Evita.

"Why Evita?"

"From *éviter*, to evade, escape responsibilities."

"Escape normal, late middle-aged routines, escape from what is expected of you. Oh, yes! I like that."

Now, a year later, here we were, chasing our dream, in La Rochelle.

Chapter 3
Surprises

We now had until September to explore our adopted country. Instinctively we headed southwards, stopping at a town called Périgeux, the second, in fact, on my list of possible language schools. As we drove through endless suburban streets of grey houses, I thought how glad I was that I would be teaching in La Rochelle. This was a BIG town.

We parked near the cathedral, also grey but with a distinctive roof shaped like a pineapple. We parked and wandered past a gateway into the narrow streets of the old town.

"I don't know about you, but I think we should look for a restaurant. It's nearly twelve and I'm hungry."

When Bill says 'look for a restaurant' I know now this means comparing menus, which could mean trailing from one to another for another half hour or so. However, on this occasion we settled unanimously on one in a small square with a fountain in the centre. It was hot and as we sat sipping our *kir,* white wine with a peach or blackcurrant spirit added, the sound of water was not just soothing, but somehow cooling.

Bill's choice of salad with *gésiers,* (gizzards) followed by cervelles à la génoise, (calf brains fried with tomatoes and cheese), didn't tempt me at all, even though he said they were absolutely delicious. I preferred goat's cheese on tiny rounds of toast amongst a variety of salad leaves followed by lamb cutlets. When my main course arrived I felt I should photograph it for its artistry: two bundles of green beans tied with a sliver of bacon so that the whole resembled a sheaf of wheat, the cutlets tastefully sprinkled with fine shreds of carrot, coriander and cherry tomatoes, a heart-shape of puréed carrot and a block of potato slices in a creamy mixture. Neither of us realised at this point how typical all this attention to presentation is to well-served French meals.

Replete, we continued wandering and found workmen placing barriers between the historic centre and the rest of the town.

"*S'il vous plait, monsieur,* is something happening here?"

"*Mais oui!*" he replied. *"La fête de la musique!"* Realising I was looking puzzled, he added, "It's the 21st of June today, music in the streets of every town in France to herald in the summer. You mustn't miss it, *madame.* Come back around five."

We duly returned just after five to find a band playing at the first barrier. Precise, regimented and in impeccable navy and white uniforms. We stood, arms round each other, listening appreciatively, for a while before moving on.

Turning a corner, we were surprised to see a boy of about eight standing playing his violin. A rather anxious-looking lady stood behind him holding a sheet of music.

"Probably his mum," I whispered to Bill.

His playing was simple. I don't imagine he had been learning long, but he played confidently, not looking at the people gathering around, concentrating on his bowing.

Round the corner was a square with a stage. 'Joshua fought the battle of Jericho, Jericho, Jericho' sang out a choir, swaying to the rhythm. We tapped our feet and enjoyed several other spirituals before moving on.

In our lunchtime square sat a chamber group in black ties peacefully playing, probably Vivaldi. It could have been incongruous, but the respectful hush was akin to being in a concert hall.

Every space, large or small, or just a shop doorway, was occupied by people making music, a seemingly never-ending round of surprises: three young girls – eleven perhaps – played recorders, young men playing blues and rag time, and an accordionist attracting a crowd. Bill swept me into a waltz, to the smile of people around, then others joined in until there were quite a few of us dancing, smiling as we passed each other.

Somewhat reluctantly we left to see what else there might be. But what was this? The unmistakeable sound of castanets. And yes, there were flamenco dancers in their long flounced dresses, arching their backs and twirling their hands way above their heads while stamping imperatively with their feet. This we had to stop to watch. Suddenly my attention was caught by a plaque on the wall announcing that here in September 1944 five Resistance members were shot by the occupying enemy. This sent a little chill down my spine. I pointed it out, quietly, to Bill who read it and shrugged, his eyes fastened on the slim body of the nearest dancer.

Around midnight we felt sated, so we wandered back to Evita. The first band was still playing, but now the beat was ragged, the uniforms no longer pristine, and the trumpeter's face purple from exertion. As we unlocked our door, I said, "And to think, *chéri*, we have this to look forward to every June for the rest of our lives!"

Two days later, it was so hot we decided to stop at a campsite where there was a swimming pool. The evening was balmy so we wandered towards the village.

"Listen," Bill said stopping. "What can you hear?"

Cicadas, thrumming busily in the dry warm air. "A marker we're in France!" We looked at each other excitedly.

A very different sound emanated from the square: the sound of revelry. There was a table laid for perhaps seventy or more people all ages sitting eating together. An amazing sight. An old lady, seeing us standing watching, beckoned us over.

"Bonjour. Anglais?"

We nodded. Yes, well, Scottish…

"Welcome." She beckoned a young man over and offered us a glass of wine. "*Santé!*

"How kind. Thank you, *madame*. But please tell me, what are you celebrating?"

"Our village. Being together."

As we left Bill said, "I wonder if one day we'll be celebrating being part of our village, wherever that may be."

"Oh, I do hope so."

CHAPTER 4

We Search for Ibex, Marmots and Egrets

We needed to be at Albi, home of Toulouse Lautrec, one week later because we had arranged for my contract to be sent there, poste restante. From there we would wind our way across to the Mediterranean, heading up into the Pyrenees.

We studied my contract carefully. In it I noticed a strange loyalty clause that stated that subsequent to the end of my contract, which was from September to the end of June, I would be unable to work within a perimeter of twenty-five kilometres of La Rochelle. Since both of us found this disturbing, we arranged to see a notaire or solicitor.

When presented with the contract, he laughed and threw it down on the table.

"You're worried about that final paragraph, yes? Well, I can assure you there's no way that would stand up in court. In fact the whole contract is laughable as a legal document. This –" he jabbed with his forefinger, "And this, for example – you cannot arrange people's lives like this."

"What about the pay? It's ridiculously low."

"That is something you'll have to negotiate with your employer, madame. What she's offering is indeed low, but not below the minimum rate. So it is not illegal."

"You're absolutely certain it's okay for me to sign it? And I won't find myself in an impossible situation? After all, we may well settle in the area if we make friends and like it, we are not just passing through."

"Certainly you can sign it. No harm in that at all. And as I've said, no court would uphold it if your employer tried to make trouble."

We left, partly reassured. But my image of my new boss as a charming, friendly person was undergoing review. She obviously had a strong business side.

I was not clear about the average rate of pay for language school teachers. I remember being warned that it was low, but the equivalent of six pounds an hour seemed pitiful. After all, although I hadn't taught English as a foreign language before, I had years of teaching experience, including running courses for adults, so I should be able to adapt easily. I decided to ring her and discuss it.

Her reply was, "Sure you've had general teaching experience. But I have to count you as a beginner. However," she conceded, "I understand your concern, so let's say, at the beginning of February, I'll review the situation. If you turn out to be successful, and I'm sure you will, I'll increase your pay."

At least that sounded better and, unable to move her further, I accepted.

Now we felt free to explore Albi. First the cathedral, which was a surprise, being a red-brick building I thought rather ugly from the outside, but richly and decoratively painted on the inside. Next the museum dedicated to Toulouse Lautrec, with his saucy, riotous drawings of Parisian life in the 1880s. But, as much as we enjoyed this, the mountains were calling us.

We stopped late one evening at Pau. Up until then, although we knew we were approaching the Pyrenees, we had, strangely, seen no evidence of them. The following morning, strolling along the promenade on the south of the town, we suddenly saw a row of peaks, just like fairy-tale mountains, some snow-capped even in the height of summer. Magical. We stopped and stared. Our only desire now was to get there, so we turned and went back to Evita.

It was strange, I'd always thought mountains started with foothills, but not the Pyrenees. One moment we were driving across a flat plain of hay fields, and the next climbing steeply. As we drove higher, the hay was no longer in the usual plastic covered bales, but piled round tall poles creating cones, presumably because tractors were impractical on the steeper slopes.. The houses, built of granite with the dark colour broken by window boxes of bright red geraniums, were built in clusters at odd angles to each other, perhaps to fit into the pockets of more level ground. The overall impression was one of green as there were many trees. We wound our way higher and higher, following the course of a wide river rushing over boulders and stones. Eventually the road simply stopped, in a car park, one moreover designated for camping cars. We were in fact on the edge of a deserted ski-station, eerie with empty flats, shops and bars and silent cable-cars. At the end of the car park were massive, dark-grey peaks looming over us. In startling contrast were gleaming white glaciers tucked into the niches of the granite.

Having always been passionate about nature, I had read up about all the mountain flowers, bearded eagles, ibex and marmots that we might see, but first glance I was disappointed. Boulders and scree dominated the landscape, no trees, or bushes, let alone mountain flowers. I couldn't imagine where the marmots could have their burrows. However the rocky terrain made seeing an ibex a more likely possibility.

We set off straightaway to explore the nearest glacier, but the air was furry in the heat and it was hard going. Suddenly Bill seized my arm and put his finger to his lips. He pointed ahead and mouthed the word 'ibex'. So I was going to be lucky! I stared ahead. Sure enough I could see a part of a black animal behind the big rock to our right up ahead. It didn't move. Very cautiously I tiptoed forward, bit by bit. It moved out of the lee of the rock – a black billy goat. I was so disappointed. I looked at Bill and saw him laughing.

"You rotter!"

"You should have seen yourself," he crowed.

I turned away from his laughter in disappointment and carried on up the mountain. As we got closer to the glacier, it disappeared from view, the moraine, stones and boulders, the debris pushed down by the glacier, obscured it. We scrambled up, then Bill stopped dead in his tracks.

A great white arch rose in front of us. What had seemed a solid mass of snow from below had, in fact, an immense cave-like opening.

We stood there, panting, hot in our T-shirts and shorts, facing snow and ice. Why didn't it melt when it was so hot? As though disbelieving that it genuinely was ice, we both leant forward to touch it. Yes, genuine snow. From below it had seemed a brilliant white, whereas it was in fact dirty, covered in mountain grit and plant debris.

Bill just had to try walking on the glacier, prodding carefully with his stick before putting down his foot.

"Give me the camera so that I can take a photo of you on it."

I'd hardly put the camera back in its case, when I was hit by a snow ball.

"So that's what you want, is it, okay, here we go. Just remember, you're in the more precarious position."

It was an odd feeling to be having a snowball fight on a hot summer's day.

From there, we continued to climb up to the pass above us, although there were times when I wondered why we were making the effort. The backs of my calves were protesting, the heat was intense and I was thirsty. The view from the top, however, was impressive. To our left, a small lake was cradled in the rocks, the water black and sinister looking, to our right, peak after peak of hard grey mountains, directly ahead, a small clump of dark fir trees.

We decided to picnic on the rocky ledge above the path, the very highest point. Our conversation was nil: we were both reacting in our different ways to the scenery. For Bill it was magnificent, but to me it was oppressive. I prefer to see more green. We ate in silence.

Suddenly, a cold sensation swooped over my shoulders, sinister. I ducked, grabbing Bill's arm, then looked upwards. So close I felt I could almost touch it, was an eagle, no doubt one of those bearded eagles I'd been reading about. I could see its feathers and the way they separated at the end of its wings. It turned and passed over us again, silently. Once more I felt the air pass: an eerie feeling.

After lunch, halfway down again, where at last there was green grass and some low scrubby bushes, Bill, leading as usual, froze and whispered, "Quick, look! Over there." I could see nothing at first, but then a flash of brown as something disappeared into a hole.

I looked at him suspiciously to see if he was having me on again. But he was obviously fascinated.

"So that's a marmot," he said.

"I didn't see it properly."

We positioned ourselves on a boulder a little way away, from where we could clearly see its burrow. We sat waiting for it to reappear, staring at this little hole for ten minutes before eventually a face appeared, outlined by the burrow's entrance, just as though it were in a doorway. It looked in all directions, fixing us with its stare, even from that distance.

We sat as still as we could, hardly daring to breathe, but it refused to emerge. Every now and again, it would advance a few inches, only to retreat again with its eye fixed on us. For another ten minutes this pantomime was repeated before it disappeared completely.

Regretfully, we got up and moved on as quietly as possible. Every now and again we would catch a glimpse of a marmot whisking into the safety of its burrow, but we couldn't see one in the open. We continued to inch forward, one foot gently and silently after the other.

All at once I saw Bill spring into the air, comically, with a surprised look on his face.

"A snake," he cried "I nearly trod on a snake!"

While he was still going on about his snake, which we later discovered was probably a grass snake and therefore harmless, I noticed a marmot nibbling on a patch of grass some way ahead. I put my hand on Bill's arm and we froze, but it was too far away to see any details. Then it disappeared.

Keeping an eye firmly on that cluster of boulders, we advanced. Here was an area of soft, green grass and under every boulder around it was a marmot hole with an entrance and clearly marked runways.

"Marmot city," I whispered.

That sound was enough to produce a response. From under a boulder, right beside our feet, a marmot shot out, thumping a warning heavily as he did so and emitting a cross between a chirp and a whistle. It was close enough to touch.

"It's enormous."

Indeed it was: it had a big bushy tail, and was a good fifty centimetres in length. We were amazed. Until then we had imagined they were a lot smaller.

As we wandered back to the car park, Bill joked, "One down, two to go. We may not have been lucky with the ibex, but −"

"We have seen a marmot!"

For five days we explored and enjoyed these fabulous mountains. We walked past lakes hidden in bowls on plateaux, along rushing torrents crashing over boulders, past silent pine forests, and jumped over small streams tinkling down grassy ledges, but we did not see an ibex. We got used to the mellow sound of cow bells, clanging as the animal moved, the tinnier sound of the rarer sheep bells, to the sight of eagles soaring above and of coming across small mountain refuges in the middle of nowhere, a haven for the long distance hiker or one caught in bad weather. Above all we enjoyed the magnificent vistas that rewarded us for our arduous climbs. I had got to the point of deciding we would not see any ibex, and then on the sixth day, we were lucky.

We had walked up to a mini-plateau totally encircled by grassy mountain ridges. On our map a path was clearly marked going north. Nothing was as clear on the terrain. We did find a narrow path zigzagging upwards in approximately the right direction, but without a footpath sign. I was certain it was not our path, it was too narrow, but since we didn't see any other, we started off. Almost as soon as we left the plateau, the weather changed. We could see right in front of us, but the rest was shrouded in an eerie damp, mist. We were struggling on, slowly, when we heard a cough. My stomach lurched. Who was there? We hadn't seen anyone. It sounded like an old man.

We stood still, straining our eyes to see through the mist. Another cough. This time right beside Bill. We stared at each other. The mist lifted fractionally and we found ourselves face to face with a sturdy black animal with large curving horns and a beard. I'm not sure who was the more surprised. It coughed, then turned and leapt off up a virtually vertical mountainside, dissolving into the mist. We stood staring at where it had disappeared, before looking at each other.

"Two down, one to go," I crowed

Common sense made us turn back, even though I wanted to continue in the hopes of seeing another ibex, but the mist was too thick. In fact it was now so dense that we had to pick our way down extremely carefully. Having reached the comparative safety of the plateau, we realised we had probably been walking on an ibex or goat path, rather than a human one.

We had heard egrets could be seen in the shallows of the *étang*, a lake just inland from the coast, a few kilometres north of Perpignan. Along this area of the Mediterranean coast there are several inshore lakes or *étangs*, a bird-watcher's paradise. We chose to camp close to the shore of the largest, having bumped down a rough cart-track to the water's edge. Here was an obvious place to see these milk-white, wading birds, like herons, but smaller and more delicate that were intriguing me.

In the evening we cycled along the track hopefully, but it was an exercise in the skill of keeping our bicycles upright, to the extent that it was impossible to birdwatch. The wind was so strong that we actually had to lean our bikes diagonally into it, at about 45° to the ground, to avoid being blown across the road. As I pushed my legs down onto the pedals as hard as I could, I was startled to be overtaken by a jogger. Once we were in the lee of the hills, the sun shone warmly and the ride was idyllic.

At one point the lane led right across the *étang*, with water on both sides of us. Excitedly I pointed, "Look. Flamingos."

A flock, perhaps a hundred or more, was wading at the far side of the water. Occasionally one would take off and we could see the pink and black tints under its wings. We stood entranced for a few moments, but then continued, still searching for those elusive egrets. After all, I'd seen plenty of flamingos when Bill had taken me to Kenya.

On our return, the flock had moved closer to the lane, heads dipped, busy sifting the water, they were all wading in one direction. How, if the bill is under water, can they make so much noise? It sounded as though they were all chatting incessantly and yet their heads were, definitely in the water.

That evening I said regretfully, "No egrets...Never mind, we'll wake with the dawn and then..." I left the phrase unfinished as my imagination raced ahead with a vision of the scores of egrets I would see in the first flush of dawn. The more practical Bill is always saying I'm an incurable romantic.

Our camping place couldn't have been better, a rocky outcrop sheltered Evita from the force of the wind. Fifty metres in front of our windows was the lake. As we were facing east we would also see the full glory of the dawn. So we went to sleep with the windows open and binoculars ready.

We were woken in the night by the van rocking in the wind, which had frivolously decided to change direction. The camping car was solid, but it was as though we were a boat on water.

"Quick. Shut the windows."

This eased things, but did not eliminate the movement. Somehow, we managed to sleep, fitfully, and dreaming of sailing on choppy water.

"Dawn, *chérie*, wake up, you said you wanted to see it."

"Not any more, go away," I groaned.

"Come on. Wake up."

"Okay, so I've seen it. Now let me go back to sleep." Moments later, remembering our plans, I surfaced and stared out of the window.

The apricot sky and pink tinted baroque clouds were worth waking for. But still no egrets. No birds at all in fact.

"Too early," I grumbled.

"Too much wind," Bill contradicted.

After the usual early morning cup of tea, I noticed a small flock of flamingos paddling close by, and coming our way. I nudged Bill and grabbed the binoculars. I could see them dibbling backwards with their beaks curved back and upwards. Then first one, then another raised their heads and within minutes the flock was in the air. Their triangular wings beat regularly, their necks sticking forwards and their legs backwards – a strange but magnificent sight. Why couldn't it have been flamingos we were interested in? We would have to wait for our egrets.

CHAPTER 5

Work or Play?

A sense of excitement and new adventure filled me as I walked towards the language school, not far from the harbour at La Rochelle, on my first day at work. The site was an attractive one, with an ex-dock pool on one side and a courtyard filled with flower beds on the other. There were three classrooms, a language laboratory and a library, as well as Barbara's study and a staff-room.

To my surprise I found I was to be neither teaching nor preparing classes, but translating at an international boat show and later a marathon. At my interview my boss had mentioned translating, but I had imagined this would be paperwork, but what she was proposing was jumping in at the deep end! Her words filled me with both excitement and apprehension.

"*Le Grand Pavois* at La Rochelle is the largest boat show on the Atlantic coast, so there will be lots of big companies, many of which will need a translator."

Could be exciting, but would I be up to it?

"Meet me at the entrance tomorrow at nine thirty, and I'll introduce you to the organisers. Right now, we'll go through your teaching programme."

Fortunately, I'd spent a lot of time messing around in boats, so I didn't think the boating terms would cause a problem, just to be sure I checked out one or two, then crossed my fingers. What I didn't like the sound of was 'big international companies'. I reassured myself: I was not translating a contract, merely explaining, and for that my French was perfectly adequate. Obviously the job I thought would be teaching was going to be more exciting and varied than I had thought. When I told Bill his eyes widened, but, fortunately for my confidence, he didn't question my ability. Instead he said smiling, "I'll have to come and ask some awkward questions, won't I?"

"Bill, I'm not there to answer questions, only to translate."

"Oh well, I'll still come, could be interesting. And I'd like to see you being 'professional'. A different you!"

The show was centred around the marina, in that part of La Rochelle which, I had seen from old photos, had originally been sheep fields and marshland opposite the town itself. Now it was 'the wooden village', because all the original houses were built of wood, with the aquarium, geology museum and the new and growing university colleges. However, all this was obscured by the traffic crawling slowly towards the area while police were directing them towards the car parks (thank goodness I had a member's ticket) and already, half an hour before opening time, cheerful queues were forming in the sunshine outside the gates. This was certainly a big event.

"Okay, so this is the *Grand Pavois* of La Rochelle, the biggest international boat show on the Atlantic coast," Barbara, explained again in her American drawl, "and you are here to translate for any company that is concluding an international transaction, which will, of course, be in English."

Barbara introduced me to the organisers, presented me with my identity badge then suggested we had a coffee before she returned to the language school.

"So what brought you to France?" My boss fired question after question. Despite being at the administrators' table at the entrance to a boat show, we chatted as if at a pavement café. Barbara was easy to talk to and the more we talked the more I liked her. I told her briefly we were only just married and the reasons why we were in France. It wasn't until much later that I realised she had not told me much about herself, nor why she had established her school in La Rochelle, particularly as she said she found the people cold.

Just before the show opened she left me saying, "Remember, if nobody comes to you, you go to them. Walk around, introduce yourself and let them know you're here. I'll be back later to see how things are going."

Nervous at first - who wouldn't be? - I nonetheless enjoyed looking around and introducing myself. I found it was indeed an enormous show, part on land, part in the marina, where line after line of white boats were moored, flying gaily coloured bunting and flags with the companies' logo. The white against the blue of the water was stunning and the brightly coloured flags created a festival atmosphere. First there were rows of enormous gin-palace yachts, then specialised yachts for passionate sailing enthusiasts lined three other pontoons with large banners proclaiming their boat-builder. However, the area that intrigued me most was the section where enthusiastic artisans explained the art of wooden boat-building. It is hard to resist touching, caressing, the smooth lines of these boats and I was not the only one doing so.

Inside the two huge marquees were the essential accessories for boaters, ranging from compasses to clothing, insurance to inflatable dinghies. Here the atmosphere was infinitely more business-like.

Introducing myself produced polite responses, but there seemed no great interest in my services, so, having completed my tour, I returned to the organisers' tent. By the end of the morning I had dealt with such serious matters as directions to toilets and helping a man who had lost his poodle.

It was a surprisingly long day, waiting for someone to require my services. Then Barbara was back.

"Well, how have you done? Any translations?"

"I've just translated a fax that came through, reminding them of our service," I said tentatively.

"Oh well, early days yet. Let's get back; we'll take the bus."

To my surprise we turned to the marina quay. The 'bus' was a boat bus which took us from the marina into La Rochelle harbour, a pleasant half hour ride down the entrance channel towards the old harbour, with its towers and a glimpse of the town beyond. I sat back in the sun and relaxed. It had been an interesting day.

It was the harbour with the towers guarding the entrance, a boulevard of trees and the mass of pavement café's sprawling the length of the water, that had made me fall in love with La Rochelle - and here I was right in the middle of it. I'd been told they used to close off the entrance in case of attack, but right now I was not interested in the history, merely enjoying the picturesque scene.

Having passed between the massive towers, the boat turned abruptly towards the pier by the boulevard of trees and there, at the end of the gangplank, stood Bill, a bunch of flowers in his hand – the romantic lover.

Barbara insisted we went up to her flat, only one minute away, for a celebratory drink. The apartment was three floors up, with a spacious main room, and functional kitchen. It was sparsely furnished because she had only just moved in. Instinctively we moved to stand on her narrow balcony, leaning on the graceful wrought iron railings to look down on the boulevard and harbour. Through the leafy branches we could see the heads of people strolling below and beyond that, the water of the harbour and the boats. Gulls wheeled and mewed overhead. I breathed a sigh of contentment.

We moved indoors for the celebratory drink. I sank on the sofa and watched Bill chatting with her. He seemed to like her too. However, we didn't stay long because I found I was surprisingly tired.

"Well?" I said as we left.

"She's lively," he said, simply. "How do you find her now you've seen a bit more of her? You said you liked her."

"Yes, I do."

On the second day at the boat show the atmosphere at the show was totally different. The wind was strong, the clouds menacing and it had turned cold, despite being mid-September. I did my tour of the stands to remind people of our service but found no-one was interested. The festive air of yesterday was a thing of the past. Visitors were moving briskly, clutching their raincoats to their chests and stallholders talked with one eye on the sky. I returned to my position to find the organisers looking worried. At mid-morning the committee called a conference. Around the table, the organisers were talking quietly, shaking their heads and glancing at the way the marquee was flapping wildly as though it might take off any minute. I heard phrases like '*ce n'est pas normal*,' as I sat, shifting my feet to try to avoid the draughts coming through the entrance, and listening to the howl of the wind.

The committee returned looking even more worried and put out a call for all organisers. "We're going to have to shut down because of the gale force winds."

People exclaimed all around. "Close the show!"

"It's a difficult decision. Two more days… losing time and custom… but we cannot guarantee these marquees in what is virtually a hurricane."

Stupefaction and concern. Then the need to organise took over and practicality ruled. Safety was paramount.

A loudspeaker announcement followed.

'Would everyone take notice, participants and the general public: for safety's sake this show is regretfully having to close due to freak weather conditions and gale force winds. Would everyone kindly make their way to the exit. The area must be clear by 12.30.'

It was now 11.50. I expected a rush towards the exits, but no, people continued as before and the stallholders simply increased the speed with which they talked but with a wary eye on the straining and flapping sides of the marquees and the wildly bobbing boats.

Somehow the site was evacuated and it was at this point that frenzied activity took place, with stallholders securing what was immovable and packing away what they could. Since there was nothing for me to do, I left this chaotic scene and took an exceedingly choppy ride back into the harbour to Bill.

He was looking out to sea anxiously, but his face lit up when he saw me disembark. He tucked my arm into his, and heads down against the wind, we set off clutching each other and bent at an angle of forty-five degrees, towards Evita, our camping car.

"Gale force winds, you say? That's strong."

"Strong enough to close the show."

I was thinking of the camping car, our home for the moment. "Where should we put the camping car that would be safe? In the lea of a building?"

"Yes, but if tiles blow off the roof, they could land on us."

"And if we're on open ground, we could be blown away," I said casually, little realising this could be a reality.

We were passing the harbour where boats were tugging at their mooring ropes, when we saw a row of cars standing 30cm deep in water. The cobbled quay-side was a designated parking area but was now flooded.

A distraught looking young lady splashed her way out to her car. We watched fascinated. The water was lapping just below the sill of her door, fortunately not yet reaching the exhaust pipe. She stood there, water way above her high heels, her keys in her hands, panic-stricken. Was it her shapely legs or chivalry that caused five men to wade out towards her?

"Don't start the engine, *Mademoiselle*. We'll push her out."

She handed over her keys then hid her face in her hands. The men called for aid and others rushed to help. Slowly, bit by bit, they pushed the car back and nosed her round into safety.

"Shall I try her?" the leader of the group asked, a big man with a flowing moustache.

"Oh, please do, *monsieur*."

By now a crowd had gathered and we all watched breathlessly. The car sputtered and coughed, then faltered. Repeat. Eventually, with much coaxing, Monsieur Moustache got her started. Shaking, with tears in her eyes, the girl kissed him on both cheeks and thanked him profusely. Then she climbed in, visibly pulled herself together and cautiously drove off.

The others clapped the hero on his back and the crowd applauded. As the men turned to go for a welcome drink, Monsieur Moustache turned and pointed to a Volkswagen with water halfway up its exhaust.

"There's no way *he'll* get out."

Thoughtfully, still fighting our way against the wind, we continued, but were drawn by excited voices to a wildly gesticulating crowd that had gathered on the wall of the second harbour, where the large pleasure boats are moored. As we arrived on the scene a diver emerged from the water clutching a teddy bear, then another, clutching a lady's high heeled shoe.

Aghast, I turned to my neighbour. "What's happened?"

"A car was blown in. A blue Peugeot. It was parked here, but suddenly took off, right over the side."

"Anyone in it?"

"I don't imagine so. But perhaps that's why they have called in divers."

At that moment a crane drew up and now we realised the purpose of the divers: their job was to attach the hooks and chains for a salvage operation.

We watched fascinated. The water heaved and swirled for several minutes before the car suddenly emerged, empty, and was swung clear into the air, water streaming from it in all directions.

"Someone will have a nasty surprise when they return," Bill remarked glumly. "I think we'd better go back and secure Evita."

Bill decided we should stay where we were, in the lea of a very solid looking building. He placed bricks on both sides of the wheels and pulled the handbrake up so hard I thought he'd pulled it off, but his efforts kept us safe, despite violent rocking from the wind which kept waking us in the night. In the end, I was so tired that I slept soundly. Not so Bill, who lay awake worrying.

The gale lasted three days, continuous buffets of wind and frequent lashings of rain. What had happened to that lovely summer weather? It returned but too late for the *Pavois.*

We had a week of preparation with a few individual classes, a week of calm. This gave me time to get to know my new colleagues, all of whom I liked. There was Anne, chatty, lively and very friendly. She was French but had spent a year at Cardiff University and would be my partner in English teaching. Then there was Elske, the German teacher. She was small elegant with longish curly brown hair and eyes that sparkled. She spoke English well but with an inflection that made everything sound either mysterious or ironic. Carmen, the Spanish teacher, seemed friendly but was rarely in the school. The Russian teacher, who only came in occasionally and was not communicative, floated around in black and red, with high boots and a wide brimmed hat. Maybe she wanted to dress the part.

We were sitting discussing our classes one afternoon when I heard a commotion outside the window. Shouts, the sound of – could it be? – a tractor and altercations. Being closest to the window, I peered down.

"Just look at this! There's a tractor with a trailer full of fish and the man's throwing the fish all over the road and pavement." The others crowded round the window. Someone came out of a door and started haranguing the fish thrower. Others gathered by, laughing tolerantly. Whatever was going on?

"Ah," said Barbara, "the fishermen demonstrating again."

"But why?" I said naively.

She shrugged. "The usual. Not enough pay. Too many restrictions. It happens every now and again."

"But what a waste of fish."

"Those fish aren't fresh. They stink. You'd better close the window."

They certainly did. Well, I suppose a fisherman is not going to waste fish he could sell.

We settled back to work, wrinkling our noses and grinning like naughty children from time to time. But within half an hour we heard a new sound. This time it was the municipal cleaners removing the fish and washing the streets.

"That's quick," I said.

"Well, I guess they're used to it," said Anne. "You say you want to know everything about the French, well, you'll discover, Gillian, they have a passion for demonstrating."

Classes started and I began to really enjoy myself. The key pleasure was that every student, whether they were retired people, youngsters of business people, were there because, for whatever reason, they <u>wanted</u> to learn English. Gone were discipline problems typical of school teaching, you could almost say gone was the necessity to motivate the students, since they were self-motivated. Somehow this made me want to do my best for them. So one evening I decided to take one of the textbooks home with me to get better acquainted with the way it worked.

"What are you putting that book in your bag for?' Barbara said sharply. I explained.

"Well, I provide a certain amount of preparation time here, and no book, ever, goes home. Is that clear, Gillian?"

Fine by me. There's more to life that working. I didn't want to get caught up with work being the be all and end all of my life. And Bill certainly wouldn't want that.

CHAPTER 6

A Search for a House

We had presumed, erroneously, that we would be able to stay on camp-sites until the end of October or so, when it would start getting chillier. However, in much of France, certainly around La Rochelle, the camping season finishes with the start of the Autumn school term, so, the sites close in mid-September. I felt I needed a daily shower if I was going to work, so we needed to find a house to rent, which was not difficult as there was plenty of choice. For some reason, I can't think why, we thought it more logical to live out of La Rochelle itself and so chose a cosy house near the beach at Chatelaillon Plage with three bedrooms, suitable for the family at Christmas. I would be able to take a bus to work as we were only ten minutes from La Rochelle. Chatelaillon itself was not a picturesque seaside town, but it was a delight to cycle to the market on a Friday morning alongside the beach. I would pause to look at the sea, a grey, slick sea, rarely with any waves, protected as we were by three islands. When the tide was out, it retreated almost to the horizon, leaving, beyond the stretch of golden sand, a brown sludge that glinted in the sun. To one side boulders edged the beach, rubbed smooth by the movements of the sea, and above, lone gulls wheeled and turned. Out at sea the white-sailed yachts from La Rochelle tucked and wove their way across the bay.

Much as we loved the situation of our house, we had to find somewhere to buy for Bill to renovate as he needed something to do. He was finding being a tourist on his own boring.

We had drawn up a list of what we would like before we left Britain and number one on the list was 'on a hill with views'. Impossible around La Rochelle. A flatter area I have yet to find, unless it's Holland. Number two was a garden big enough to grow our own produce. Number three was to be accessible to theatres, cinemas and concerts. Armed with our list, we went to an estate agent.

He considered it. "A hill and views, not possible. A garden for vegetables, quite possible, but in the country. Cinemas etc., perfectly possible, but within La Rochelle. So, which is the most important?"

"Something to renovate with a garden," we both said unhesitatingly.

"Aha, now we have it." He pushed aside the list. "Renovation starts here." He drew a ring round La Rochelle. "And here," he drew another ring even further out. "Renovation is cheap. The further from the coast, the cheaper it becomes. But if Madame works in La Rochelle…" he left the sentence unfinished and looked at us enquiringly.

"Up to half an hour away," Bill temporised.

"So… and how much do you want to renovate?"

"Something habitable, that has been started and needs finishing. Nothing too drastic, but nothing that can't be changed."

Our guide, *Living in France*, failed us in the first essential endeavour of finding a house to buy. It did not tell us that, here anyway, the estate agent does not give you details on a sheet of paper, but drives you to the house or houses he thinks will interest you and shows you round. Time and again we asked if we could read the details, but no, we were always assured, this would be house we would really like.

We learnt the art of being patient and saying polite things to owners whose house we had no intention of even considering. In one at least we could genuinely admire the new, spotless, 'American' fitted kitchen.

The old lady swelled with pride. "My son installed it. Isn't it beautiful?" She then showed us into what looked like an adjoining garage. "And this is the kitchen where I cook."

Here was an old free-standing gas cooker, a table and an old china sink. So much for the 'American kitchen'.

We began to enjoy our house hunting as an outing, although we were beginning to wonder if we would ever find one we wanted. Then one day we saw a photo of a drab, shuttered farm-house with land, at a truly ridiculously low price, only 10,000 francs. Whatever could one buy for so little? Intrigued, we decided to look at it, particularly as it was still within our half hour radius.

As we got out of the car, I saw a house partially covered in ivy which sagged into a field, at the bottom of which stood a tall tree. For some reason I felt a thrill of excitement and I whispered to Bill, "This is it. We'll have this one."

"Don't be silly. We haven't even seen inside yet."

The agent said cheerfully, fitting his key in the lock. "Here we are. This is somewhere where you can live while you renovate. He struggled a bit but finally swung the doors open.

Before us a tractor and old farm machinery were stacked so tightly it filled the entire space in front of us. With no windows, it was dim and smelt decidedly musty. Behind a wooden partition was the kitchen – an earth packed floor, a sooty corner under a chimney with a medieval ratchet hook for a cooking pot. Even so my enthusiasm was not dampened, although I could see a downward turn to Bill's mouth.

"And the living area. . ." The agent flung open a door, which was practically off its hinges and stepped forward, banging his head as the doorway was so low. We followed him, ducking carefully into a long dark room with an enormous mantel piece. Instinctively I wrinkled my nose, a fetid smell. Rats. Then I noticed the earth floor was riddled with burrows. I moved to open a window. What window? I realised there were no windows, only shutters, sometime in the past they had either rotted or been taken away.

"Have you noticed the fireplace? True Charentaise this," the agent said, as though it were an Adam fireplace in perfect condition. True it was large, shoulder height, made of creamy-coloured stone, but apart from its size, I saw little to recommend it.

Up a ladder was a hayloft deep in stale hay. The other two rooms showed a similar neglect: the roof in one place had been leaking and the rain had pitted the floorboards beneath.

We looked at each other. This was virtually a ruin. Much more work than we had bargained for.

"Electricity?" quavered Bill.

"No, no electricity. But no problem, it's in the road outside and will be easy to link up." He watched our faces carefully, then added brightly, "But you have got water, er… at the bottom of the garden."

"Out of the question," Bill declared as we drove away. But a few minutes later he added, "Well, at least we certainly couldn't live there now, as he suggested."

"What sort of people does he think we are?"

"I think he'd never been there before. He was simply going on what he'd been told. You know, it's got a roof, therefore it was habitable, but no-one in their right mind could imagine anyone actually *living* in what we saw."

"I liked the garden."

"What garden? Do you mean the field?"

I let it lie.

The estate agent rang the following day to explain they had only just put it on the market and if we were interested we should decide quickly.

"Exactly what we won't do," Bill stated firmly.

However, being a tourist was definitely beginning to pall. He had already cycled all along the coast and explored all the villages. He was finding that when I was at work he had too much time on his hands, and he was desperate for the motivation of a project of some kind. So we found ourselves putting in a ridiculously low offer, which, to our great surprise was accepted.

"We can always back out," I said helpfully.

But that, apparently, is something you can't do in France: the initial agreement is binding. If you do back out, you lose your deposit. Nor, we were informed, is it customary to have a house surveyed.

"It's a bit like buying a pig in a poke," Bill commented.

With mixed feelings, we drove back to look at it again. We could not even remember the exact name of the village. As we approached Bill saw the sign. "Chambon. That's the name."

"That means 'good field', Bill. Perhaps it's a good omen, we can create a lovely garden."

"Ever the romantic."

We noticed practical details as we approached – we were in the village, but on the edge of it, so we overlooked fields on two sides. A thick, evergreen hedge covered in small red berries ran down the roadside giving privacy. A kind of open barn structure stood at the bottom of the land, through which we could see the next field. On the other side were two ash trees and open land. We certainly didn't have the view from a hill we had dreamed of, but maybe we could put in a balcony. Just as at our first visit, as I stood looking at the huge ash tree which dominated the land furthest from the house, I felt a surge of optimism, which even I recognised was ridiculous as the house looked truly desolate.

Watching us from his yard was our future neighbour, a man in a flat cap, the typical blue workman's jacket and trousers with galoshes. He was probably in his late seventies but robust. We introduced ourselves and Jacques, we quickly discovered his name, opened his gate and stepped forward.

"So nice to have neighbours again. I'm so glad. When will you move in?"

"Move in? We haven't signed the contract yet."

"But you're going to?"

I looked at Bill, smiled at Jacques and said firmly, "Oh, yes."

"*Alors*," Jacques instinctively put out his hand and touched my arm. His blue eyes showed his pleasure. "I'm so pleased."

"There's a lot of work to do. I can't wait to get started," Bill said, suddenly enthusiastic.

"Well if there's any way I can help, let me know."

As usual, 'Scottish' drew an exclamation of delight from Jacques. "We French always like the Scottish. It's a beautiful country, or so I've heard, I've never been, *mais*", he gestured dramatically, "I have been to Morocco, you know, when I was in the army." He turned to include me. "You'll find the village very friendly. We all like to help each other. I'm sure you'll like living here."

"I'm sure we will," I enthused, warming to him.

"How long has the house stood empty?" Bill asked.

"Well, *Grandmaman* Jeanne was the last to live there, must be over thirty years ago. She used to drive her geese down the road every morning . . ."

"Thirty years. I can imagine it," Bill was continuing his line of thought. "Well, it won't be empty much longer if I've anything to do with it."

"Eh? That's the spirit. So, Beel and Gilly-Anne, that's right isn't it?" We nodded, a good enough approximation. "*Bienvenus à Chambon*!"

We quickly adapted to the French versions of our names; it seemed the first step to becoming integrated in our new life.

Over the next few days, Bill's views of the house varied from exhilaration and a desire to get started, to worry over what we were buying. I tried to be encouraging but realised it was Bill who would be doing the work. I'd only be the occasional helper.

"You always told me that whenever any of your employees came to tell you they had a problem, you used to say that it was not a 'problem' but a 'challenge'…" I didn't continue as I saw Bill's quizzical look. "Well at least our neighbour offered to help," I finished lamely.

"Jacques? He's well over seventy."

Wandering round a market one weekend, we saw what were undoubtedly leek plants.

I turned to the vendor, a young man in a flat cap, a cap that seemed to be the typical headwear rather than the beret we British associate with Frenchmen. "These are leeks, aren't they? Can one plant leeks in October?"

"*Bien sûr*, if they are spring leeks. You plant these now and eat them in the spring."

He saw my doubt and continued, "You are English, yes? Well, remember it's different here with our mild climate."

"You mean…" I hesitated, I hadn't even discussed this yet with Bill. "Well, I want to plant fruit bushes, blackcurrants and gooseberries. Do you mean I don't have to wait until the spring?"

"No. You can plant up until frosts and even then sometimes. So how many would you want?"

"Hang on, *chérie*, we haven't dug the ground yet."

"Look, my nursery is at the entrance to the town, on the road from La Rochelle. Why don't you come to see me when you are ready. I can give you not just the plants but advice."

We bought the leeks in a rush of 'The Good Life' enthusiasm, coupled with the thought of eating our own vegetables around Easter time. What a thought!

"They'll last till Monday, when we sign the contract. We can put them in afterwards." Bill was in his optimistic, positive phase.

However, the solicitor rang to say there was a last minute delay and we couldn't sign until Thursday. Would our bundle of leeks last that long, even if we kept them in a bucket of water? We asked if we could have permission to plant them. Our vendors replied that by all means we could start on the land and get our vegetables in, particularly as it was the right season for planting, but we were not to touch the walls of the house.

The bottom part of the land would be the sensible place for our vegetables. Later we could plan out the area nearer the house. We started to dig with an eagerness that waned rapidly as we realised what an arduous task was ahead of us. The land hadn't been worked for forty odd years so was as hard as a brick and thick with evil rooted weeds. After half an hour we'd made no noticeable headway. We moved nearer the house, where the earth was easier to dig.

"Our first plants in our own land." I stood back and admired the line of leeks as though we had created Wisley Gardens. What satisfaction.

CHAPTER 7

A Pig in a Poke. What Have We Bought?

Signing the contract was an incredible ceremony. Nine people sat in the solicitor's office, one brother, six sisters and two grandchildren, all with a share in the property. Under French law, land and goods has to be divided equally among <u>all</u> children, legitimate and illegitimate, which I understand has caused shock and embarrassment on more than one occasion, when a grieving widow finds her late husband had been unfaithful. The solicitor reads aloud the document, checking not only that all the details are correct, but that everyone understands, in particular, of course, us foreigners. Each person had to read and sign every page, so that the twelve page document took an hour to sign. The family kept commenting in patois, interrupting the solicitor. Finally it was signed and sealed, followed by handshaking all round. Just as we were driving away, feeling elated at being the owners of an eighteenth century farmhouse, I noticed Monsieur Lavergne, the only son, rubbing his hands with obvious glee. What had we bought?

The sobering thought was, an earth floored ruin, with no windows and a leaky roof, which had no water, no electricity and no sanitation.

We went straight to the cottage. Bill turned the key and flung open the doors. Without the farm machinery, the barn area looked enormous. We walked through the empty house in awe. Upstairs small cracks ran the length of one wall and another was falling away in one corner.

Finally Bill said, "This is no cottage, it could easily be a four-bedroomed house. It's far too big for just the two of us."

Intimidated, we wandered outside and stared at what we had bought. We wandered to the corner facing the land. The south wall was covered in ivy, which we both began to rip off. Now we realised why we had been told not to touch the walls: an enormous crack almost split the wall in two, twice the size of anything we'd seen indoors. We stood appalled.

"If we'd had a surveyor like you do in Britain, this wouldn't have happened," Bill grumbled.

"But it's not the custom in France. We asked, remember?"

Bill spent the next few days worried that we'd bought something that was likely to fall down.

A couple of days later, we were meeting some acquaintances for drinks in a bar. Claude was another estate agent and he listened to Bill's woes with interest and offered to call round at the house after work the next day to give us his opinion.

He was able to date the house more precisely from the way the stone was cut. Even though we had the date 1848 over the entrance, he pointed out that this was to the barn, which had obviously been added later; the actual house would have been built between 1720-25. Regarding the cracks, he said he knew a fail-proof test.

"The outside crack is only superficial even though it looks bad. The walls are double walls and the inside one is okay. For the others, do the lime test. Slap a lump of lime cement onto the crack and leave it for a few days. If it splits, the crack is moving and could be serious. If not, don't worry. It could be a crack that's three hundred years old and won't bother you."

For two long days we waited for our lime lumps to dry. Then returned to observe.

As we climbed the ladder to the upstairs. I crossed my fingers.

"I don't believe it. No movement."

"Hooray, now you can relax, Bill."

But he didn't relax and after three more sleepless nights he asked another estate agent we had been dealing with to come and look at what we had bought.

Cautiously he offered, "It's not bad, not a real bargain, but I reckon the price was fair."

"I want to sell it."

"But you've only just bought it. What do you want to sell it for?" he said astonished.

"I'm worried about the cracks … and it's too big. We didn't realise it was so big when it was packed with machines. So the best thing to do is to sell it."

The estate agent considered Bill thoughtfully. "Well if you're serious, I suggest you put in the basics – water and electricity, re-roof it and put in windows. Then put it on the market as partially renovated. Whatever you do, don't do anything personal. That could put buyers off. When you've done that, contact me and I'll see what I can do."

Bill was now reassured, and couldn't wait to tackle such a challenge. The first thing we decided to do, probably the least sensible considering it was November and rainy, was to strip off the grey rendering covering the stones. We were delighted to find, under such a grim exterior, cream coloured stones. However, never having done anything like this before, Bill lost confidence in his ability to make the right judgements. He rang a friend in Britain who had renovated houses, who promised to fly out the following weekend.

"That's fantastic," I said, "but how come he can drop everything just like that?"

"Ah, that's a story. He owes me a favour." He would have stopped there, but he could see my curiosity would lead me to persist. "A couple of years back, he and his wife had a row and she threw him out. At about ten in the evening he knocked at my door and I took him in. For about five days I listened to his tales of woe, then I decided to go and see Gloria. She used to work for me, some while back, so I knew her and we'd had a good working relationship. I hoped this would help now. It turned out she felt she'd acted over-hastily didn't want to make the first move, but if I would act as intermediary… And all became rosy again."

Steve was tall, well-built and with an easy smile. He spoke with a slight northern accent which lengthened his vowels, adding weight to what he was saying, and he spoke knowledgeably. I left the two men to talk technicalities while I walked around the 'garden', trying to imagine it as it might be one day: a mass of daffodils under an apple tree, something more exotic to be seen from the south-facing windows, oleander perhaps, or bougainvillaea considering we were so far south? I stood, lost in dreams. Overhead a ragged line of gulls, flapped slowly back to the sea. In the hedge, a constant chirping, probably of sparrows.

I glanced back towards the house. They were sitting in the sun on a pile of logs drawing plans and talking endlessly. I realised Bill felt inexperienced and welcomed Steve's strength and confidence. Bill told me later that the more he listened, the more he realised he would be working from a practical instinct. Finally Bill stood up and stretched, so I wandered over.

"Don't worry, Gillian," Steve said. "I know all about stresses and strains, what size timbers to buy for the beams and how far apart they should be. I've given Bill a shopping list because we'll both come over at Easter and help get you started."

Not only was Steve's reply reassuring, but he was promising two helpers he and his wife. What couldn't we accomplish? I went to Evita to get the champagne.

Walking back, I saw Steve was drawing again, but now they were both laughing.

"Here you are." Steve offered me the paper. "A little drawing of your new house."

A house with a small tower with a conical roof added at the south-eastern corner, from which flew the Scottish flag. Underneath he had scrawled, 'Bill's *château* for Gillian'.

CHAPTER 8

Marathon or Purgatory? And – Oops!

Big excitement. Barbara announced that the following week was the international six day marathon, *Les Six Jours de La Rochelle*. The aim was for the competitors to cover as many kilometres as possible in six days and nights. Afterwards I thought endurance race might be a better term than marathon. Our job was to translate for the runners from Britain, Anne and I, Germany, Elske, and Spain, Carmen.

Barbara instructed us to go to La Rochelle's main square, Place de Verdun, at three o'clock. Here I saw a strange crowd of track-suited runners mixed with well-dressed others waiting by a gaily decorated bus covered with balloons. I found John, the runner for England I was to translate for, and introduced myself. Eventually we all boarded and the bus drove slowly through the town, tooting its horn, for publicity and deposited us outside the Town Hall, the castle like structure I'd so admired on our first exploration. Today the gates were open and I stood staring spell-bound at the cream-coloured walls with crenellations, ending in two delicate towers, half suspended at each corner. However, I was here to work, not to gawp. Our group of athletes crowded into the courtyard where a crowd of stylishly-dressed people were taking photos of a bride and groom who posed on a balcony above us. Of course a town hall was the equivalent of a registry office - and what a picturesque place to get married! The photos finished, the wedding party filed out through the gateway, laughing and exclaiming, scattering rice and confetti, and we moved in. Now I could see the interior of the courtyard more clearly: the building was probably mid-sixteenth century.

Barbara nudged me. "For your information, since you're so obviously open-mouthed in admiration, those statues represent all the virtues a leader of this town should possess. And that," Barbara continued, pointing a statue of a man with a ruff, short puffed knickers and hose like an Elizabethan, standing where the bride and groom had stood, "is Henri IV. He gave this architectural gem to the town."

She said this sarcastically, but truly, it was a gem.

We went inside and up to a reception room, where we were offered nibbles and *un pot d'amitié,* a drink of friendship. Then the speeches started. No French event, we now know, can occur without speeches, often long and frequently involving many people. I sensed the runners were tense, waiting for it to be over.

When we eventually left, we drove to where the marathon was to be held in a large exhibition hall on the outskirts of the town. At first sight the hall seemed filled with bars, stalls and a restaurant. People were sitting drinking or wandering about greeting friends, children were chasing about screaming and a band was playing.

Already the air was filling with cigarette smoke. (This was before the no smoking in public places law was passed.) In the centre of all this was the track. I was amazed that the floor was concrete, as I couldn't help thinking it surely couldn't be a good surface for running.

I turned to John and asked why he would want to run round and round a hall for six days. He looked at me in surprise and told me it was the highlight of his year because it was the best organised running event of its kind that he knew.

"But … it's so stuffy in here. I bet you'll need some of fresh air."

"Oh, that's not possible. One step through the door and we're immediately disqualified."

I thought fleetingly of the glorious blue sky and sunshine outside, then asked, "One thing intrigues me, where on earth do you sleep?"

"We each have a cubicle, where we can lie down if necessary. But naturally I keep it to the minimum, because time out for sleeping is time lost for kilometres."

When it was obvious he didn't need my help any more, I wished him luck and left him to eat his energy giving meal of pasta to return to the language school. Frankly, I was glad to get out into the fresh air and sunshine.

That weekend the weather was so glorious we couldn't resist setting off to explore a little further afield.

Reaching the river Charente, and it being twelve o'clock, we decided to picnic on the banks. We found a spot beside a clump of cream and pink comfrey along the bank where someone else at some time had flattened the grass for their picnic. The river here was wide and flowed quietly. The only movement was from the cows lazily chomping the meadow grass the other side of the river. Perfect.

We spread out our rug and settled down to a leisurely lunch of olives, *charcuterie*, and a variety of cheeses with fresh baguette and, of course, some red wine, Bergerac I think. When we'd finished, I lay back against Bill, watching the wisps of white cloud and wondering if they were actually moving.

"Here we are, enjoying the sunshine and the peace all around, while those runners are pounding round that hall. I still can't believe anyone would do that for pleasure."

"Everyone to their own taste. Come closer, *chérie*. I know what my tastes are at this moment." He eased my t-shirt off and started caressing.

Having chosen an isolated spot and not a soul being around, we moved into a gentle love-making. We were just reaching the climax when a car chugged along the track and, believe it or not, parked just a foot away from Bill's head. A fisherman got out and set up his rod as though we didn't exist. This car was followed by four others, also fishermen, also with their chosen spots along the river.

Surprised I looked at my watch and realised what had happened. It was now ten past two. The lunch hour was over. Barbara had said something about the French lunch break of twelve to two still being respected in this area.

Grabbing our clothes, we retreated to the camping car, all without a word from the fisherman beside us. There, we collapsed in laughter. Oh well, we wouldn't forget the lunch break again.

The penultimate evening of the marathon we teachers were to return to the hall for a dinner. This involved the local councillors and business sponsors, so Barbara saw it as an opportunity to promote the language school. Anne, Elske, Carmen and I were told we were not to sit together but to mix and be sure to mention the school.

The restaurant was on a raised platform at the side of the track and despite being temporary structure was pleasantly laid out with linen cloths and green plants. From there I had a perfect view of the runners, except they were no longer running but limping their way round, barely moving forward and one looked as though she might keel over at any moment. Their singlets and shorts looked stained. Their legs were covered with grease, which my neighbour informed me was to keep them from chafing, and yellow ointment stained their thighs where they'd been rubbing together. To me it looked more like a bad movie about slaves than a sporting competition. Only six were left and John was not among them. I thought what determination they had to keep going. I wanted to ask my fellow diners which nationalities remained, but it was obvious they were not really interested in the race, although they were bandying distances varying between six hundred and a thousand kilometres. This seemed an in immense amount. Was it possible?

I couldn't help contrasting our haut-cuisine, elegant clothes and cultured conversation with the grim determination and suffering below. I turned so that I could no longer see the 'runners' and concentrated on the conversation. Their main interest was politics and an interesting documentary on Tibet recently shown on television. I did my best to introduce the school. They listened politely then continued with their discussion. Oh well, I'd tried.

I enjoyed these translating events. Were they going to be typical of my new job? I rather hoped so.

CHAPTER 9

The House on the Corner

The village we had chosen to live in was not particularly attractive. On our travels we had seen hundreds of prettier villages, in particular the honey-gold stone with dark brown roofs of the Dordogne, half-timbered rambling farm-houses of Normandy, and the dark granite with red shutters and red geraniums of the Pyrenees. All that our village offered was the impression that once it had been bigger and more prosperous.

Many of the houses looked as though they needed the woodwork repainting, the shutters re-hung and the rendering cleaned. None had been renovated leaving the stones showing, as we were planning to do, all had been covered with a uniform roughcast, which often had turned to a dull grey. Yet, there was something appealing: a large green, lined with dark red prunus trees, the occasional stone trough at the side of the lane filled with flowers, and a rather grander house, overshadowed by a huge cedar tree, at the end of our road.

Sometimes in the evening we wandered round the two lanes that comprised Chambon. We found a small cottage, totally unlike the other houses, with red honeysuckle covering the porch and rose bushes filling the front garden. Another had stone carving above and round one window, reminiscent of an ecclesiastical building, and yet another must have been a forge because of the row of horseshoes nailed up along a lintel. When we had more time, we would explore the history.

Meantime, like good law-abiding citizens, and as our book *Living in France* instructed us was essential, we had drawn up and put in plans to renovate.[1] However, at the time, we did what we had understood was necessary which meant waiting before starting work, as the permit took several weeks to come through and nothing major could be done until it had. Worse still, it was going to cost us twenty two thousand francs in two instalments. This seemed an inordinate amount of money! We discovered that the book obviously wasn't going to be the essential guide we had expected. It had been delightful to read in anticipation but not one to follow letter by letter.

Because ours was an old building, we were given detailed instructions as to what type of small-paned windows we were to install, the precise measurements and the colour of our shutters, the regional colour of Charente Maritime. What colour was that, we wondered. Most people in Chambon had brown shutters, a nearby village favoured green and yet another pale blue. So which was the colour of Charente-Maritime? We hoped not brown. In

---

[1] (Two years later, when we were friendly with the mayor, he told us we hadn't needed to since we weren't altering the exterior and we could have saved ourselves a lot of money.)

fact it was grey, not a colour we'd seen anywhere except on the château in Surgères, our nearest town. Confusing.

The accompanying letter said that the permit had to be posted up outside the house for everyone to see. This caused a stir. We were surprised to see how many people stopped to read it, but Jacques explained why.

"*Eh bien*, it wasn't necessary, you know. Nobody bothers. Who's going to know in a little village like this? Ask Guy and Bernard, they'll put you right."

They were our other neighbours and were cousins. Bernard was well-built, curly-haired with brown eyes and was a mason. Guy was tall, angular, with prominent cheekbones and piercing black eyes and was a carpenter. Both had renovated their houses and seemed friendly and ready to give advice.

Conversation between Bill and these two was funny to watch as they had no English, and he very little French. Bernard would listen with his head to one side, and Guy couldn't keep still, but was full of restless movements while keeping his eyes fastened on Bill's face. The conversation went along in leaps and jerks with much miming and gestures. Within a week Bill had picked up an amazing range of gestures such as rubbing the side of his nose to show he knew something special, seizing his elbow and bringing up his hand sharply to show strength and a twist to the nose to show tipsiness. Fortunately they were patient and seemed to enjoy his pantomimes.

Bernard recognised Bill's worries about the cracks. "Beel, what you need is double walls. Basically that's the answer to everything."

"Double walls? What do you mean?" I asked, puzzled because all the walls of the house were two stone walls with rubble in between.

"Come. I'll show you."

He took us into his house. Every original wall had been covered by plasterboard to give a more modern look.

We nodded politely. "Very good."

"Clean, hygienic, and gives you neat right angles."

Bill tried to explain that we wanted to keep the rustic effect and that we liked our stone walls, in fact they were one of the reasons why we had bought the house.

"Oh, now I understand, Beel. The stone wall effect. Look in here to see how to do it."

He took us through to his living room and pointed to his stone wall with pride. Our hearts fell. Wallpaper.

"Basically cleaner, no dust, no problems," he beamed.

He saw our faces and said he'd send a friend of his along, another mason, who would give us his advice.

We returned to our bulging walls and our cream-coloured, rough stone.

Two days later Bernard arrived at the house with his friend the mason, a big chap with a round face, frizzy hair and beard, all rather uncontrollable. He took charge, Bernard trailing respectfully behind, inspecting while talking volubly about the village, cars and his horses.

Finally he said, "So you've got a bulging wall?" Shrug. "Most of these houses have bulging walls. If you're worried though, I can fit a *ceinture*."

"What's that?"

"A *ceinture*…? A lady who is too fat wears a *ceinture*, and *voilà* she has a beautiful figure again." He was leaping around, showing the shape of the woman with expansive gestures. He saw Bill's amusement at his description and seized him by the elbow. "You have to come and have *apéritifs*! We'll fix it."

In fact both the idea of the *ceinture,* and the aperitif invitation, came to nothing because Bernard took Bill for a walk round the village, pointing out the number of houses with bulging walls and impressing on him a *ceinture* was very expensive and not really necessary. Bill stopped worrying about his walls.

Couch grass, threaded through the brick-hard earth like the strings of a fishing net, makes digging a nightmare. A half hectare nightmare, to be exact. When we bought the house, we had bought an extra plot of land to extend our garden and to include an outbuilding that would serve as our garage. It was this area we had designated for our vegetables, but at this rate the land would never be ready. Bill had started digging as 'a relaxation' from the heavier work of the house, but it was so arduous even he grew dispirited.

"If we don't pull out every bit of these couch grass roots, they'll multiply and we'll be back where we started," he said gloomily. "But what is worse, there's not a single worm, and worms mean good soil."

"Perhaps we could collect some? From our garden in Chatelaillon and bring them over?"

"Not a hope. They only live in *worked* soil. We'll have to persevere, but right now, I must get back to work."

Bill was in the process of retiling the roof. We had decided to use the old tiles as we liked the range of colours, cream, orange and brick red. When we had taken them off, we had sorted, cleaned and stacked them well clear of the house and possible breakage. It was now my job to carry them, a few at a time, up to the house and up the ladder to Bill who was waiting on the roof. He placed them carefully in position, one underneath curving upwards and one on each side curving downwards over it. What surprised the uninitiated me was that these were only secured at the ends, under the ridge and above the guttering, the rest simply lay one on top of another in rows.

I was returning for another load when I saw a tractor pull into our bottom plot and start ploughing.

"Bill!" I yelled, racing into the house. "Someone's ploughing our vegetable patch. Do you think he's made a mistake?"

"Farmers don't make mistakes about their land. We'd better go and see."

He strode down the garden and signalled to the man, still busily ploughing.

"*Bonjour monsieur*," he said politely.

"*Bonjour*," The man leant out of his cab to shake Bill's hand. Bushy hair and a flowing moustache almost obscured his face. "Jacques told me you needed this 'ere ploughed – too hard to work by hand. Well it certainly hasn't been worked for a good forty years. I was on my way to plough my fields and thought I'd stop off and plough it."

"That's very good of you," I said.

"Can't stop, *Madame*. Too much to do. Any more you need ploughin' while I'm here?"

"Er – no." We were both too bewildered to think clearly.

"Then I'll finish and move on." His head disappeared back inside the cab. With an "*Au revoir*" and a wave he disappeared down the road, leaving us appreciating the rich smell of newly turned earth.

"We don't even know his name," I cried.

Years later we still don't know who he was.

The following weekend, when we were once more at the house, Bill was drinking a well-earned coffee in Evita when a car with a trailer pulled into the drive. We looked up in surprise.

A stocky man got out and came across. It was Bruno. On one of the many occasions when he was round with Bernard offering advice, Guy had introduced us to his father-in-law. Now Bruno greeted us and looked around.

"*Bonjour* Beel and Gilly-Anne," he said. "You've got plenty of work here. I don't envy you."

"We enjoy working on it. Yes, there's a lot to do, but then I like doing practical things," Bill explained.

Bruno turned to look at where the land was newly ploughed.

"Ah, I'd heard someone had ploughed your land."

I told the story and explained we did not even know who he was.

"Could have been Lupon, but he doesn't have a moustache, so probably it was Pinson from the top of the village. Anyway, I've come to help you with my cultivator." He led the way to his trailer which held a machine with four shiny discs ready to turn earth.

"Great," Bill cried. "Exactly what we need."

"Guy told me how you'd hurt your back, Gilly-Anne, because the earth was so hard."

"Oh, it's okay now. But I can't dig this anymore."

Bruno kicked at then earth and stubbed his toe. "*Zut*! That's hard alright. Come and help me unload it, Beel. At least, I presume you would like me to give you a hand?"

"Definitely," we chorused.

As Bruno set his machine to work, I darted behind picking out the dreaded couch roots, white against the dark earth, while Bill hoed.

After an hour and a half, Bruno said he could do no more and he and Bill loaded the marvellous machine back into the trailer. But that was not the end of the surprise. Bruno dived into the car and pulled out two carrier bags.

"The best way to clear your earth and get rid of the weeds is with potatoes. This lot," he held up one carrier bag, "Are whites, and this lot," he held up the other, "are reds."

Now we were amazed. First he had come unexpectedly and transformed our field into a garden, and then he had presented us with the seed potatoes that would continue the process.

"But that's awfully good of you," Bill mumbled.

"*Bof.*" (A local expression that can mean anything from 'don't mention it', to 'so-so', according to the context.) "But I must be off now – time for lunch."

From potatoes to beans and these came from Bernard. In this rural area, your crops are so important that, for our neighbours it was inconceivable that we could not be anxious to get in the basics, onions, potatoes, beans and tomatoes. It was too late for onions and the earth was too tough for tomatoes, but between them they had ensured we had our potatoes and beans. Apparently they had been most impressed that the first thing we had done was to plant leeks.

We were learning the extent to which our neighbours believe in mutual help. Up until now these had been odd gestures, but once Bill had done all the basic preparations, they were there ready to help in earnest. They said they'd arrive first thing on Saturday morning with their concrete mixer to lay the floors, and at eight a.m. prompt they stood on the doorstep, tall lanky Guy, and the more solid Bernard with a tall young man we discovered was his son, all three dressed in overalls. After the usual greetings they got to work.

Around half past ten I decided to make coffee and asked how they liked it.

"*Merci*, that's very good of you, but we don't stop for coffee when we're working."

Bill grimaced. He was ready for a break; laying concrete is back-breaking work.

They arrived for three successive Saturdays, always promptly at eight a.m. When the concreting was finished they helped erect the double walls we had agreed would be sensible for the outside walls in our '*salon*'.

Guy was lively and constantly quipping as he leapt around organising. Bernard worked thoughtfully, responding to Guy with nods and the odd comment, the son worked in virtual silence. Bill struggled to follow the instructions he only partially understood and I could see the onslaught of the French was almost as exhausting as the physical work. As the Saturdays progressed, however, he became less of the apprentice and more of an equal. He was learning fast.

When Bill, concerned at the amount of time they were giving, wanted to pay them, they were firm.

"Absolutely not. We're neighbours and neighbours help each other, *'le coup de main'*. One day we may call on you for help, but now, your need is greatest."

It was not just, the help, that was useful, but the knowledge and skills that Bill absorbed. This meant that later on he was able to do these jobs himself. Everything they did, was done expertly and efficiently.

It was during this work that we learned a strange, but practical, custom. Greetings are important in France, men always shake hands. But if you've been working and your hand is dirty, this would be discourteous, so the wrist is shaken instead. We quickly got used to shaking proffered wrists.

On Sunday afternoons it became the custom for the villagers to go for a walk after lunch. Our group took the route to see what *les anglais* were doing now. It was through the women that we learnt a rhyme:

'Petit par petit
Oiseau fait son nid'.

Little by little the bird builds his nest.

This was a rhyme we were to hear frequently. Another phrase that was used all the time when people were with us, was '*Courage!*' The equivalent of 'good luck', and is used, in particular it seems, when the odds are against you.

"Do they know something we don't know?" Bill kept musing.

One Saturday when they arrived they issued a strange invitation It seemed to be the custom that the cousins ate together every Sunday, a family get-together. Now they were inviting us to join them for dessert. Come at two, they said. The same thing happened the following weekend. After that we were simply included in the family Sunday lunch.

These were fairly noisy affairs. The men sat one end of the table and the women the other with the children somewhere in the middle. This meant there were two simultaneous conversations as the men talked cars and 'manly' things and the women talked mainly about recipes.

Jacques had told me that Bill had gained respect in the village with all the work he was doing, both on the house and the garden. He was a familiar sight now, in his dungarees and wellies and the villagers would stop and pass the time of day. One of these was a little man with a limp and a rosy face with dimples. He walked past our house every morning and we began to wonder where he went. There was no mystery, as he went to feed the cats in an empty house down the road. He would stop and comment on what Bill was doing.

"Putting in your *patates* then?" asked the little man with a limp. In the country potatoes were not *pommes de terre* but *patates.*

"Yes, the red ones." Bill.

"Not in rows like that though. It's best north to south."

"Really? Why?"

"We just always do it that way. It works best."

Another time the conversation went like this:

"This used to be all vines round here."

"Here? In our garden?"

"Yes. But not just here, the whole area."

"What happened?"

"Disease, phylloxera. Killed the lot. 1875. Terrible year, that."

"I might put in some vines," Bill was thinking aloud.

"Takes a long time to mature."

The conversations were never long, but Bill began to enjoy these short exchanges. Then the man stopped passing.

"What's happened to the man who feeds the cats?" Bill asked Jacques.

"He's too busy. You see old man Perrot's gone into hospital, so we're looking after his farm for him. With cows you can't just stop, they need to be milked twice a day, you know. He's taken over the lion's share and we others help out. It's my turn for the milking tonight."

So that was what was happening. For one week the villagers ran the farm and then continued to help out as much as possible when the farmer returned from hospital to give him time to recover.

CHAPTER 10

A Strange Invitation

It was shortly after this that we received a strange invitation.

While we had been touring in the summer, we had made friends with Juliette and Pierre at a campsite near Narbonne, close to the Mediterranean. They had had a tent not far from us on one of the campsites, and we had been fascinated by their evening routine. Pierre would sit cross-legged in front of a small table and paint. Later he would brush his wife's long hair. When they went to the toilet in the evening, they each took a book, and disappeared for at least half an hour, explaining later they had no light for reading in their tent so used the electric light of the toilet block. They told us that they had been attracted to us because of our laughter. We learnt that he had been a philosophy teacher and was now a forester, doing a summer period of firewatching, and she was an unenthusiastic Classics teacher.

Shortly after we settled in Chatelaillon, we got an invitation from them with an intriguing post-script, 'The mushroom season is in full swing so don't wait too long'. We were not sure what the connection was between the mushroom season and our visit, but we were soon to find out.

We set off the last weekend of October in brilliant sunshine. They lived near Arcachon, west of Bordeaux, the other side of the Gironde River which effectively cuts the south-west in two. The Gironde has always been an important river strategically as its wide estuary leads to the port of Bordeaux, famous for its wines since Roman times.

There is a ferry that goes across the mouth of the estuary, a half hour trip, so we decided to take the evening crossing. That night we slept in the forest, calm and tranquil, with nothing but the sound of the occasional owl. We were woken by gunfire, our peace was shattered. What on earth was going on?

Bill peered through the window.

"A group of loonies – no probably *la chasse*. Right by our camping car."

He pulled on some shorts and opened the door and we saw a dozen men, guns in hand standing round Evita. Bill raised his hands in mock surrender and called out cheerfully, "Ok. I'll come peacefully!"

The men laughed, lowered their guns and called back a *bonjour,* some making a mock salute.

We learnt it was the hunting season and we had parked in a favourite hunting area for deer and boar. The men thought it a great joke to have woken us up by firing their guns and were delighted we'd taken it in good part.

Juliette met us exuberantly in a village not far from where they lived to lead us to their house, because, being a forester, it was well off the beaten track. In fact it was set in an open space on a sun-catching knoll deep in the forest, with a terrace all the way round. What immediately caught my eye was a large table piled with mushrooms, bright yellow and white. Pierre assured me we would find plenty for ourselves before we went home.

That afternoon, they did the tourist act, taking us to first to Arcachon Basin with its blue water dotted with small yachts, and then the sand-dunes that were engulfing a row of houses. Apparently these had been built and sold, but the owners had never been able to move in, as the dunes began moving towards them. Over the last fifteen years there had been an ongoing battle between owners, builders and the insurance companies as to who was liable. He finished by saying how important the forestry's work was to stabilise the dunes by replanting. Apparently a type of tough grass was the best stabiliser as it multiplied by sending out runners beneath the sand, but he showed us a small, inconspicuous flower that looked as though it had been covered in fluff, that was planted first to start the process.

I sensed an undercurrent of excitement when he announced that we would go mushrooming the following day. It evoked the same feeling as the promise of a birthday treat had when I was a child.

At dinner that evening, they proudly put on the table a large platter of seafood, piled high with whelks, shrimps, prawns and some kind of bivalve. We have always been fascinated by these platters and the way a French person will nonchalantly use the array of dentist-like tools to pick out the meat. Now it was our turn.

Bill attacked it with gusto, but I was more cautious. I was happy to try the prawns and even the tiny shrimps, but not the whelks and bivalves. All of a sudden Pierre said, "Shut your eyes and open your mouth, Gilly-Anne; this is something really nice." He made the typical gesture of kissing his fingers with a moue of his lips.

So it must be delicious. Trustingly I did as I was bid. A lump of rubbery, salty something, was popped into my mouth, impossible to swallow without chewing and loathsome to chew. How do you discreetly remove such a thing from your mouth when your kind host is beaming at you and watching your reaction?

The next morning, we set off on bikes, single file down a forest path lined with heather. Bracken grew under the silver birch and a variety of mushrooms had pushed their way through the light soil. I wanted to stop at every mushroom I saw, "*Non, non*, Gilly-Anne, come on, follow me. I'm taking you to the best places."

A couple of times Juliette wanted to show me a type of mushroom, but each time Pierre's impatience mounted.

"Julie, don't I walk these woods every day of the week? Don't you think I don't know where to go?"

Submissively we got back on our bikes and followed.

Suddenly he stopped, laid down his bike and led us into a mossy area under the pine trees. He looked like some wood elf who was about to reveal a treasure.

"But where are they?" I was disappointed as all I could see was dense moss.

"Watch me," he said with glee and bent down to part the moss. Inside it was thick with orange stalks with small velvety brown heads, about five centimetres high. He picked one up to show us, fingering it reverently.

"*Chanterelles modestes*, excellent in stews and soups, or a classic dish is to cook them in a sauce with olives go with your steak. They are one of the few mushrooms that are equally good with fish - hake with *chanterelles*, mmm." He put his fingers to his lips and kissed them in appreciation. "You find them all along the Atlantic coast in the pinewoods, in fact their other name is *chanterelles jaunes des pins,* yellow pine chanterelles. Anyway, help yourselves. Pick as many as you want, because you can dry them and keep them to use during the winter."

I picked and picked, then stood back. All around was soft green moss and yet, with my newly trained eye, I could see the occasional yellow stalk. *Chanterelle Modeste* … a good name, hiding away and with a deep brown hat modestly hiding the body.

After a while, Pierre said that was enough, to get back on our bikes and he'd take us somewhere else. This time we headed straight for the dunes. Leaving our bikes in the sand, under the last pine trees, we walked forward, but I felt I'd stepped on something so looked down. Unbelievable. I was walking on a carpet of saucer sized mushrooms.

Pierre laughed at my expression. He had been standing watching our reactions. Bill was already on his knees, examining this new find. I was just staring amazed and even Juliette was surprised.

"No wonder I never find many of these. I've never come far enough."

They were an extraordinary colour, being a brilliant, custard yellow underneath, and dusty yellow or white on top.

"These are *Tricholome equestres,* known as such because they used to be reserved for knights. Locally they are called *bidaux*. They grow where the pine forest meets the dunes, again all along the Atlantic coast. One problem is the sand, so be careful with them and clean them thoroughly."

This was a warning we were to remember well when, the following day, back in Chatelaillon, we fried them with shallots in butter. Munch, munch, grit, grit and more grit.

We had returned from this weekend with four carrier bags of mushrooms. This was the beginning of a growing mania for mushroom-hunting.

CHAPTER 11

We Learn – Sometimes from Mistakes

I was not only thoroughly enjoying the teaching, but also the company of Anne in particular. I found her very easy to be with; she 'flowed'. Preparing work in the staffroom together included sharing confidences and joking about the foibles of our students.

Barbara, my boss, however, was not someone who 'flowed'. She had a very variable temperament, one moment lively, witty and intellectual, and the next the hard, practical head of the establishment. Despite this we got on well and she invited Bill and me several times to her flat. I liked stepping out onto her tiny balcony with its typical wrought ironwork and its perfect view: first the tree-tops of the boulevard of trees, and then the harbour, framed by the towers.

"Beautiful, yes, but noisy in the holiday season with the buskers and tourists. And as for the Francopholies, all those summer concerts blasted out on the edge of the harbour - well, you know how water magnifies sound."

Maybe, but for the rest of the year, a view unparalleled.

She got on particularly well with Bill, who went round twice to put up shelves and new curtain rails for her. Gradually I became irritated by her attention to 'dear William', a name he actually hated being called, but accepted from her.

It wasn't long before she invited us over for dinner.

"I've bought some beef especially for you. How do you like it, William?"

And Gillian? Obviously she didn't count. Throughout the evening. I said exactly one sentence. I began to think things were getting crazy. When, at the end of the meal, I heard Bill, who was getting more and more eloquent after an excellent bottle of Bordeaux wine, say, "Barbara, you look more and more attractive as the evening goes on," I jumped to my feet and stated it was time to go home.

I stomped down the stairs, hands deep in my pockets, shoulders hunched. Outside I turned to round on Bill, but saw him physically shrug himself, like a dog shaking off water. "She does go on, doesn't she? How do you stand it all day?"

"You don't think she's like that with *me*, do you? It's *you*! And you egg her on atrociously."

"Hey, *chérie*! Calm down. I tried to be charming because I thought it would make your job more assured… You don't think it meant anything?"

I studied his face. Open and genuinely concerned. How could I have doubted?

"She's lonely. And you know I like to make people feel special."

"You mean, make lonely *women* feel special." I was not ready to give up feeling jealous and grumpy.

"Well, yes, you could put it that way. But it's no more than that. Anyway, I think she's not only a lonely person, but very insecure too. So if it gives her a bit of pleasure…"

He saw my look, and did not finish the sentence, just put his arm round my shoulder and gave it a squeeze.

I recognised what he was saying but still couldn't shake off my mood that easily. Instead I simply said, "I'm tired."

He turned me round and kissed me gently. As we wandered back to Evita, past the harbour and the moonlit boats reflected in the inky water, my irritability slowly evaporated.

I got on so well with Anne that she often popped over to see us, either in the evening or at the weekend, for a chat. Bill and she got on well too, helped by the fact he could relax and talk in English. So we were not too surprised when she said her parents would love to meet us and would like to invite us over for *apéritifs*.

This is a far more elastic institution than the British 'drinks': it can vary from simply peanuts and crisps with a drink to a series of elaborate nibbles, becoming more and more substantial, even pizzas and quiches, anything so long as it can be eaten with fingers.

Consequently our evening at Anne's parents, which we thought would last roughly an hour, lasted three. Anne explained afterwards that the hot nibbles were waiting in the oven and when she saw her mother switch it on, she knew that meant they liked us.

Since it was late October, we took with us a beautiful golden chrysanthemum plant for our hostess. We had found the florist shops were suddenly bursting at the seams with these flowers, spilling out onto the pavements in a riot of glorious colours.

When I presented it to Edith, I was surprised, as she barely said thank you, leaving it by the door instead of enthusing and bringing it in to the living room. The following day I learnt why.

"By the way," Anne said, "In France you never give chrysanthemums when you go out somewhere. They're for All Saints Day, November 1st, when we put them on the graves."

I stared in amazement. "Oh no! And I gave one to your mother. No wonder she looked a bit confused."

"Well, she didn't want to say anything, she realised, of course, you didn't know the custom. But for us, *chrysants* are only for cemeteries."

"I'll remember in future. So that's why the shops are so full of them now."

"You'll see, the day after All Saints', the cemeteries are magnificent." She smiled mischievously. "And be careful, don't let Bill give anyone carnations."

"Why? What do *they* mean?"

"Love!"

So we had managed to commit our first social blunder. We decided to check in our *Living in France* to see if it offered any other advice. We read in it that taking a bottle of wine when invited somewhere for dinner, as one would do in England, is not customary. In fact it is tantamount to implying that you do not trust your host's choice of wine – and that ability is something every Frenchman prides himself on and we quickly learnt that it is an indisputable fact that French wine is the best. I have watched Bill more than once say to a group of friends how good Spanish wine is, in particular the Rioja. It is like throwing a fox in among chickens. First there is physical recoil and then everyone launches simultaneously into a heated explanation of why it cannot be as good as French wine. A Pavlovian reaction.

Bill worked on the house while I taught in La Rochelle. The weekends we spent doing things together on 'our' house, making it a joint project.

For me work was a real pleasure as I simply had to teach, none of the aspects of being a head-teacher that I had found so tedious. Nor were there any disruptive, problem children. The language school students were all adults and highly motivated, so all I had to do was to kindle their enthusiasm and make their learning a pleasurable experience. Some of the classes were people who needed English for their work, but many wanted to learn English to help them when they travelled, and many of these were retired.

With the beginners, it was as much encouraging them as teaching the grammar, because many had such bad memories of English at school. With the advanced groups it was more a matter of stimulating them to get a discussion going. We discussed anything topical, travel, films and books. I shamelessly asked them to recommend authors, as my first visit to the local library had left me feeling helpless.

I had gone in, explained to the librarian that I was English, wanted to read novels in French, but didn't know any French authors, except for the classics, and wasn't sure where I should start. I would like to read historical novels to fill me in a little with the history I didn't know and some family sagas. She had stood up and said to follow her. She pointed solemnly to the first shelf inside the door and said,

"We start here with authors beginning with A and work round the room to Z, over there," and then had walked away.

My story led to the students animatedly discussing, all in English of course, what I ought to read and arriving the following lesson with books for me to borrow, Colette, Françoise Sagan and the first volume of *Les Rois Maudits*, set in the twelfth century.

Sometimes the French attitude surprised me, in particular over sex and relationships. One day, with an advanced group, of retired ladies, most of whom had been teachers or school inspectors, so were well educated, we were discussing the news. In Britain, a member of parliament had just resigned when his affair with his secretary became public knowledge.

"But why did he resign?" The class sat looking at me blankly as I struggled to explain … 'honour' … 'duty' …' doing the right thing', 'the expected thing'. The blankness did not change.

Finally one of them said firmly, "It's a lot of nonsense. Everyone knows people have affairs. It's a matter of keeping it in perspective. It's one's private life and does not concern work."

"Look at Mitterrand," added another. "Everyone knew he had a mistress, but it was accepted. It didn't make him a better or a worse politician."

They decided the English must be a strange race to be so concerned over such a natural matter.

On another occasion, with an average group of middle aged and retired people, I had given them pictures of things that usually either scare or delight, to get them talking.

"Try to give your reactions. Don't consider too long, simply tell your partner how you feel about what you see."

An older man picked up a picture. "A baby ... I don't like babies."

One of the other men, overhearing, called across the room in a loud voice, "But I bet you like making them!"

The class collapsed with helpless laughter, but no-one was embarrassed.

Doing a similar exercise with a more fluent class, I was suddenly aware of instead of couples talking to each other, there was a hush. I looked round to find the cause. Everyone was listening to an elderly, elfin lady.

"The most frightening thing in my life was the day the Germans arrived in Paris and the mass exodus. I had to get on that last train, or I knew I'd be arrested. But it was full to overflowing. I managed to get one foot in the carriage, but only one, the rest of me was hanging out of the door. Strong arms held me all the way till we were well into safety." Before anyone could comment she quickly said, "Now it's your turn, Robert."

One thing that struck me through the year, was that all the retired students took two holidays, one in autumn and one in spring. The autumn one seemed to be to a far-off place, Turkey, India, Thailand, Egypt, South Africa or China, and the spring one, associated with the snow. One went on a five day trek across the *Massif Centrale* on *raquettes,* which are a kind of snowshoes, and others went to the mountains to enjoy the views with snow, but most went skiing.

I got the impression that for them retirement meant the time to travel. I discussed this with Anne, saying that perhaps they got a better pension than the equivalent in

Britain. Even so I was surprised when she said they got about seventy percent of their salary, quickly adding when she saw my face, that they'd had to pay a lot into that over the years. If only I'd been teaching in France!

Both Anne and I believed classes should be fun and social occasions as far as possible, particularly for those who came in tired after a day's work. This was lucky, because, for organisational reasons, we alternated teaching classes weekly. By the end of the autumn term the second year English learners had gelled as a group. Perhaps it helped that they were all young, late twenties and early thirties, and all keen to progress professionally.

When stuck one evening trying to explain *'fondue'* in a discussion of favourite foods, flamboyant Philippe, an executive from the electricity board, threw down his pen.

"It's easy. I'll show you what is *fondue*. We all go to the Swiss restaurant for a *fondue* meal. What you think?"

We needed little encouragement and arranged to go the following week after class, the last of term. It was also a farewell to Anne as she was leaving because she did not get on with Barbara.

It was a good evening and Bill's limited French forced the students to use their English, at least initially.

"This is my husband, Bill."

"And I'm not English, I'm Scottish."

"What *ees* the difference?"

"Difference?" he said dramatically. "We're a different nationality, a different culture."

"Scottish eh? So where's your skirt?" joked Philippe.

"My kilt you mean. I used to wear one, but I've decided I'm European, so I dress like a European."

"He *can't* wear it. It's full of moth holes, in all the wrong places."

Later in the evening, Isabelle, blonde with large brown eyes, whom Bill obviously found attractive, asked the inevitable question. Unfortunately, as her English was limited, it came out as, "What you have under your kilt, Beel?"

"What every young girl dreams of." But seeing her bewildered face he corrected her English, "What *does* a Scotsman *wear* under his kilt? Traditionally, nothing."

He then told the following story. Having heard it before, I watched the group, leaning towards Bill over the table, puzzled yet fascinated.

"A Scot was in London and a woman approached him in the street. 'Tell me Scottie, what do you wear under your kilt?' He replied, 'If ye put your hand up, ye'll find out.' The woman did so and drew her hand back quickly, saying, 'It's gruesome.' To which the Scotsman replied, 'Aye and if ye do it again, it'll grew some more.'"

"Really, Bill!" Anne was the only one to burst out laughing. She attempted to explain the joke to the baffled students.

By this time Isabelle was blushing furiously, through her laughter. It was obvious they decided Bill was a great joker. It certainly set a note of hilarity for the evening.

The effort of speaking English was dropped fairly soon after this, except for easy phrases. I have to admit, I enjoyed the company better than the *fondue*, feeling it is a dish that is over-rated. As the wine flowed, we swore friendship and that this should be the first of many meals together. A picnic, a cycle ride and an evening at the bowling alley were enthusiastically arranged.

CHAPTER 12

A Christmas Visit from the Family

Our children joined us, in our Chatelaillon house, for Christmas, Bill's son Henry, training as an interior designer, my son Gareth, in publishing in London, my daughter Rachel, back from her voluntary work in Kenya with Brian, the American boyfriend who she had met there doing Peace Corps work. We were keen to show them the neighbourhood. But what was best in mid-winter? Obviously La Rochelle. We didn't say anything but simply said we were going to go to the Park and Ride. They were delighted to find the 'ride' was by boat, the boat bus I'd taken all those months ago after the boat show. It seemed more than just three months ago.

As we approached the harbour entrance with its towers, they all rushed forward, cameras at the ready. The shadow of the Saint Nicholas tower fell on us and I looked up at the tiny windows high up and the French flag fluttering from the roof, then down at the green seaweed clinging to the solid base. The boat swung round sharply, pulling into the quay and we found ourselves at the boulevard of trees. Already they were looking around admiringly.

First I took them to the Town Hall. It really fascinated Brian, who kept shaking his head and saying there was nothing like this back home in Arkansas. Then we separated to do some Christmas shopping, arranging to meet up at a café beside the harbour in an hour and a half's time. I dished out town plans I'd got from the tourist office previously, then left them and raced round getting my last presents.

When we met up again, I could see from their faces that they had enjoyed their visit. We sat outside in the sun to have our coffee, loosening our coats and lifting our faces to the December sun. Even though there were no fairy lights, no buskers and no Peruvian pipe band music floating across the water, they all fell in love, as we had expected, with La Rochelle.

Obviously the family were curious to see the house we had bought. When we had shown our photos in Britain, my brother-in-law had said, "Did you pay or did they pay you to get it off their books?"

And that rather seemed the unspoken attitude.

However Bill and I were full of enthusiasm and were determined to christen it as 'our home' by having a family lunch there. Admittedly, the floors were still earth floors, and the lack of windows would make it draughty, but we could eat with our coats on. For us it was to be an occasion.

The first job on arrival was to light a fire in our beautiful Charentaise fireplace, but we paused to watch their expressions as we went in to what we were optimistically calling '*le salon*'. On their faces were clearly written their reactions.

"They surely don't intend living here, do they?" Gareth.

"Looks like it ... but why?" Henry.

"Hang on, maybe it'll be okay," Rachel.

While Brian obviously thought, "Hell, they're nuts!"

All this was so clear. They might as well have spoken their thoughts out loud.

The day was saved by Jacques arriving to say hello and meet the family, closely followed, of course, by his wife Louisette.

"You're having lunch here? But where?" she said despairingly, looking round at the dark, damp room, cold still, despite the fire.

"We're christening our house. Join us for some champagne," Bill said waving a couple of glasses in the air.

"Just a moment, *mes amis*," said Jacques, "We've got exactly what you need. You young'uns, come and give me a hand."

Gareth and Brian returned a few minutes later with a big trestle table, which Louisette and Henry quickly covered with a roll of paper tablecloth.

"The candles! Light the candles!" I pulled them out of my basket excitedly.

With the fire blazing, the candles lit and a sprig of holly stuck in the middle of the table, it looked more festive.

"To the house!"

"To Mum and Bill!" "To Dad and Gillian!" "To Beel and Gilly-Anne!"

"To all of us!"

Jacques shepherded Louisette away, still muttering about it being a cold place to eat, leaving us to enjoy our lunch. And I'd made sure it was an especially good lunch.

Later in the afternoon, I suggested showing the family the village.

"You go, *chérie*. I think I'll stay here," said Bill.

Thinking perhaps he needed a break from the family, I didn't query it and we set off for a tour of Chambon.

When we returned, he was standing on top of a large pile of stones in the *salon*, covered in dust and looking triumphant. We had a new window, or rather a huge hole that one day would become a new window.

"Thought the room was a bit dark. Needed a window this end. After all," he added as he saw my expression of incredulity, "we've got our permit through now."

"Yes, but it didn't include a window there."

"It doesn't affect the side on the road. No-one can complain they're overlooked. Anyway, don't you think it's a good idea?"

The family agreed, as, in fact, so did I. But the speed with which it had happened disturbed me.

We knew Gareth, being something of an expert on naval life at Nelson's time, having written a book about it, would certainly be interested to see Rochefort, half an hour further south of us, a town built specifically as a naval dockyard in the seventeenth century. Everything therefore had developed around the naval buildings, the provision store, the armoury, the naval hospital and of course the dry docks and the *Corderie Royale,* where the ropes were made for the rigging.

We parked near the marina where the small boats are moored, not far from the *Corderie Royale*. We set off briskly along the river path, past rushes and ornamental bushes. The view opened out and across an immaculate lawn we saw the most beautiful, and unusual, long building of golden stone with a grey slate roof. It was incredibly long, in fact, we learnt, three hundred and seventy two metres, but only eight metres wide, low, with rectangular small-paned windows and between these a curl like a treble clef, presumably to support the length of the wall. This was the *Corderie Royale* itself. Of course, we reasoned, it had to be so long, since it had been designed for the manufacture of ropes for the ships of that era, but the beauty of the design was breathtaking. Inside is now a museum showing how these ropes were made, but we continued on as we wanted to discover the whole area.

Brian started taking photos and I had visions of his family back in Arkansas being shown photo album after photo album. I just hoped they were interested in Europe.

Gareth became fascinated by the two dry docks, side by side, at the river's edge and started pointing things out.

"Look, this is the keel of a ship, the mid-rib if you like as all the planking is fastened to it. It's put into place and held in the shape of the curve for the prow, then kept there for months, sometimes longer, to take the required shape."

"Why did they need two docks?" I asked without thinking.

He looked at me witheringly. "So they could build two ships at a time. I've just explained that the setting of the keel takes months. While that's happening, they can be building another one."

He peered at the ledges narrowing down to the base and mumbled about their good condition. It was at that point that we noticed a sign saying the timber was the first step in reconstructing an eighteenth century frigate, The Hermione, which would be a joint French-American project, since the original had gone to the aid of insurgents in the American War of Independence.

"There you are," he said triumphantly. "I told you the docks could still be used. I'd like to see that as the project progresses."

Bill was getting restless and suggested we went into town for a coffee. While we did, I delved into my guidebook. Apparently, Rochefort was built after the original port, Brouage, got silted up. Being on the river, it wouldn't suffer the same fate. Louis XIV's ambition was to be respected at sea, and since he had only twenty ships, he needed to increase his fleet, but first he needed a new dockyard. Rochefort was ideal: the river channel was deep even at low tide, the entrance to the harbour was protected by the three islands, which could be fortified to add protection, and because it was far from the sea, it meant it was difficult to attack. In addition, inland there were plenty of forests which could provide the timber for shipbuilding. It progressed fast: in 1669 there were 2,500 inhabitants, by 1685, more than 13,000. After the naval buildings were built, plots of land were allocated for houses and the town was laid out on a grid pattern, with the most influential people having the plots nearest to the *Corderie Royale* and the river. I found all this fascinating, but no-one was particularly interested in hearing the history, so I suggested that, after our coffee, we went to Pierre Loti's house.

"What's that?" asked Rachel.

"I really don't know. It seems it's an absolute must, but no-one will explain why. Every time Barbara, my boss, tells me I really must go, it's accompanied by a knowing look and a wink to Anne. But she refuses to say why it's special. All I know is he was a nineteenth century marine officer who enjoyed travelling."

"Well, we'd better go and find out then."

It was well signposted and easy to find, but appeared exactly the same as all the other houses in the street, a grey painted door and two rectangular windows to one side.

"Nothing much to get excited about," Bill said disparagingly.

The first room was typical of the turn of the nineteenth-twentieth century, with the conventional dark red velvet and plush. Just another historical house. The second room was a pleasant dining room with a nicely polished table and – now my breath was taken away. Behind was a medieval hall, complete with a magnificent carved staircase, huge fireplace, a heavy oak table and a suit of armour. There was even a minstrels' gallery. We signalled our surprise at each other as the guide proceeded to explain how the ceiling had been removed to give the extra height and how Pierre Loti had entertained here, medieval fashion, in costume with a period menu. I thought this was amazing, in the middle of a normal house, but it was nothing compared with what we saw next.

Pierre Loti had travelled a great deal to Turkey, and loved the country. He even grew a drooping moustache, Turkish style. On the top floor he had recreated a mosque, actually importing authentic, Turkish green and blue decorated tiles. As we entered I instinctively felt we should be taking off our shoes.

No wonder Barbara had had such a knowing smile.

On the family's last day we decided to go to Saintes, on the river Charente, about an hour away. Once there, we separated to do some shopping, leaving the young ones to explore the narrow streets lined with cream-coloured houses. We would meet up at the Roman arena.

It started to rain and my anorak was quickly getting soaked. I held my umbrella out at an angle to protect myself.

"It would rain on their last day," I grumbled to Bill.

"Well, we've been very lucky. This is the first bad day in a week. Come on, the amphitheatre is just up the road. Cheer up!"

Despite good intentions, we'd not yet visited this and were completely taken by surprise at how enormous it was. We were up above, looking down on a vast oval space surrounded by tiers of stone seating and huge ruined arches. And there, standing in the middle, well muffled in her anorak, was Rachel, apparently totally lost in thought. I spotted the other three huddled under one of the arches, shoulders hunched against the rain. I called, but got no response.

"Come on, Bill," I said impatiently and started off down the steep steps.

"Hi, Rach." She looked up, startled. "Whatever were you thinking of?"

"Just imagining... what it might have been like. You know, the important people up there, ready to give the thumbs up or down for the gladiators, the entrance there," she continued, turning, "through the tunnel. Imagine standing here and seeing lions charging up it towards you."

"Lions or gladiators?"

"Gladiators mainly, but lions too perhaps from time to time, although they probably didn't have lions in France."

I looked with her. Yes, it was almost possible to imagine it as it must have been in its heyday, probably because there was so much still standing.

"You two like talking in the rain, do you? Come up to where the others are, in the dry." Bill was being practical again.

The wet was killing enthusiasm. Even Brian wasn't taking photos. Definitely time for lunch.

By two o'clock it had stopped raining and the sun was shining fitfully through the clouds, so we decided to stop on the way back at the château of *La Roche Courbon*, built in the seventeenth century. As we approached, Rachel said, "It looks like a picture from a fairy story book."

It really did – square with pointed turrets at each corner. Unfortunately the château itself was closed for renovation and we could only walk round the gardens, which were formal and typically French. Small beds were surrounded by a neat box hedge, with conical, carefully clipped yew trees. We walked to a reed covered lake that had obviously been drained where three workmen were busy driving huge poles into the ground vertically. Whatever were they doing?

"We're going to put the lake on a platform of oak, *Madame,* to protect it from the surrounding marshes."

I must have misunderstood. A lake this size – impossible! "You mean…" I gestured helplessly, "you are going to put the lake on –"

"*Tout à fait*, exactly," he said, standing up and easing his back. "Look how the lake is being taken over by rushes. It needs containing."

"Yes, but on top of a platform... "

"*Ah oui*, Most of the buildings in the nearby marshes were built on a type of floating raft and though the lake looks big, it is in fact very shallow."

I tried to imagine houses built on a raft, but couldn't.

"Come back next year, *Madame,* and you'll see a beautiful lake."

"But not the raft." I laughed

"Naturally, it will be underneath, invisible. But this shallow water was designed to act as a mirror."

Certainly, it would provide a perfect reflection. We looked back at the château. Wide, double curved flights of steps led to the first floor with its lines of windows and the turrets. So exact. So charming.

"Wouldn't I like to live in one of these," enthused Brian.

"Next time you come, we'll have to visit it, presuming the renovations are finished," I said cheerfully.

CHAPTER 13

Drunk at Work? And Bon Appétit!

The first day back, after Christmas, I was amazed to see the students of my nine o'clock class walking in carrying four bottles of champagne and some kind of tart.

"*Bonjour, Gilly-Anne,* Happy New Year! Put three bottles in the fridge and we'll open this one," they said.

Whatever was going on? The students were taking over. After the usual greetings and enquiries about Christmas, they cut up the tart and passed it round, then poured the champagne.

The tart was called a *galette des rois,* flaky pastry with marzipan. These were made apparently in remembrance of the coming of the three kings. We sat there munching and sipping, discussing the New Year celebrations. Suddenly I bit on something hard and discreetly put up my hand to remove it from my mouth.

"Aha! She's got the *fève!*"

General excitement.

I had a tiny china figure in my hand, no bigger than the first joint of my little finger.

"That's the *fève,*" they explained, "it used to be a genuine broad bean, but now it's a china figure, often from the Christmas story." (Sure enough, I had the Virgin Mary, unmistakable in her blue dress.) "And the person who gets the *fève* has to provide the next *galette.*"

They looked at me gleefully, and I had the impression my getting the *fève* had been rigged. I was even more sure of this, when I found one in each of my slices, in each class, throughout the day, because they had all arrived with champagne and *gallettes des roi.*

Later I learned that the person who gets the *fève* is crowned and can choose a partner for the evening. Since it is up to this person to invite everyone to a *galette* party, when someone else will find the *fève,* the celebrations go on and on. The following year in our village we were going to two or three parties per week, for the four weeks of January. Perhaps part of the original idea was to distract people in the coldest month or to overcome the January blues. Whatever the reason, it makes this month a busy one socially.

On that first day of term, I emerged in the evening after six classes celebrating in this way, a little tipsy.

"Thought you went to *work*. Whatever have you been up to?" Bill asked.

"Celebrating the New Year."

He looked half unbelieving and half amused.

"*Galettes* and champagne, six bottles."

Now he did look surprised. "Six bottles? Of champagne? Surely sparkling wine?"

"Sparkling wine then – but champagne sounds better."

I flopped on the sofa and explained the custom.

To continue, I now was faced with the expense of buying sufficient *galettes* for each class, plus the wine or an alternative.

Bill's answer was simple. "Why be French? Why not give them English mince pies?"

"That's not the custom; what about the *fève*?"

"You've come home with enough *fèves* for every class. Put them in one mince pie in each batch, but mark it in some way so that you know which it is, and whatever you do don't eat it yourself. Forget the champagne, why not go down to the café bar on the ground floor for a coffee?"

"Brilliant idea, thank you, Bill."

My students were delighted with the English fare and reluctantly agreed English cooking wasn't so bad after all.

The school secretary laughed when she heard what I'd done. "They try it on every year if they can. They measure you up by how you respond, joining in or not. John (Anne's replacement) didn't, you did. But that was a neat idea to call the tune with your mince pies."

"But will it continue? When does it stop?"

"When the boss comes back. We've never had a week of it like this before."

Barbara had been away for the whole of the first week, having gone back to the States for Christmas and the New Year. When she returned I was given a stiff lecture that I should not socialise with the students, not in the school and certainly never outside. This seemed incredible, and I said so, pointing out that it was the students themselves that had initiated it.

"It doesn't matter what your opinion is. I'm the boss and my word counts."

This was the beginning of the end of our friendship.

I had a different kind of surprise in those first classes after Christmas. I thought I had by now begun to understand the French culture but obviously I hadn't.

"Did you have a good Christmas? What did you do?" I asked my students, expecting to hear about family gatherings, skiing and outings, but every single one replied in terms of food, what they had eaten and how they had cooked it. Recipes were shared and the lesson ran itself with little intervention from myself. I made a mental note, that if ever I ran out of material or was tired, all I would have to do would be to mention food and the class would take over. Obviously cooking is important, French people pride themselves on their culinary reputation, but also I realised that Christmas here is a family affair, so perhaps the students felt easier talking about food rather than anything else.

A typical Christmas dinner in this part of France, I learnt, starts with oysters, followed by *foie gras*, (made from the engorged liver of a goose or duck that has been force fed with maize) followed just as often by salmon as by some kind of poultry, salad, cheese and a Christmas log, a light sponge roll covered in a thick layer of butter cream and chocolate, although, because this is so rich, the new trend is to have the same shape in ice cream. These *buches de Noël,* as they are called, are very tempting and are beautifully decorated with small figures, reindeer or trees. There's no equivalent of Christmas pudding, and nowhere did we see any crackers that we would associate with an English Christmas dinner.

My students' response got us thinking why food is central to the traditional French way of life, because it certainly is. Everyone we've met jokes about English cooking and, often because they may have had a bad experience as a schoolchild in a family in Britain. Perhaps because the meal comes in so many courses, or perhaps simply because mealtimes are social occasions, meals take longer than in Britain, notably Sunday lunches, which can last from twelve thirty to three or even four, with plenty of chatting between courses. TV meals horrify our French friends, who ask when does the family talk, when do parents find out about their children's day at school, or their problems? We were also learning that it is nothing unusual for a French hostess to seat fourteen or even twenty round her table. We had wondered why in the antique and junk shops dinner services came with such a large number of plates, and this, obviously, must be the reason why.

One evening Françine, one of my colleagues, invited us to dinner. Her husband Guillaume was a local councillor and fully involved with environmental issues in their area. She had spent some time in England as an English teacher at a school in Rugby, so felt she knew quite a bit about English customs.

As a starter she served what she said was soup, but what looked to me when it was put on the table to be more like a pie, having a solid top. This, in fact, was a thick crust of bread over a rich broth with onions. "*Bon appétit.* Just a traditional onion soup," she said when she saw our faces.

"No, I never had a good onion soup in England. Even the soups there seemed different."

We started talking about the difference between French and English meals.

"I think the main difference is the way of eating a meal," Bill said. "A French meal consists of various courses."

"Of course. To get a balanced diet. Even in schools we have the same thing, starter, main course, salad and dessert," Françine interrupted.

"Even in schools?" This really surprised Bill.

"Of course."

"I suppose they're used to it." I was thinking of the regrettable change to snack meals in our school just before I left. "But we talk about a lot of courses, but they are relatively light. I mean, one can be just vegetables, which you tend to serve separately from the meat."

"You're wrong!" Françine was quick to correct me. "Of course we serve a vegetable with our meat or fish, either rice or potatoes."

"Ah, well, we don't count those as vegetables, so I was thinking of other vegetables, carrots, cabbage, leeks, Jerusalem artichokes, that sort of thing."

"Oh, you English," she laughed, "you're so pedantic! Anyway if by Jerusalem artichoke you mean those knobbly roots, we don't eat those because in the Occupation that was about all anyone could get. You'll find your neighbours feed those to the rabbits." She paused, turning to offer us more soup. "But in a way you're right. Heaping all your savouries on one plate, as you do in England, seems disastrous. You can't savour the tastes."

When we reached the cheese course, Françine returned to the subject. "That was something I never got used to in Britain - and perhaps I ought to say, that I did grow to like English food – but eating cheese after the dessert…."

Guillaume looked up in surprise. "Cheese after the dessert? *Quelle horreur!* But what about the wine? That would be totally illogical. The dessert requires a sweet wine, therefore the cheese course must follow the main course and continue with red wine." He toyed with his wineglass and sipped reflectively. "And you, Beel, you like your cheese after your sweet wine?"

"Not me. I like the French custom."

CHAPTER 14

A Dispute at Work

February, the time for the review of my pay. As Barbara had already told me she was delighted with my work and how pleased the students were, I had no hesitation in asking for the promised increase. To my surprise, she hedged. First she was too busy to discuss it, next it was the wrong time and finally she said she would only give me an increase if I signed another contract for a further year. This I was loath to do, partly on principle and partly because the situation seemed to be changing weekly. First there was the lecture I had been given about not socialising with the students and then Barbara was beginning to put an increasing amount of restraints in my way. The second reason was that my new colleague, replacing the vivacious Anne, was stodgy and completely lacking in humour, for example, his reaction to the *galettes* with *fèves* was to say what a stupid idea it was to put something hard into a *galette* because you could break a tooth, and that would result in a costly visit to the dentist.

However, I did not dismiss her offer out of hand as I liked the teaching and the students, but two things finalised my decision to say 'no thank you'.

One day Barbara, very much in her role as the boss, asked me to explain why my students laughed so much in my classes.

"I try to make my lessons fun."

"Fun? Learning English is not fun, it's serious. Less laughter please."

As Elske, my German colleague commented, "The honeymoon period is over; it doesn't last long. It's the same with every teacher. I survive because I'm here so little and because it's hard to find German teachers. Gilly-Anne, why don't you apply to the Ecole Supérieure de Commerce? I work there as well as here and I happen to know they are looking for an English teacher."

Four days later I went there for an interview. When I returned home I felt fazed.

"What's up?" Bill asked. "Didn't you get the job?"

"Yes and no. I've been offered a job alright, but it's not teaching English. They want me to teach Ethics in Business, a post-graduate course for international students, and advertising."

He stared, open-mouthed.

"They picked up on my MBA. They didn't seem to realise my MBA was linked to education, not business. They seemed keen."

"In French?"

"No-o, in English."

Bill thought for a moment then asked the inevitable question – salary?

"I'd get more than four times what I'm getting now."

Now he did stare in amazement. "So what's your hesitation?"

"I'm not sure if I can do it, if I'm up to it."

"Course you are. You could do anything if you put your mind to it." He seized my hand, looked at me lovingly and kissed it.

Advertising I could mug up, but Ethics in business intrigued me. Without committing myself, I began reading ethical case studies. The *Harvard Business Review* graced our coffee table. But my two children hooted with laughter at the idea of their impractical mother lecturing in a school of commerce.

I had been told that the level of English was such that all lecturing was done as though the students were English, and to get an idea of this level, I was invited to participate in the entrance interviews. It was hard work and I enjoyed both the challenge and the respect that I was shown. However, I was horrified when the organiser told me at the end of the afternoon that Barbara had sent a *huissier de justice,* a legal agent, down to see the director to complain of my being there.

"Pardon, *Madame*, but what does that mean?"

"It could be serious… Maybe it's in breach of your contract? Or maybe she just wants to scare you – you know her best and what the situation is. As far as we're concerned, the director isn't bothered."

I went home worrying about exactly what a *huissier de justice* was. I was amazed at Barbara having taken such a step. It seemed threatening. Bill took my hand comfortingly when he realised how alarmed I was at this turn of events.

"Don't worry about it. I've always said Barbara was insecure… this is an example."

I looked at him. I could not follow his train of thought.

"Look, you're a good teacher, at least I believe so, and probably she doesn't want to lose you. Just forget it. After all you've only got another term before you finish there."

I frowned. "Easier said than done."

I went to work the following day wondering how Barbara was going to react, but she stayed in her office and I had no contact with her. I, therefore, tried to put the whole matter out of my mind. However, two days later I received a registered letter which threatened me with having broken my contract and informing me that I belonged to the language school. It sent a cold shiver through me. Bill exploded.

"This is ridiculous. Well, that settles it. You don't want to carry on there, do you?"

"No-o. Probably not." I couldn't imagine working in a place with a hostile atmosphere.

"Well then."

"But what am I supposed to do?"

"Nothing."

But the atmosphere at work had changed. Barbara went around with a bitter face and one day I even found her listening at the classroom door. All trust between us seemed to have disappeared. I thought it best to try to talk things through, so plucked up my courage and went to her office. She remained seated behind her desk.

"Barbara," I started, "things aren't going well between us at the moment. Perhaps we could talk things through."

"There's nothing to talk through, as you put it. I find your behaviour disloyal."

I flushed. That was a strong word.

"And while we're at it, I want no more talk in this school of your personal life here. I've heard you chatting to the students about your house. That's to stop."

"But they ask how things are going!"

"I reiterate. I want nothing of your personal life in the classroom. You should be more professional. I've warned you before. This is a workplace, and you are not to socialise with the students in any way whatsoever."

I boiled with frustrations. But it seemed there was nothing I could say that would change her attitude, so turned to go. Nonetheless, I seethed with hurt at the injustice of her accusations and embarrassment at the conflict situation we'd reached. I also realised how unpleasant life could be at work in the future.

When Bill saw how upset I was, he said "This is getting ridiculous, *chérie*. I'm not having you coming home upset over your work. Pack it in – after all we're not put on earth solely to work, you know. We're here to enjoy life. In the long run, we can manage without your salary. The idea was that your teaching would be a stimulus, give you contacts with people and be something you enjoy. If not, well…"

"I can't just pack it in, as you say. I have to work through my contract," thinking at the same time that if I was unprofessional, as Barbara said, I wouldn't be concerned about this.

"As you like. Just don't let Barbara get you down."

It was a great pity that something I had enjoyed so much had gone so sour, but it clarified things. I accepted the job at the Ecole Supérieure.

I had the rest of the summer term at the language school to finish my contract, two months to prepare. The more case studies I read, the more fascinated I became. This was something I could enjoy and I set about creating a booklist and compiling a reference manual of the case studies I wanted to use. Bill began to complain that these days my head was always buried in a book, but I had become enthralled.

One afternoon, when I opened my book of case studies, I found a different bookmarker, a slip of paper with the following written on it:

What about the ethics of marriage?

I went hot and cold. Bill. I had not taken into account how he was feeling, had not even thought about it. I ran outside. There he was hoeing away at the bottom of the garden. I raced down calling, "Bill! Bill!"

"What's up? Something wrong?"

"Yes, very wrong. I'm sorry, *chéri*, I got so immersed..."

His face was changing from concern, to diffidence. He prodded the ground with his hoe, and muttered, "Oh, that..."

"Yes, 'that'. It's important Bill. My work shouldn't come between us, and I never meant it to."

He was still looking at the ground. "I'm not as intellectual as you,' he mumbled.

"I'm not as practical as you." I tried to make light of it, but realised he was more deeply hurt than I had imagined, so I added seriously, "I couldn't be doing what I am without your backing. Surely you realise that."

"It seemed to me I didn't matter to you anymore."

Now I was astonished. "However could you think that? I *need* you and I love you."

He looked up at last and saw my eyes. "That's alright then," he said, apparently non-committal. Then dropped his hoe and gave me enormous hug. "Because you mean *everything* to me."

CHAPTER 15

Village Life

Village life, we soon learned, is punctuated by the sound of a variety of horns. In our village there is a middle toned one for the baker's van, high for the fishmonger's and deep for the butcher's. Since Jacques and Louisette opposite us, rarely leave the village (and certainly not to go shopping) all of these stop right outside our gate. Each hoot is greeted by a frenzy of barking. Somehow, Pepito, their dog, knows which is the butcher, because long before he arrives, he barks in excited yaps and wriggles in ecstatic anticipation as the butcher frequently brings him a bone.

Jacques and Louisette have a house with a huge yard in front of it and a series of ramshackle barns that are bigger than their house and twice as high. These house the rabbits, usual in rural France where they provide a standard meal, with the cages stacked on top of one another containing perhaps a total of twenty, an enormous wood pile, a small dilapidated tractor and an old Citroën from the fifties with beautiful curves, covered by a carpet that had been gathering dust for years.

"Boy, wouldn't I like to renovate that." Bill's love of cars made him covet this antique and caused him to reminisce about his first car, a three wheeler BSA, 1932. According to him, he had driven all the way from his home in Edinburgh to his RAF base in Norfolk without any brakes, using the gears instead. I'd heard the story before but suggested it was just the thing to interest our neighbour Guy, who is mad on cars.

"You could even work out the vocabulary and practise it," I teased.

Next to the barn is the chicken house and beyond that a walled vegetable garden the size of a field. Every morning the chickens are let out to scratch the earth and every evening is marked by Louisette's 'Phew, Phew,' as she ushers them back with a long stick to lay their eggs, exactly like a goose-girl of story books.

One night a strong wind buffeted the house. Bill was concerned about our roof, which he had only recently finished, but before he could get out his ladder to check, he noticed Jacques struggling to place his against his barn. We stood mesmerised. We could see a sheet of corrugated iron had come adrift on the roof. Surely at nearly eighty, Jacques was not thinking of climbing up there? As he put his foot on the first rung, Bill shot across the road.

An hour later the sheet was refastened and they were both on terra firma, Jacques busy shaking Bill by the hand and Louisette trying to get him to accept some eggs.

That was how our friendship was sealed.

Next came the life stories. First it was Louisette, who collared me at the bottom of our garden. "I was sixteen, unmarried and with a baby. I didn't like living with my parents, so I looked around. I saw this farmer, with a lot of land, four children and no wife, and I said to myself, 'He'll do' and that was that. Yes, 'He'll do', I said to myself."

A few days later it was Jacques' turn. He wandered over when we were sitting in the evening sun and sat down. Bill offered him a glass of wine.

"*La patronne* is out so I can talk. I know she told you her life story, so let me tell you mine. I was happily married, you know, with four children and a lot of land. I had the farm on the other side of the village with the white shutters, do you know it? One morning my wife was working with me planting potatoes, that same evening she was dead." He paused. "She was pregnant, number five, you see. Didn't tell me, decided to get rid of it, went to the old woman in the village and that was that. Died of haemorrhaging. Nothing I could do."

Even after all these years, he was still obviously moved. We waited till he was ready to continue.

"But what was I to do then? Four young children and no wife. I hired a live-in maid, Louisette. And for some time it was fine. But I was a healthy young man, certainly not a monk, and she had the bedroom next to mine ... so what can you expect? And *voilà*, that's how it happened."

And what had happened were five more children. Jacques is now the grandfather of eighteen grandchildren.

Once the two stories were told, there were no further confidences. It was as though each had simply wanted to set the record straight.

They live a life close to the earth, virtually self-sufficient; anything you want to know about planting, Jacques has the answer. Their lives are governed by the seasons and *'la lune rousse'*. We are still not sure exactly what this is, but Louisette will wag her finger at us and say it is not planting weather because it is *la lune rousse*. She is full of sayings and proverbs like the best day for planting is Saint Catherine's Day, 25th November:

A la Sainte Catherine
Tout prend racine, (Catreen and raceen, rhyming.)

Frequently in the evening, Jacques will sit under his weeping willow tree, half-hidden under the curtain of green, playing his accordion. He used to play in a band, all over south-west France, but now only plays locally. He prefers to play sentimental songs from the fifties, such as "*La Vie en Rose*", which drift across to our garden.

As a well-loved figure in Chambon, Jacques is always referred to as Père Brumon, we are the only ones who call him Jacques. He refers to her as *'la patronne'* and she him as *'le chef'*. He is a real character. Whenever he sees us, he has a quip. He'll stand to attention and salute as we pass, or present arms with the broom or spade that he happens to be holding or he'll hold up his hand as though it were a mirror and comb what's left of his hair to it. As he wobbles off on his bike for his evening milk from the local dairy farm, he'll say 'I'm off to find a pretty girl in Rochefort', (approximately twenty kilometres away). He frequently asks if the girls in England are as cold as he's heard and he loves describing those entrancing coloured girls he met when he was in the army in Morocco.

Probably his way of life has not changed greatly since he was a youngster. Once every two months is feet washing time. Despite having a modern bathroom, he washes his feet in a tin bath outside the kitchen door.

Louisette is more down to earth. If you want to know anything about anybody, she knows it. The village busybody? Definitely, but without malice. Whereas Jacques is Père Brumon, she is not Mère Brumon. She is tolerated rather than liked. She is incredibly good-natured, to the extent that sometimes people take advantage of her, but occasionally her good-nature can be irritating. The following is a perfect example.

After having tried to dig another patch of our brick-hard garden, I had hurt my back and was supposed to rest. I was asleep in the *salon* one afternoon when Louisette arrived. Since we didn't yet have a proper front door, she had taken to just wandering in.

"Hello, Gilly-Anne. I had to come to see you."

I struggled awake. "Yes, Louisette, what is it?"

"I've come to say how important it is for you to rest and to sleep. Yes, to sleep," she said importantly.

I thought, but I was asleep until you woke me up. "Thank you. That's a good idea."

"When my Christophe had a problem. . ." She started a rambling, repetitive and somewhat incoherent account of when her son had strained his back at work.

"I think I'll sleep now."

"Yes, you do that." She went off nodding wisely.

It was not very long before we began to suspect that the afternoon siesta is drinking time, and by around five o'clock she is usually happily pickled.

The following morning she was back with another suggestion.

"Gilly-Anne, we have a faith healer in Chambon."

I wondered where this was leading.

"I'll ask him to call, shall I?"

"Call? Hey wait a minute, Louisette. I don't understand."

"The faith healer ... he'll cure your back. In 1982 he cured Madame Paton's backache, in '89 he helped Yvonne who lives down the road when she fell off her horse, in '91 it was my niece ...

It amazes me how the French remember dates. I think of 'two years ago', 'when the children were at junior school', in generalities, but unless something is corroborated by a date, it is as though it is not authentic. Louisette was continuing with her list.

"… and he can certainly help you."

"But who *is* he? And how does he work?"

"Who is he? Why Robert who lives in the house next to the post office. Don't you know him?"

"I don't think so," I began, but as usual, Louisette was in full flow.

"He lays his hands on the part with the problem. It works. I promise you."

After two days of pain, I was ready to try anything, even a faith healer. So I agreed to see him.

Robert was an unassuming man. He stood holding his flat cap in his two hands in front of him. He was slightly bald and had mild blue eyes.

"Louisette told me to come. I hear you have a bad back, yes? I can help, if you want. But if not, I'll go away again. I don't mind; it's up to you."

I decided in favour. I lay on my stomach as directed and he gently started fingering my back. The fingering changed to stroking which was relaxing. I was just at the point of thinking the stroking was venturing further and further into regions I had definitely *not* said had any pain, when I heard 'Cooee!'

My friend Yvette peered through the window, looked startled and hastily withdrew.

Robert equally hastily withdrew his straying hands and an embarrassed moment ensued before he muttered that he was sure that would help me feel better.

I called for Yvette to come in, introduced them and thanked Robert for his help.

"Hmm," she looked at me quizzically. "I didn't know a faith healer lived in your village … but then of course I don't know everyone," she added hastily.

I explained Louisette knew him and his reputation.

"I'm glad you get on well with your neighbours, but I've known Louisette a long time and – well, don't believe everything she tells you."

And was there a miracle cure? Not one I noticed.

One morning, as we were having breakfast, I noticed a new arrival next door, a large grey goose with a drop belly.

"Look, Bill, they've got a goose."

"So what?"

"It's simply standing there, in one spot."

"You're getting just like Louisette, curtain flapping. Don't be so nosy."

"I can't be a curtain flapper," I grinned, "we don't have any curtains. We have only just finished putting in the windows!"

By the end of the day, the goose was still in the same spot. But the following day it started following Jacques like a faithful dog.

When I saw Louisette I asked if it was for their Christmas dinner.

"Christmas, no. It's for my *rillettes*." (A type of rough pâté) "But not if Jacques gets too attached to it …Oh no, then I guess it'll have to join the menagerie," she sighed.

It appeared Jacques was the soft one of the two. One morning I met him wandering down the road with tears in his eyes. Concerned, I stopped him.

"What's the matter?"

"It's killing day today. Now we've got a young cockerel, it's the end of the old one. I won't hear it crow any more. I can't kill them, you know. S*he* does that, the rabbits, the chickens. I just keep out of the way until it's over."

And he carried on down the road.

Progress in our garden. Our neighbours were curious about our numerous soft fruit bushes we were planting. But for us they were a necessity because soft fruit, apart from strawberries, is always sold here in tiny punnets and is so expensive that one could not think of buying several kilos to make jam. As well as our vegetable plot and soft fruit, we had now planted a cherry, three apple and two pear trees. They were all very small but in my eyes our garden was thriving.

For me flowers are very important so I had planted, clumps of daffodils and narcissus in the grass at the bottom of the garden and red and yellow tulips in the bed outside the front of the house. Jacques came over one morning to admire them.

"But tell me, why do you plant them like that?" he said, lifting his cap and scratching his head.

"Like what?" Bill queried.

"In groups. We always plant ours in lines."

Bill and I looked at each other, but he was being perfectly serious. Bill shrugged. "Ask Gillian, she's in charge of planting."

"I like them like that. It looks more natural."

"Ah," he said thoughtfully. "*Les Anglais*… They're known for their gardens."

A few days later he arrived with some friends. "May I show them your garden? I like it so much."

"Feel free." I said surprised.

As he left, he said, "I'll tell *la patronne*. Next year we're planting our flowers in groups – no more lines."

CHAPTER 16

Such Experts!

The week Steve and his family arrived was the week of the worst weather we had ever had. Each morning we woke to a grey sky piled with ominous clouds. There was not even a glimmer from the sun: good working weather, as there was no temptation to go sightseeing, but nonetheless I felt somehow guilty, particularly having spoken so much about the glorious weather we'd been having. The grass became a soggy quagmire, the views of the sea we had hoped to show them were simply shades of grey water merging into a grey sky, nothing to inspire the use of the pastels that Steve had optimistically brought with him.

However, we greatly appreciated the speed with which things started to move. The new beams for what was to be the dining room and kitchen (the old barn and kitchen) went up in a rapidity I wouldn't have believed possible. Having put in thirteen of the fifteen beams, we realised with horror that the height of the beams was too low for the height of the kitchen window. It was such an obvious fact, but far too late now to take out all those that had already been cemented in place. The result? A change in ceiling level in the kitchen, which means the toilet we later installed above genuinely truly is a 'throne', as it sits on what is effectively a platform. Steve's expertise wasn't foolproof!

Jeanne, Guy's mother-in law, who was so often in their house that we had mistakenly thought she lived there, insisted we all came to lunch on Easter Sunday. And what a lunch! *Foie gras* and *rilletes, confit de canard* (preserved duck), cheese then hot grapefruit with raspberries inside topped with meringue as well as the ubiquitous *tarte aux pommes*. Steve got on with them immediately, his sense of humour helped where his vocabulary was lacking. Simple basic humour is understandable without many words and the jokes flowed with the wine.

The last cognac was finished at around five and we went back, supposedly to finish some work. We marched into the house confidently. Within five minutes Steve was sitting on the floor, cradling his sledge-hammer and singing cheerfully 'Old Macdonald Had a Farm' in a cracked voice, while Bill was slumped over the trestle table adding tiddly-poms and beating out a rhythm. We females looked at them: there was going to be no further work today. So we decided to take a walk down the road in a brief patch of sunshine, to admire the mass of cowslips growing all along the verges.

By the time Steve and Gloria left, we had our new beams installed, the floor of the utility room concreted and the walls there roughcast. Steve had also insisted we needed to dig out the floor of the *salon* so that it was lower. So out came the heavy, almost solid, earth and down went a layer of stone which had to be pounded to make it settle evenly. The renovation of the house had leapt forward and we couldn't thank them enough.

Every Saturday Guy and Bernard continued to turn up at eight o'clock, frequently with their cement mixer, to give *un coup de main.* However, Bill was determined to do things as far as possible for himself. His resourcefulness never failed to amaze me nor did his inventiveness. I arrived home one evening to find he had a slight cut over one eye.

"It's nothing. I was just lifting a beam into place and it fell on my head. That's all."

"A beam? Let me look. Anyway how could you possibly lift one into place single-handed. It took two of us to carry each inside, and they were heavy." I thought of the size, 10x10 and six metres long, good oak.

"There's always a ways and means if you can work it out."

"But how? Why didn't you wait and ask one of our neighbours? Or wait for me? *Chéri*, you're so *têtu* - so stubborn!"

"And have to wait for the weekend? Not likely. No, it was simple: I put two ladders, one on either side against each wall. I lifted the beam onto rung one on ladder A, then up to rung two on ladder B, and so on, until I got it into position."

I stared at him amazed. Part of me admired him for his ingenuity; the other part felt he was foolhardy for risking an accident. However, he looked so pleased with himself, like a dog that has fetched a ball for his master and is wagging its tail in anticipation of the praise it will receive, so I refrained from haranguing him.

After having reroofed the old part of the house where it had been leaking, one of the first things we had to tackle was the installation of our sceptic tank.

"This is absurd." Bill had come in from working and was sitting at the campervan table in his socks, studying the leaflet detailing the regulations. "We have to have three trenches fifteen metres long – that will cross the whole top garden. I don't believe it. How do houses in towns manage?"

"They're probably on a different system." I was busy cooking the supper.

"I don't believe every house here has fifteen metre trenches. What about Bernard? If *he* had, they'd end in our *salon*."

He went on grumbling and commenting as he read further. "Think I've got it," he finally said. "It's a question of how often it's emptied: with the trenches it's less often." Satisfied he looked up and added, "And how much you put in it – what about that house on the corner that empties its washing machine water into the road?"

"And the smell of drains."

"Even the most picturesque villages smell of drains."

"Not surprising, if household water is emptied onto the road."

Even the mammoth task of digging the pit and trenches, Bill decided to do himself and set to work with vigour. Each day he disappeared a little further in the pit until only his waist upwards was visible.

"*Salut*, Beel!" called Guy as he passed. "Digging your swimming pool?"

"No, my sceptic tank pit."

"You must be joking. You'll never go that deep. You'd better ask Gérard. He's got the machine to dig graves, so he could do it for you."

Having hit a layer of rock, Bill gave in and asked the said Gérard, who replied he could come, so long as no one died in the meantime and he had to dig a grave. No one did, so he turned up, as expected, with his spider like grave-digging machine and began excavating. The job, which should have taken a few days, became the saga of the mud. Just as Gérard started, the rain came, day after day, which created complications. Each morning Bill had to get into the trenches and shovel out the earth, which had slid in during the night before from the side. By the end of ten days the area looked like the battlefield of the Somme and Bill had developed muscles he never had before. Eventually the rain stopped and the mud dried out.

We connected the tank and laid the piping and lining fabric in the required manner. Then it was time to fill in the trenches again. Once more, hard shovelling. But here we hit a problem; there was more earth than would fit back where it had come from. And we were left with long mounds marking the lines of our trenches.

Jacques came up with a solution. "*Eh bien,* leave it with me," he said, tapping the side of his nose, "I know just the person to help you."

Two days later I was standing in the garden wondering whether to attempt some more digging of our brick earth, when a man on a scooter roared across and pulled up beside me.

"*Bonjour,* I'm Stephane," he said, shaking my hand, without getting off. "Jacques sent me. I hear you've got a problem."

He could have seen if he had looked around, but he was busy looking at me. I introduced myself and explained.

"I see," he glanced in the direction of the mounds. "I'll return with my tractor tomorrow."

"You'd better come in the afternoon if you can, because Bill won't be here in the morning."

"That doesn't matter. Will you be here?"

I nodded.

"Then I'll come in the morning."

He sat on his scooter chatting. He was between forty and forty-five, lively with an appreciative eye. As we talked, he absentmindedly revved his scooter from time to time but made no move to go. I found myself responding to his easy charm and humour: he made me laugh at jokes that in themselves were not that funny but suddenly seemed enormously so.

Bill emerged from the house and I introduced them.

"Must dash now," was Stephane's sudden response and he roared off.

"What was all that laughter about?" Bill stared at the receding scooter. "Who is he anyway? And why did he go the moment I appeared?"

"That's Stephane. He's coming with his tractor tomorrow to level the earth."

"Great. Just what we need. The afternoon I presume."

"No, the morning." I found myself beginning to blush.

Bill looked at me thoughtfully, before turning to go back inside.

The following day Stephane was business-like and had the earth rolled flat and had waved goodbye all in a matter of half an hour. Bill miraculously was able to change the time of his appointment and had decided to oversee the levelling.

One of my students, Martine, lived in the next village and was excited to find we were moving so close. She invited us over for *apéritifs* to meet her husband, Luc.

Although Martine's English was excellent, Luc's, wasn't, but he had a great sense of humour, so he and Bill quickly got on well. He lounged on a bean bag and they talked disjointedly about pop stars, our village and English food – suddenly hilarious subjects - with interventions from Martine or me when the conversation stuck through lack of vocabulary. From time to time he leant forward and drummed a rhythm on the coffee table unconsciously as he talked and I understood why some people called him Ringo. Their joking grew more adventurous then turned to our ruin of a house.

"Yes, a house with no water. We wash in the trough where the cows drink –"

"No!" Luc did not know whether or not to believe him.

"He's exaggerating. But it's true we have no water.' I added.

"Luc can fix that; he's a plumber."

"A plumber, eh? Then you'd better plumb our house."

Another crow of laughter. But they arranged it: Luc would do our plumbing.

We left them feeling they were likely to become good friends.

The following evening, when I got home from work, Bill said casually, "I was dancing on the roof today, singing while Luc danced on Bernard's and whistled an accompaniment." He said it as though it were an everyday occurrence.

"You what?"

He disappeared to the kitchen singing 'Hello, Dolly', which, I learnt, is Luc's favourite tune.

It appeared that Luc had been doing a job for Bernard, opposite, and had whistled across to Bill. Jacques told me afterwards they were like a couple of schoolboys, capering about on their respective roofs, singing their heads off, vying with each other with their antics.

CHAPTER 17

The Killing of the Pig

Up until now, we had been using what's called a working line for our electricty, but this could not be for ever. Following his English DIY book, his Bible these days, Bill took hours laying out our electrical system. At the end of the day he asked Bernard's opinion. He and Guy solemnly looked at the layout and then at each other. There was silence for a moment before Bernard spoke.

"*Non*, Beel, we don't do it like that in France, basically it's quite different. What's more, someone from the electricity board comes to check before they change your working line to a domestic line. So it's got to be right. But don't worry, I've got a friend who'll help you."

So we engaged, or so we thought, Henri to install our electricity. Henri's greatest feature was the Gauloise that stuck permanently to his bottom lip and wobbled up and down as he spoke. It was not that he smoked a lot. I don't think I ever saw him light it. He was big, round-faced, with a clipped moustache that seemed disproportionately small. When you asked him how he was, his standard reply was, "*Bof!*" with an accompanying gesture to show he did not know where he was with all the work he had got. He talked constantly, both to himself and to us, but as some of this was in patois, and the bit that wasn't, was mangled by his cigarette, he was difficult to understand.

We grew frustrated as we never knew when he was coming or for how long he would stay, sometimes it was two hours, sometimes only half an hour.

"This is an odd way of working," Bill grumbled.

However, the job was eventually finished. Now started the business of trying to pay him, which went on for several weeks. He would call, check everything was all right, have a drink and a chat, but would leave the moment money was mentioned. Finally, the day came when Bill sat him in a chair and said, "Henri, you're not leaving until you tell me how much I owe you."

Henri grumbled and talked of a thousand other things but not money. An hour later, after several glasses of Pineau, the local *apéritif*, he scribbled a figure on a scrap of paper and pushed it across the table. I saw Bill's eyebrows rise.

"But this barely covers the materials you used. What about your time?"

"Beel, we are friends," Henri mumbled, embarrassed. "I don't work to make money from friends. They help each other, and maybe one day you can help me."

So, it appeared we had not in fact been employing him. No wonder his work pattern was erratic. He had simply been fitting us in whenever he had the time, yet another example of the *'coup de main'*.

We decided to buy him a case of wine and some whisky, which by now we knew he liked, and to deliver it personally. But what a day we chose. As we bumped down the track to his house we sensed activity. Several cars were parked higgledy-piggledy outside and voices emerged from the garage. We knocked. No answer. So we opened the garage door cautiously, wondering why Henri was entertaining here. Dante's inferno. The whole of his double garage plus workshop was laid out with trestle tables and on each table was a part of a pig, cut into bits. Fortunately, the actual killing of the pig had taken place before we arrived. It looked like a charnel-house with the parts of the body laid out in rows. About six women were busy with some substance – perhaps better left unknown – in a bucket. The men, who had helped with the killing, were standing around talking, while Henri himself, Gauloise still hanging from his mouth, waggling as he talked, was chopping up a leg. I had never seen anything like it.

Henri put his chopper down, wiped his hands on his bloodstained apron. We were presented with a hairy wrist to shake and a beaming smile.

"*Mes amis,*" Henri cried, waving his hands expansively, "you are welcome. What would you like, chitterlings, a trotter, a cheek – or maybe some black pudding when it's made?" He turned proudly to everyone else. "These are my Scottish friends."

I took a step backwards at the thought of closer contact with these animal parts. I had been vegetarian before coming to France so disliked being reminded that meat was part of an animal. There was nothing worse in those first weeks than being drawn to a restaurant by the succulent smells emerging, restaurateurs saying they were happy to provide *madame* with a vegetarian dish, then being presented with a plate of carefully laid out vegetables, almost invariably two florets of cauliflower, four green beans a handful of peas and a few carrot rings

– all with no sauce and for which I paid the same as the rich, savoury dishes Bill ate. Obviously *madame* was on a very strict health diet! So I slid into trying those savoury dishes Bill was raving over, principles forgotten.

Bill explained to Henri why we had come, showed him the drink and handed him the envelope with our payment. While he still stood gazing in amazement, his wife, Babette, quietly relieved him of the money.

When Henri finally realised the crate was full of wine, and this and the whisky were a present for him, he immediately opened a bottle of wine and served it all round, liberally. Babette looked highly embarrassed at our gifts. She cut slices of the Bayonne type ham that was hanging up, already cured, insisting we tasted it.

I hesitated but Bill had no hesitation.

"*Superbe*," he said appreciatively, quietly helping himself to my slice as well.

After several rounds of wine, and much disjointed conversation, mangled as usual by the cigarette, Babette appeared with her arms full. She thrust into our hands one freshly plucked chicken, a jar of homemade hare pâté and some wrapped ham slices.

With many thanks, we staggered back to the car, clutching as much as we had brought, thinking, it's a good life, this of rural France.

Bill's reputation for flirting with the girls grew rapidly. It was not that anyone took his flirting seriously, probably they guessed he would have run a mile had they done so, but he couldn't help making appreciative comments or telling someone how attractive she was.

His attitude caused amusement. When first our friends dropped the usual kissing greeting, four perfunctory pecks on the cheeks, changing it to one, Bill asked why.

"Now we know you, Beel, we kiss you once," explained Martine. "It's the custom – four times for people you don't know so well, and one for good friends. You are a good friend, aren't you?"

"Yes, but I don't like this rule. Now we're good friends, I want to kiss you more, not less. It should be six or seven."

"But that's not the custom."

"But I like this kissing business. Why don't we change the custom?"

"Oh, Beel, you're crazy."

The girls played up to him. Didier's wife, Lysiane, was one of these, Lysiane with the wonderful eyes, trim figure and who, as Bill put it, sent a quiver up his loins every time he looked at her. She would brush past Bill almost close enough to touch, or stand sideways consciously showing off her figure, then turning with a teasing look to ask Bill a question. It was all very playful.

Luc decided to take advantage of April Fool's Day and set Bill up – except that his joke misfired. On the morning of April 1st, therefore, while I was at work, he phoned Bill.

"Beel? I have a message for you from a girl who wants to meet you. She wants me to give you her phone number and says please will you ring her this afternoon as it's her day off and her husband is working late."

"What? What's all that?"

Luc started again, but Bill interrupted him.

"Luc, I don't understand a thing you're saying. My French isn't good enough. You'll have to speak to Gillian when she comes home." And he hung up.

Later that evening he remembered the call.

"*Chérie*, Luc rang. Can you ring him back. I think someone wants to meet us, but I didn't understand what he was going on about."

I rang. "Luc? Bill says someone wants to meet us – is that right?"

"Heavens no! I'd set up this really good April Fool, but I'd forgotten that Beel wouldn't understand… and it was such a good joke … You see I had set it up so that he would ring Lysiane and she him. Good, no? What do you think would have happened?"

"You're impossible, Luc! Whatever will you think of next?"

He was still chuckling at the April Fool's joke he had thought up as he rang off. I put down the phone thoughtfully. Had Bill genuinely not understood? Or had that been a convenient way out of the situation?

CHAPTER 18

Wrangles at Work and Moving In

One morning when I was teaching the door was suddenly flung open and Barbara said curtly "Out."

Wondering what on earth could be wrong I joined her in the corridor.

"I have told you not to talk about your personal life."

"I haven't been," I said bewildered.

"Oh yes you have. I heard you talking about packing and moving house."

"Oh yes. But it was for Michel. He moved house on Saturday."

"Well, I am giving you warning."

I returned to the classroom highly embarrassed. As the students left Huguette whispered to me, "We are so sorry you are having problems. Don't worry. We all think you are a good teacher. And," she added smiling, "it's almost the end of term."

Barbara listening at the door. I had never experienced anything like this.

The promised warning arrived by post. Yet another recorded delivery letter reiterating the command to keep my personal and professional life separate.

"This is getting ridiculous," Bill said. "Pack it in now."

"No. I want to finish the term. It's not the students' fault."

He shrugged. "Up to you. I always told you she was insecure."

Barbara was waiting outside the classroom after every lesson that last week to make sure there was no fraternising. Little did she know that several classes had invited me for a farewell meal in a restaurant. But I couldn't help feeling regret that something that had started so well had ended so bitterly.

I looked forward to the last day of term so I could say goodbye, that I wouldn't be seeing her again. Well, that was what I thought.

Somehow our neighbours were all there the evening we moved in to Chambon. The furniture had been delivered from Britain on the Tuesday of my last week at the language school and I had come back to a stack of crates to be unpacked and a store of furniture covered in plastic sheeting, but to 'a home', or to be more precise, one room which was furnished, the *salon* To me it looked beautiful and spacious. Fleetingly I thought of Bill and Martine working side by side, nails in their mouths, banging the boards into place, while I had been relegated to yet more jointing, at which, they said I had become expert. Now with the three piece suite we'd bought at a local antique shop in place, it looked very French.

I'd hardly arrived when our neighbours burst through the doorway holding high a couple of bottles of sparkling wine. *"Bonjour! Bonjour!"*

Of course they were welcome: a moment such as this needed to be made into an occasion. So we toasted our neighbours, the house, the village and ourselves until we were light-headed.

When they finally left, calling *'à demain'* till tomorrow, Bill turned and ran towards me with his high-spirited clicking of heels in mid-air.

"*Chérie*, we're in! Our own house!"

Seizing me round the waist he waltzed me round and round our wonderful room until we collapsed on the newly installed sofa in giggles.

Finally we would be sleeping under our own roof, Bill's roof to be exact. Cooking would still have to be done for the time being in the camping car and the large *salon* would double as both living room and bedroom, but we joked about how romantic it would be to sleep watching the flames of the fire on cooler nights.

On our first morning, Bill leapt out of bed, threw open the shutters and sang out, in true Robin Williams style, 'Good morning Chambon!"

There was a further surprise from one of our neighbours: on our doorstep we found a freshly cut lettuce and a bunch of radishes.

A great marker in our life in the village was our big lunch party. Over the working months, our neighbours had invited us for Sunday lunch. This was in fact a mixed blessing as being in the country the men sat one end and the women the other, so Bill was without his interpreter and at this stage his French was rudimentary. Our neighbours' goodwill was therefore expressed by pouring extra wine into his glass and clapping him periodically on the back as a good guy, *"sympa, Beel"*. Effectively this stopped our work on the house on Sunday afternoons, because by the time we returned, Bill was both exhausted by so much non-stop French and by the wine. Long siestas were the result.

Now the time had come to repay our neighbours' hospitality and to thank them for all they had done to help. When I invited Bernard's wife she said, "So, you're going to *pendre la crémaillère.*"

"What does that mean?"

"You know the ratchet in the chimney you hang your pots on?"

"Ah yes. We actually have one in the chimney corner of our so-called kitchen."

"You do? That's *la crémaillère*, so literally it means you are ready to cook in your house."

"It'll be a while before we can do that. But you mean a house-warming. I like that phrase. I'll use it."

Which I did when inviting everyone else.

Bill and I also realised this was the first party we had given as a married couple.

"Should we cook something typically English?" he asked. "I mean, if you were still in Britain, what would you cook?"

"Curry," I said without hesitation.

"That's funny, so would I."

Bill is an excellent cook. Having managed hotels and restaurants, he was full of ideas and adored trying them out. One of the first surprises in our developing relationship was arriving at his house for the first time, him looking very serious and saying, "There's something I want to make clear (my heart had plummeted). I don't want you in my kitchen." (Imagine it. He had thought he was depriving me of a pleasure!) But on this occasion he was happy for me to help him cook, since there was so much to do. We had eight adults plus four teenagers, two children and ourselves. Between us, we created a variety of curries. My contribution was two vegetable curries while Bill's was two enormous chicken and prawn curries. His starter was melon boats, very professional looking and I made a large fruit salad for dessert. Our growing tastes in French cheeses showed in our choice displayed on a large tray.

We borrowed the Christmas lunch trestle table from Jacques, laid it out with a white cloth and small vases of wildflowers. Then we stood back. We were ready to welcome our guests.

One moment the house was empty, the next full of noise and people. After a lot of milling around and recounting the progress we had made, we eventually got them seated. We had decided we were going to avoid the usual men at one end, women at the other, but however much we guided them to a seat, somehow the usual pattern prevailed.

The meal seemed to go well, although I did hear Jacques ask Guy at one point where the meat was and I was surprised that a shrug was the only answer. There were many good-humoured jokes about *les Anglais*, the progress of our house and other people in the village. Around the cheese course, Julie, the six year old daughter of Guy and Odette, got bored and entertained us by climbing onto the bottom step of the hayloft ladder and reciting a poem and singing a song.

At the end of the meal, chairs were pushed back and everyone continued talking. No one showed any signs of leaving and I realised with horror that the usual custom was lunch, a short walk and then supper. We didn't have anything to offer them, so were most relieved when they, at length, started to leave.

The following weekend I was busy sorting out some of the boxes of things we had had shipped out from Britain, but which now appeared to be junk, when Julie arrived.

"*Maman* says to come. Now. *Tout de suite.*"

I got up. There must be some emergency.

On arriving, I saw her mother and grandmother busy at the kitchen table. No crisis. I was told to sit down and observe. Jeanne was making a cake. She instructed me how to weigh the flour, beat the eggs and so on, step by step.

"Now take the recipe, Julie's copied it out for you neatly, and if you have any problem, you can always ring me."

I was bewildered, but thanked her for her cookery lesson and returned home with the recipe. Hardly had I got indoors when Louisette arrived with a basket of baby cucumbers.

"For you, Gilly-Anne," she said happily. "Now just watch and I'll show you how to prepare them. Sit there and watch me."

As I watched her peeling and slicing, I realised either that our neighbours believed I could not cook, or else the peasant role of the woman in the kitchen the man outside was so firmly engrained that they could not understand why I allowed Bill in *my* kitchen.

However, they must have appreciated our culinary efforts because a month later, Bernard came over to see Bill one Friday evening.

"Beel, do you like eels?"

"Yes, I love them. Why?"

"Can you lend me a recipe? We've got eels but no recipe."

"No problem at all. I'll sort one out."

"*Superbe*. And would you like to join me and Guy for lunch tomorrow? The women will be out shopping, so it's just us."

A men only lunch? This was a new one. Bill happily accepted and put it out of his mind.

The following morning Bill was off to buy some timber. Around ten o'clock, Bernard and Guy arrived. They stood there exchanging the time of day pleasantly, but I noticed Bernard scuffing the ground with his foot.

"And Beel, where is he? He hasn't forgotten?"

"No, don't worry, he hasn't forgotten he's coming to lunch. He's gone to buy some timber, but he'll be back soon."

They looked at each other uneasily.

"*Mais*...It's not exactly that – you see..." Bernard tailed off.

"We want *him* to cook it," Guy finished.

"Well, basically it's like this," said Bernard. "We've been given these eels. Marie and Odette are at work all day and neither of them like them. So we thought of Beel."

So simple. Why not?

But when Bill came home, he explained that it wasn't simple at all as the eels were alive and in addition he had never cooked eels in his life. So it could be a problem, certainly an experiment.

"Not a problem, a challenge, *chéri*," I quoted his favourite saying, but quickly left the room before he could retaliate.

He told me later the scene in the kitchen was a crazy one as when he cut the eels into the right sized pieces, these continued jumping all over the table and floor and Bernard and Guy were ducking and diving for these slippery bits.

"Never again," he said with a shudder.

"But was it good?"

"It was delicious." And he made one of his favourite gestures of fingers to the lips and blowing a kiss to show just how tasty it was.

By mid-spring Bill had dug four beds ready for flowers. As he loved the rhythm of digging, there were more than I had expected. I had volunteered to be in charge of these while he was in charge of the vegetables.

"It'll cost us a fortune to stock all those," Bill said browsing through gardening catalogues.

I nearly said, perhaps he should have thought of that before digging so many, but thought better of it.

All our neighbours have big gardens, but they are devoted to vegetables. If there are any flowers there is a single line of gladioli. So we could not expect help in the form of cuttings from them.

"I know," I said brightly. "I'll ask my students, I'm sure I've got some keen gardeners in some of my classes. What a good thing I'm still at the language school and have got the contacts."

The unassuming Huguette from my advanced class invited us over to choose some plants from her garden.

"It's not the best time of year, but it'll help to get you started," she said.

We followed her directions which led us to a high wall and baronial gates. We hesitated. Yes, this was the right address. We turned in and there she was waving to us.

When we had gone through the usual formalities of greeting and introducing our respective husbands, she said, "First, Gilly-Anne, I'll show you round the garden and you can choose what you want and then we'll have a cup of tea, English style, I've even made some scones – they're really English, no?"

I looked around. Next to the house was an enormous outbuilding housing a boat on its trailer, a table tennis table and a large table with a stack of chairs for entertaining. At the end of all this was a tower with a pointed roof.

She saw me looking at it. "The pigeon house."

"Must have been a lot of pigeons," I commented.

"Two thousand. The amount of pigeons depended on how much land you owned, so the more land you had, the more pigeons."

"And the more pigeon pie," Bill said.

"Possibly, but the droppings were what was important, as they made an excellent fertiliser."

Impressed with our new knowledge, we followed her into a sheltered courtyard with flowerbeds all around. These were well-stocked and, as she pointed out, many of the herbaceous plants needed dividing. She asked her husband to get the wheelbarrow, and while we wandered along choosing the plants, the two men marked them, divided what wouldn't suffer and filled the barrow. The ones they had marked she said we could have in the autumn, the proper season.

We sat in the sun sipping tea, appreciating her scones, and feeling very grateful for her goodwill.

"I should like to think, that when my irises are flowering in your garden you'll think of me and your

English class," she smiled. "We have all enjoyed having you as our teacher this year."

That made me think about inviting some of the students from the language school to see the house they had heard so much about.

I put it to Bill. "Is the *salon* ready enough, do you think?"

"I reckon so. It's still not quite finished, but it looks good...Yes, why not?"

Bill partitioned off the other area of the house with a plastic wall so that the dust would not penetrate, and covered the newly concreted kitchen floor with flattened cardboard cartons so that there was a clear walkway through to the *salon*.

I put a huge vase of flowers in the fireplace and wished we had some curtains. Nonetheless I thought the room looked beautiful: the wood floor glowed, the doubled walls were covered in white wallpaper and the stone walls on the fireplace side I had so painstakingly jointed gave a rustic effect. It reflected our work superbly. It was with great pride, therefore, that we entertained fifteen students, including Huguette, who all complimented us on the house.

It was not until the following year that one of my new colleagues suddenly looked at me and said, "I've just clicked who you are. You're the one with the terrible house, the one with the plastic sheets for walls. My students have told me all about it."

So much for the admiration.

CHAPTER 19

The Tour de France – Well Almost

That summer the Tour de France cycle race caused great excitement in our village as it was passing through Marennes, about half an hour away. All our friends were planning to go and watch and were amazed that we weren't. However, the cult had not bitten us. Nonetheless, it's impossible to be in France and not realise how important the Tour de France is to most French people, who will travel many miles to see these cyclists flash past.

It occurs in early July and lasts about three weeks, covering almost 4,000 kilometres. The route, in twenty stages, goes around France and includes steep stretches first in the Pyrenees and then the Alps. Each year the route varies. It is not just for the French, cyclists of all nationalities enter, indeed it was won by an American for several years running. Every evening, television news covers the day's events and shows the winner of the famous yellow jersey, or *maillot jaune*, which is awarded according to timing. The overall winner of the race is the cyclist who completes all the stages in the lowest total time.

For me, not brought up with this culture, I am simply amazed there are not more serious accidents. On the television news we see a hundred or so cyclists, tearing round bends or down hills at around forty-five kilometres an hour, bunched up so close together, that if one falls, several must go over like pack of dominoes, yet accidents rarely happen. Crowds stand to cheer at the most exciting points, often downhill bends in the road, with no restraints other than self-control. One year a man stepped forward to photograph the lead cyclist, but had failed to anticipate his speed, and the cyclist crashed into him, falling from his bike. However, the cyclists are very professional, so when Lance Armstrong fell, the cyclist ranked as second, Jan Ullrich, waited for him to remount. Courtesy, or simply he didn't want to win as a result of such an unfortunate mishap?

Cycling clubs are popular. Every Sunday groups of cyclists, as many as twenty or thirty, set off early before it gets too hot, and whizz along the roads on their high-speed racing bicycles, in brightly coloured, matching Lycra outfits, each club with their own colours. Restaurants and bars at midday will have bikes outside and cyclists walking in awkwardly in the specially shaped cycling shoes. Many of the cycling groups are middle aged or retired people who devote their Sundays to this sport. Cyclists are respected, it is perhaps to the French what football is to the English, a topic for conversations and jokes. When we were cycling along the seafront with friends, a man called out to us, *"Vive le Tour de France!"* Even the bus I took to work when we lived in Chatelaillon, slowed down behind anyone on a bike until the road was wide enough to pass safely, none of the tooting to get out of the way I had experienced in England.

When we first met Albert, Martine's father, he asked Bill if he cycled. Bill said yes, he did. "*Alors,* you can come cycling with me. On my own I only go about eighty kilometres, but if you're keen, you can join our club."

Bill thought of his old Raleigh that had done him faithful service over thirty years, and felt he was not equipped to join in, so he made the excuse that, for the moment, he was too busy with the house.

Martine told us later that her father had had a bypass operation two years before and the specialist had recommended cycling as a recuperative exercise. At Albert's six month check-up, the surgeon had asked if he'd followed his recommendation. He had been taken aback to hear Albert regularly did eighty kilometres – not at all the gentle rides of sixteen to twenty he had intended.

One evening we were in a restaurant and got talking to some people at the table next to ours. The man, probably in his late thirties, said something about racing the following week in the *Tour de France.* Naturally I became interested.

"You're racing, *Monsieur*? You're in one of the teams?"

"I'm racing, but no, I'm not in a team, I'm not a professional. I'm just racing for the day, going from Limoges to Saint-Flour on Sunday, 87 kilometres."

Apparently, so long as you pass a medical test and pay the fee, serious cyclists can join for a day. Now I was intrigued, what time did they start and finish, and what did they do for a midday meal?

He laughed. "No lunch, just energy boosters and water. And we set off at 6.30am and cycle non-stop for twelve hours."

I regarded him with admiration. He must surely either be a fanatical cyclist or mad.

"Yes, I'm keen; you could say it's my passion. I've been a member of a club since I was seventeen."

Before the end of term, our friendly group of the famous fondue, had organised a day of cycling in July, with a picnic, on the Ile de Ré, which is one of the three islands in the bay of La Rochelle. (The Ile d'Oléron, connected by a bridge, and the Ile de Ré, connected by a toll bridge are the two largest, the Ile d'Aix is much smaller, there are no cars there and it can only be reached by boat. These islands take the brunt of the Atlantic weather, which is why the climate at La Rochelle is so mild.) We'd arranged to meet at the car park by the toll bridge.

We invited Anne to come too and within minutes of arriving and the usual greetings all round, everyone had lifted their bikes off the cars and we were ready to set off. Chattering like a flock of sparrows, as we had not seen each other for some while, we sped off. Not for long. The bridge is three kilometres long and the first half is, of course, uphill. It was some time since I'd done any serious cycling, but I was determined to keep up. However, my breath became short and I stopped chatting, just made monosyllabic grunts to Isabelle's steady flow. Bill, as usual, was ahead. Why did he always excel physically?

Pierre who was weaving between the front and those of us at the back, saw me looking enviously at Bill.

"You ask why is Beel so fast? Because there's no flat land in Scotland. Scots, they have to grow special muscles," he laughed.

Glancing down, the yachts passing below looked like toy boats. The bridge now swooped downward towards pine trees, with a curve of the bay to our right. Far ahead I could make out ruins of what appeared to be a church or monastery.

The cycle track took us inland, through gorse and pine trees that gave us welcome shade. The smell of resin hung heavy in the air and the heat shimmered off the track ahead of us. Small brown fritillary butterflies drifted from bush to bush of bright yellow broom. Then we crossed a road and dipped down to the first town, La Flotte. A deep rectangular harbour was flanked by tall houses on all sides, with their regular windows. Most of these are now cafés or bars.

"I think it's time for coffee," I called.

"So soon?" Bill said.

"Why not?" Anne said.

I was lucky that most of the group were not taking the cycling too seriously. We propped our bikes up and sat in the shade of umbrellas, drinking our coffee and catching up on news.

Cycling is not the best way to make real conversation. Now, despite good intentions, it was a mixture of English and French.

"This no good," Pierre said, pointing to his watch. "If we are to go right round the island, we must move, yes?"

"Hey! That's eighty two kilometres," Isabelle said.

Eighty two kilometres. I began to feel alarmed. I had thought we were having a gentle ride and a picnic. I should have remembered the French fanaticism for the sport.

Pierre looked round the group. "*D'accord,* okay, so we don't go round the island, but we must go as far as the bird reserve, at the far end. That's the most pretty part of the island."

"Prettiest," I couldn't help correcting. I must stop this, I said to myself, this is not the classroom.

"Why don't we divide into two groups, fast and slow, and meet up for our picnic?"

Good old Bill.

Pierre beamed approvingly. "We meet at the church in Ars. You can't miss it because the top of the steeple is black, to make marker for sailors."

With the details settled, the energetic group set off, heads down and bottoms in the air, while we moved off more sedately.

I was glad we had time to look around. We paused at a windmill, apparently still working as the sails were going round, at a field of donkeys that Isabelle insisted on photographing, and then cycled through row after row of vines, tight green grapes in firm bunches. Anne said the local wine was quite good.

Suddenly we were in a totally different area. We had passed a narrow neck of land joining the top half to the bottom half of the island and were now at the salt flats. Here earth banks surround rectangles of shallow water, roughly the size of a village hall. Anne explained that these flood at high tide. The sun heats the shallow water, which evaporates, leaving salt, which is then scraped to the side into small piles the shape of coolie hats.

"Is the salt actually sold?" I asked her.

"Oh yes. Have you never seen *fleur du sel* in the shops or in restaurants?"

"Bill puts that on his melon."

"It's the custom round here. But that salt is Ile de Ré salt. Originally it was everyday salt they produced here, now it's the speciality salt. In fact they're benefiting from all this whole food, healthy eating and all that."

We continued. At the edge of the salt flats were marshy pools and here I saw a flash of black and white. Intrigued, I stopped to peer at the overhanging reeds. Two black and white birds with a long curved beak. Delighted I signalled frantically to the others to hush and stop, then pointed them out, whispering reverently *avocets*.

They looked from me to the birds and smiled. "Yes, Gilly-Anne, avocets, but they're not the only ones here. We can assure you, you'll see others. These pools are teeming with crustaceans, perfect for birds. Come back in the autumn and you'll see the migrating geese."

Arriving at Ars, I was glad to get off my bike, aware of certain muscles that I did not usually use, only to find this was only the rendezvous point and we were going further on for our picnic. The fast group bragged of the speeds they'd done, how much further they'd cycled and wondered what had taken us so long.

"Well, Bill, we saw a pair of avocets. Did you?"

"What are they?"

I gave up.

"How far did you go?" Isabelle asked.

"To the *Phare des Baleines*," Pierre said.

"*Baleines?* Surely you don't get whales here?" I was astonished.

"They used to."

"There is the occasional one still. Don't you remember that one got stranded on the beach, oh, I don't know when, but I was still at school," Isabelle said. "My parents brought us to see it. It was enormous and really, it looked as though it were still alive, except of course it didn't move. The gulls were circling above it, but not one dared to approach it."

We picnicked overlooking a sandy beach, where gulls were squabbling over some debris at the water's edge and a few families sat under their umbrellas with two children playing in the waves. As we sprawled in the grass and shared our food, the braggers were forgiven. After lunch we played word guessing and miming games, laughing at our silliness, and greatly enjoying ourselves. Our energy ran out and we lay back in the grass, staring at the clouds floating above our heads.

Suddenly Pierre said, "Let's get going. We're going back through the villages and this is where you'll need you camera, Beel."

"Oh yes? Why's that? Are we passing something special?"

"Something special to the island," Anne assured him.

The first village: green shutters and rows of pink and maroon hollyhocks lining the streets. I'd seen this on postcards but had rather assumed it was a photographic spot. But no, all the houses had green shutters and hollyhocks taller than us lined every street. Bill spent so long taking photos, that I had time to break off some of the seed heads, thinking how nice it would be to have our garden lined with these stately flowers.

By the time we reached the town of Saint Martin, the main one and rather touristy, I said very firmly I was stopping in a café for a cup of tea and they could explore if they wished. In fact we all stopped at the café, though not all had tea.

"Several politicians have holiday homes on the island," Anne said.

"Here?" I asked, looking around at all the people.

"Far too touristy," Bill said. "Politicians and what not would want to get away from people, so I guess it would be somewhere more remote."

"Perhaps up near the bird reserve," I said.

"You're becoming obsessed with birds, *chérie*. Anyway it's all marshy there."

Isabelle said, "You're wrong, Beel. It's different, beautiful silver sand beaches and pine trees. It's a very chic area and lots of people from Paris have holiday homes there."

"But where is it then?" I asked puzzled.

"Further on from Ars, that bit of land that bends back on itself."

"We must come back, Bill, and explore that area."

After our drinks, we walked our bikes along the edge of the harbour. I was intrigued by the fact that the entrance led the unsuspecting, straight into the heart of the town – where a blank wall blocked further access, so any invaders would then be caught there, and fired on by the defenders. To actually reach the harbour, and manoeuvring space, the navigator has to turn the boat hard right on entering, down a channel, which is not immediately visible from the sea.

Leaving the town, I couldn't help noticing the fortifications, I'd have to look it up in my guidebook. (I discovered that Louis XIII needed to fortify an area that could protect his new dockyard at Rochefort, and so strengthened St Martin against, of course, the English.)

I found cycling back over the bridge hard going and as we reached the cars, I said, "Boy, am I going to ache tomorrow."

"Sixty-two kilometres, and you're not used to it..." Anne murmured sympathetically.

"Never mind awarding a *maillot jaune*, we'll have to award a special one to Gilly-Anne -"

"The green? Given for general points?"

"Well, not the white polka dot, that's for steep climbs and here is hardly the Pyrenees!"

"No, not the usual ones, a new one – for perseverance." Isabelle laughed.

When the laughter died down, Pierre said, more seriously "You're in training now, so next time we can go further."

"What about the Ile d'Aix next time?" Isabelle suggested.

"*Bof!* Not worth cycling it's so small. That's better for walking. No, d'Oléron is better for cycling."

"We can walk then. We're not all Tour de France enthusiasts." Isabelle was looking at me as she said this.

"Yes, we'll take the ferry to the Ile d'Aix, what do you think, Beel?"

"That sounds like a good idea."

As we drove home Bill said, "If we're going to take all this cycling seriously, we're going to have to get you a decent bike with gears."

"Definitely. Although I'm not too sure I want to take it too seriously."

THE SECOND YEAR

CHAPTER 20

Take a Deep Breath – I'm Lecturing

The Ecole Supérieure de Commerce is a modern building in the middle of the university complex. There is the state university, growing year by year, the Engineering School, (another private institution), and us. They had all been built on reclaimed land, that had been sheep fields only a few years before and was now a rapidly expanding university area, because, not only were there the teaching buildings, but the blocks of student flats, the best of which, those facing the sea, were let out to tourists in the summer.

As you come into the Ecole Supérieure de Commerce, or Sup de Co as it is familiarly called, you enter a huge entrance area dominated by a large computer screen, usually showing the logo, sometimes showing the catamarans belonging to the school, students at work or the twin towers of La Rochelle. Looking around, two things strike a visitor: first the number of computer kiosks, around which there are always students, and second an array of clocks telling the time in all the different cities round the world where our students go for one of their years of study, for example Beijing, Bilbao, Mexico City, New York, Hamburg and Newcastle. When I had worked there a while, I realised this was no chance. The director wanted to give an image of an up-to-date, international school. There was always an air of bustle and at changeover times it was like rush hour in the tube, with a crowd of students smoking outside the main door, since it was not allowed indoors.

One thing I had found disconcerting when I had interviewed for the position was the fact that the toilets were unisex, and to reach the women's toilet, you passed the men's urinals. On that day, I passed male candidates anxiously peeing, only to meet them a few minutes later in the formal interview setting. An odd sensation.

My introduction to life at Sup de Co was the beginning of year staff meeting, a far cry from the cosy lounging in arm-chairs in a school staffroom. It was held in the largest amphitheatre, capacity two hundred students, so we were ranked above the theatrical central space and computer screen, rather as Romans sat above their gladiators, but though our director was a fighter, this was of the verbal kind. He marched about as he talked, or stood rocking onto the balls of his feet, accompanied by computer images merging or being overlaid, one by another, in an effortless, sophisticated way, continuously emphasising the points he was making. He exhorted us to maintain standards, aim for the excellent because our objective was to move our school up the list of the prestigious *Grandes Ecoles*. The use of the internet by our students for their research was imperative. Indeed we ourselves should evaluate any new computer programmes that might serve as back up for our courses, because we must not only be at the front edge of our subject, but also of teaching methods. Students accepted at Sup de Co were of a high quality, our aim therefore must be to be rigorous, demanding and stimulating. Professionalism was the key to everything. He made every point with a gleeful look as though announcing ice-cream at a children's party. How such simple precepts could take an hour and a half to spell out, I don't know, but the French are past masters at making speeches. "And finally I want to talk to you about the new Masters Degrees we'll be introducing next year..." I wriggled gratefully on the narrow bench. "Finally..." but with our director I was to learn 'finally' is never the end. We sat through another twenty minutes of explanation and exhortations to rise and meet the challenge. Eventually we rose and filed out to find wine and canapés set out in the entrance hall, our reward for our patience.

My first lecturing day arrived. Steeped in ethical philosophy, and mindful of the director's homily, I turned over and over in my head what I was going to say. I walked into the building, holding my new briefcase tight with my overhead projector sheets and notes, trying to feel as professional as I hoped my appearance gave out. In fact I was extremely nervous. Apart from the language school, the last teaching I'd done was in a primary class and part of me felt I was a fraud to be addressing the eighty-four graduate students I would have in front of me in the amphitheatre. I arranged my notes in order and waited, stomach churning. Moments before the assigned time the students sauntered in, nodding a *bonjour* in my direction and filling the back rows first. As the custom is to shake hands with anyone you have not previously seen during the day, I wondered how long it would take with eighty four of them, but except for a few handshakes and greeting kisses, the rest had obviously met before arriving. Finally they were all in place, notepads out and pens in hand. I noticed a few placing their laptops carefully on the bench in front of them – this was the computer literate age group.

My turn.

With a deep breath I launched into the subject, the need for ethics in business. My voice came out higher than normal and I tried to breathe evenly. As I warmed up, I found myself walking up and down, dramatising and gesticulating on an aspect that particularly interested me and retreating to my overhead projector for the facts and philosophy that was driving us along. Before long the students knew when the interesting bits were coming and I could see them leaning forward for the next informal part, then returning to their assiduous note-taking as I retreated again.

In some ways I felt it was like a theatrical performance, I was delivering a monologue and they were a critical audience. Fortunately no-one got up to walk out, which I had been warned could happen. I kept my eye firmly on the clock, to make sure I paced myself and did not over-run. When I finally reached the end, my mouth was dry and my stomach hollow. They filed out, chattering amongst themselves, but without a word to me. How could I assess whether it had gone well or not? When I asked a colleague, the answer was simple, if they didn't like it they wouldn't turn up for the second lecture as they are not compulsory. If they think it's really bad, they'll go to the director, the same director that had been exhorting us to maintain high standards. I, therefore, turned up for my next lecture with a fluttering in my stomach and many anxious glances at the door, but to my relief, the amphitheatre was just as full.

"Are you enjoying it?" Bill asked, when I came home one day looking a bit harassed.

"I'm not sure enjoying is the right word. Basically yes. I like the stimulus, and most of the time it's fine. But I get the impression that the students don't feel it's relevant."

"I must admit when you said 'ethics in business' I immediately wondered if there *are* any."

"You see? That's precisely why there's a need for the course. But somehow I have to persuade *them* that it's important."

One of my lectures was on sexism at work. On this particular occasion I was working with a group of international students in a smaller amphitheatre, trying to explain that sexism is not always obvious, but can show itself in little ways such as when a man reads a report, everyone listens, but when a woman does, she is rarely accorded the same degree of attention. I could see they did not believe me.

"*Madame*, it might be so in Britain, but not in France," one girl assured me earnestly.

How could I get my message through?

Later, a Finnish student was describing an incident during her last work experience. That particular day, all the boys had grabbed the back benches and the girls were in front. As this student talked, the boys began to chat amongst themselves. She tailed off. The girls looked at each other, then at me, before swinging round to face the boys, silently.

Suddenly realising something was happening, they stopped talking and faced the front. They saw a sea of female faces staring at them accusingly.

"*Madame's* right," was all the girls said.

The boys looked embarrassed and fidgeted. But after that they treated the subject with a new respect.

After my first advertising lecture one of the secretaries was waiting at the door.

"*Madame,* your ex-boss is waiting for you. She insisted on staying. She says you've broken your contract."

"What?" I clutched my briefcase more tightly.

The secretary smiled. "If you don't want to see her-"

"No!"

"I suggest you don't go back to the staffroom."

When I told Bill he looked thoughtful. "Hm. It's that twenty-five kilometre clause…but you don't have to worry about that. Remember what the *notaire* said." He looked up with a cheeky grin. "Actually you could turn the tables and have her for harassment."

Unfortunately there were several more occasions when I got the message that Barbara was waiting for me and to avoid the staffroom.

There was an aspect of working at *Sup de Co* that I hadn't anticipated and I really enjoyed. Professional lunches were arranged once a week when local company directors, contacts who were necessary to the college to provide work experience places for students, were invited and we lecturers were asked to meet them and talk about our work. In fact we talked about topical subjects, travelling and any other subject of interest. I enjoyed these because of the variety of people I met, most of whom were very interesting. The meals themselves were excellent restaurant meals, elegantly served.

At one of my first lunches the main course was fish, a large platter of white seabass artistically surrounded by pink prawns. As it was passed down the table I noticed that most people took the fish and left the prawns. This was fine for me, as I had grown to love prawns and am less keen on fish, so I helped myself liberally to the former and took less of the latter.

Opposite me was a director of Rhone-Poulenc, who was interested in Scotland. We chatted amicably and then, finishing, I wiped my hands on my serviette and sat back. It was at this point that I noticed with embarrassment that everyone else was using a knife and fork to eat their prawns, whereas I had, as usual, used my fingers. I blushed and cringed inwardly. Hopefully, they would just presume it was because I was British.

When I got home, I asked Bill next time he went shopping to get some prawns so that I could practise with a knife and fork. I explained my embarrassment. "And ch*éri*, we'll have to stop the Good Life, we'll have to get a television. I can't join in conversations. I'm lost."

One of the things we had liked in our first year in France, was spending the evenings reading, listening to music, or Bill reading aloud while I sewed – back to the forties style. Now I was asking to step into the twentieth century.

Two days later Bill bought prawns. I quickly worked out the knack of holding down the shell with the fork while rolling out the prawn with the knife. As I became more adept, I felt proud of my achievement and felt confident about trying it out in company.

As it happened I was able to use my skill the following week when one of my ex-students from the Language School invited us to dinner.

She and her husband were rather a pretentious couple, once having spent most of the time we were with them for *apéritifs* discussing when it was appropriate to use *'tu'*, you singular and familiar, and when *'vous'*, either you singular formal or you plural, a vexed question for the unwary in France.

I got tired of this endless debate and said, "If I make a mistake with *'tu'* or *'vous'*, it really doesn't matter because people will only think it's because I'm British. So I'm not too bothered."

However, I could see from their expressions that I should not dismiss the question so lightly.

When our starter turned out to be prawns I wondered fleetingly how Bill would cope. I, the new expert, stabbed with my fork and rolled back the shell expertly with my knife. I accomplished it neatly and started on the second.

"Gilly-Anne, for goodness sake," my hostess cried, "Use your fingers. There's no need for a knife and fork."

When would I get it right?

CHAPTER 21

Rachel Springs a Surprise

In fact we didn't explore the Ile d'Oléron with our friendly students, but with my daughter Rachel and her boyfriend Brian. He was spending some time in London with her and they had rung suddenly to say they wanted to come for the weekend. From their voices I guessed there was something special about this visit, and I was right.

"We're going to get married," Rachel burst out almost as soon as they were through the door and they had our full attention. She was standing holding Brian's hand and at this point a beautiful, loving smile spread over his face and he folded her in his arms.

"But that's wonderful," I said rushing to embrace them.

"Calls for a celebration." Bill clapped Brian on the back and hugged Rachel. "But we haven't any champagne. Oh, you should have told us and we could have got some in."

"That was the whole point, we wanted to tell you in person."

"And we've brought the champagne." Brian produced a bottle out of his rucksack. "I'll put it in the fridge, shall I?"

"Try the freezer, it'll cool quicker, then we can celebrate."

Question followed question but they had no answers to any practical questions that parents ask, when, where, what type of wedding. Finally Rachel wailed, "Hey! We've only *just* decided to get married. That's a big enough step. We can think about everything else later. We're in no rush."

I asked where they were planning to live.

Rachel looked thoughtful. "Don't know. I'm not sure about living in the States –"

"And I don't want to live in Britain." Brian sounded definite about that.

"What about France?" I looked excitedly at Bill, but Rachel just gave me a quizzical look and shook her head.

"Actually... we were thinking about looking for jobs in Kenya."

That sounded logical, since that was where they had met, but I was already thinking how far away it was.

"Great," Bill said, "we'll come and visit you."

"We haven't actually decided yet," she said firmly.

When the excitement had cooled down, we discussed what they'd like to do during their visit.

"Cycle," Brian said immediately. "Can we hire bikes somewhere?"

"Easy, either at the Ile de Ré or d'Oléron. And we could go in Evita and stay the night. It'll be a bit of a squash, but what do you think?"

They agreed enthusiastically and so that was how we came to explore together the biggest of the three islands. Since it was a gloriously hot day, we headed for the sandy beaches, which we knew were perfect for surfing. They decided it was warm enough to bathe and we lost the two lovebirds in the water.

"Fancy it being hot enough in October," Rachel said when they finally emerged.

It may have been sunny, but I felt they both looked a bit shivery, so we set off back to Evita and something hot to drink. Then we drove up towards the far end where we found a lighthouse overlooking the rocks and that the land was wilder. Here we started cycling, along a coastal path near the edge of the cliffs. Stretching out into the water, there were stones arranged as walls in the shape of a flower petal. An information panel explained that at low tide these hold back the water and had been built as mini locks to catch fish.

We based ourselves at this far end, with excellent views back across the bay to the mainland with the Ile de Ré outlined in the distance and the solid oval block of the Fort Boyard in between. The young lovers disappeared on their bikes, and we smiled knowingly.

The evening was spent celebrating yet again with good Bordeaux wine. When we finally climbed into our respective beds there was a lot of joking about no hanky-panky, and that every sound could be heard by everyone in such a small camping car.

"It's not just us," Rachel protested. "You two are just as bad."

The following day, we spent cycling along tiny tracks that criss-crossed the marshes, wiggling our way through the small traditional villages, with the squat one story houses set higgledy-piggledy causing sharp right angled bends in the road, then back through the woods that skirt lovely sandy beaches. We stopped for a coffee in Saint Pierre one of the largest towns, although still small by mainland standards, in the centre of the island. We sat outside and, though it wasn't as sunny as the day before, it was still warm. The bar was in a bend of a pedestrian street set with small paving blocks, planted with plane trees, the leaves beginning to turn yellow, in a little oasis of quiet in the busy street. Even though it was a Sunday, there were many people wandering along window shopping. One shop that was open was a *patissier,* and we noticed how many people were holding the little cartons filled with the delicacies. Of course that made us decide we ought to sample them too. But what to choose? We finally chose a beautifully laid out apple tart (my favourite) *une réligieuse* – a nun, odd name for a choux pastry with cream and chocolate (a childhood favourite of Rachel), twists of pastry dotted with pips of chocolate, glazed and topped with large grains of sugar for Brian, and a luscious croissant oozing with almond paste topped with flaked almonds, which became a firm favourite with Bill. All finger-kissing scrumptious!

    Heading back towards the bridge, we decided to stop at Château d'Oléron, the main town. It grew up round the huge fort built to control the narrow straits between the island and mainland. We were keen to go round it, but found it was not open to the public. Instead we wandered round the grounds, marvelling at its size and solidity. Suddenly Bill swooped on something on the ground.

"Look," he crowed, "inkcaps! Shaggy inkcaps, just perfect for cooking. Come on, who's got a bag?"

No-one. We stared, fascinated by his excitement and saw a type of mushroom about twelve centimetres high, and looking a little like a furled umbrella, about ten or twelve of them.

"But we can't leave them! They're far too nice."

"I know, my headscarf, we could put them in that. They won't stain will they?"

"Oh, it'll wash out," Bill said airily.

Back home, as Bill was cooking them in butter with a touch of garlic, I heard Brian say to Rachel, "Is it safe? I mean aren't they poisonous?"

"I guess they know what they're doing. They seem to."

At that moment Bill said, as if to the frying pan, "Just perfect, it's only when they're exuding black that they're poisonous." Instinctively, I checked my headscarf. No, no black stains. So we were safe.

In fact we all agreed they were delicious.

The following morning Brian and Rachel left with assurances they would send frequent emails and keep in touch concerning any ideas for the wedding. But it was obvious they were in no rush to fix details

When they left, life seemed very flat, so the following weekend we set off in Evita to explore Cognac, approximately an hour to our south-west. We knew little about it except that it was the centre of the brandy-making business, had a river and the surrounding hillsides were covered in vines. We packed our walking boots and the maps, planning a hiking weekend.

We had parked on the Friday evening on the banks of the river Charente, and were just enjoying a leisurely breakfast, when a flourish on a trumpet interrupted us. All ideas of walking vanished with that imperious call. We peered out of the windows, but could see nobody, yet the trumpet sounded again. My curiosity was aroused: the only way to discover what was happening, was to find the player and ask.

The musician was one of a group of fifteen or so young men wearing white tee-shirts and jeans, wandering out of a car park, chatting and laughing, with many trumpetings and drum rolls.

"Excuse me, *Monsieur*, but are you playing somewhere today? Is there something on?"

"Most certainly. The *'fête des Vendanges'*, the grape picking festival." Tarantara! A high spirited blast, a little close for comfort. He continued, "This morning, we're playing in the streets, but this afternoon there's the carnival procession, and naturally we're performing in that."

Back to Evita. Finish breakfast. A quick tidy and off. Our spirits were high - we have always loved carnivals.

The first streets were deserted, not a soul, not a sound, let alone the music of a band. These were the steep, square-paved streets leading up from the river, past the old, impressive, merchant houses with blackened stones making them look a little sinister. (We learnt later that the black colour is the result of the evaporation of the alcohol and is called *'les pas d'anges'*, footprints of angels.) But on this occasion we were not interested in buildings nor in history. At the top of the slope we heard the 'oompahs'. Urging Bill on, I headed towards the sound. We saw the reflections of the bright brass in the shop windows. There was our band, followed by a small crowd. We caught up with them and tailed it into the square, humming along happily.

French bands, we had decided long ago, love the rhythm beaten out decisively with the brass bellowing above. Spirit lifting. This band was no exception.

They formed a circle in the central square and, with great enthusiasm proceeded from four-time to three-time, each piece being met with toe-tapping and applause. By now a crowd had gathered, parents with children in pushchairs, lads with Rastafarian locks, and older folk, all caught by the cheerful sounds rocketing around the square.

After ten minutes or so the band moved on and we wandered off in another direction. At one junction, we heard our original band 'oompahing' to our right, but approaching from the left was another with a different rhythm. It reminded me of the bull-running festival at Pamplona, where bands had paraded through the streets from all directions and at all times of day and night, even in the early hours of the morning, and when two bands thought nothing of playing from opposite sides of a square, the only acknowledgement of each other's presence being an increase in volume.

This new band was smartly dressed in cream satin shirts with full sleeves, laced at the neck, with well-pressed, black trousers and wine-red, long sashes. We followed alongside appreciatively. Noticing our enthusiastic comments, in English, the leader signalled to his group to change the tune. They swung into 'When the Saints ...' We clapped happily and he nodded to us over the top of his trumpet. We sang along, our voices totally, and probably fortunately, drowned by the volume of the brass and beat of the drum.

Eventually we left them to go to the market in search of bread, some prawns for me and the traditional oysters for Bill. At the *boulangerie* we could not resist a patisserie specially made for the festival, sweet pastry filled with cream, topped with grapes.

At the oyster stall we were deafened. Band number three was playing full volume in the half-empty covered-market. The colour of the trumpeter's face matched his wine-red anorak. Their enthusiasm reduced conversation to sign language, smiles and shrugs of the shoulder.

We retreated to the camping car to have a quiet lunch. But it was not as quiet as we had anticipated as the lining up area for the carnival floats was along the same street. As we ate and watched we made a running commentary.

"Just look at that enormous toadstool with butterflies."

"Looks like they're having a bit of trouble keeping them flying above it."

We watched as ladders were brought and the attaching wires were refastened.

"What is a Spanish toreador doing in a grape harvest festival?"

"Maybe someone wanted to dress up as a toreador," I suggested brightly.

"Thwarted ambition, perhaps."

"The closest he'll ever get to a bull-ring."

Most of the floats were connected with the grape harvest and country life, such as the enormous cornucopia spilling out hundreds of bunches of grapes, or rural life generally, a giant goose with her goslings and, typically, the snail so much loved by the Charentais. However some were fanciful – a Venetian masqued ball, Paris and dancers from *Le Moulin Rouge*, or the Viennese waltzers with their string quartet. As they lined up we could see those concerned giving a last twitch to a canopy or anxiously smoothing out a ruffled green grass carpet.

We chose a good vantage point a little way up from the river where the procession would have to turn right. In this way we would see them advancing, but certainly they would stop at the junction and perform whatever they were going to do before moving off up the hill.

The procession was lively. It started of course, with a band. A traditional group of grape pickers of yesteryear followed, with their children, pushing their barrows and bicycles, loaded with baskets, one with a goose. The men wore smocks and coloured neckerchiefs and the women long skirts, shawls and large bonnets. Another band. They were followed by the barrel runners, a group of young men, also in the traditional costume, who, with a twist of one hand and great agility, rolled their barrels swiftly in and out of the marching bands.

There were two showstoppers. The first were the Tahitian dancers. How the young girls moved their hips the way they did, I'm not sure, but the movement was fascinating as they swayed and rotated, and moved their arms in a sensuous manner. Immediately Bill was busy taking photos.

The second were the *Lanceurs de drapeaux,* or flag throwers, from Poitiers. They had almost missed the show, their coach arriving after the parade had started. It drew up with a screech on the bridge, right by the junction. We saw them tumbling out, still fastening buttons of their costume or twisting a string of pearls around their necks as they headed for their place in the procession. Immediately they went into their routine. They were a group of about ten, gentlemen and ladies, all dressed in the rich brocades of the fourteenth century, accompanying their flag throwers. These athletic young men carried enormous silk flags, about two metres square on poles a good four metres long, which they wove and twisted, periodically throwing them high in the air, catching them again deftly with one hand.

When the parade had passed, scattering its confetti and goodwill equally, Bill said, "Quick, let's follow. If we overtake them, we can see those Tahitian dancers again."

We were not the only ones, there was a flow of people walking faster than the procession and stopping at a suitable place, swelling the crowds and gazing once more at whatever had taken their fancy. In due course we reached the square, where the VIPs sat on their stand, the organiser announced each group in turn, and the crowd was so dense it was difficult to see.

But where was our friendly band of the morning? Gone were the white tee-shirts and jeans: they were replaced by scarlet satin shirts and neat black trousers. Every band had its uniform, one military-style with white peaked caps, and each preceded a float, the music from the previous band echoing down the street as the succeeding one arrived.

The last band of all was perhaps the most surprising, in puffed sleeves, turquoise jackets, cream hose and long suede boots, kettle drums at the knee.

"Wherever have *they* come from?" I said in surprise.

"They certainly don't look French," Bill commented.

Later, as the bands were dispersing, I asked one of them where they were from.

"From southern Germany," was the surprising reply.

"All that way? But why?"

"Is good," he explained. "We often come, *they* like *us* and *we* like coming. So they invite us."

CHAPTER 22

La Rochelle Unveiled

Every time Bill and I went to La Rochelle we discovered something intriguing. There was the house with a turret that leaned backwards, the house with the cat on the roof, hidden courtyards of cobbled stones and oleander, the pillory square, or the tiny château and impeccable gardens squeezed in between the usual tall, gabled houses. In the end I asked my students so many questions, that one of them brought me in her guidebook and said I could keep it for as long as I wanted. I took it home like a prize and told Bill we'd start exploring properly on Saturday, but I quickly discovered that, though he was keen to explore markets and curiosities, following a guidebook around a town, even one as fascinating as La Rochelle, was not something he enjoyed. I therefore dipped into my guidebook in the evenings and applied my knowledge as I shopped or during my lunch break.

There was a time when I had to cross the main square regularly and was intrigued by the local archaeological society's activities as they were unearthing the vestiges of a castle. They had been given six months to do so before the present underground car park was built. I paused each day to watch in fascination as first a series of walls, then a well, archways and the base of a chapel gradually appeared. But I couldn't understand why there would have been a castle there, as it wasn't a particularly high point of the town and neither was it anywhere near the harbour. I asked Victor, a barrister and local historian who was desperate to learn English and I had taken on as a private pupil. He was keen to answer my question, but the problem was he had only just started, so his vocabulary was limited. Nonetheless he explained that the castle had been English, and when it was built, it was at the entrance of the town. He saw my puzzled look.

"The *leetle* river in *zee* park, it was big, very big. Enough big for big ships to come to *zee* castle."

I thought of the little stream meandering through the park and wondered whether I should be correcting his English or the facts, until I remembered we had seen lock-gates at the mouth of this river, which obviously controlled the flow. Even so, the thought that ships of the eleventh and twelfth century had once sailed up this stream/river, took some imagination.

"I take you for a walk in La Rochelle. I show you *zee* history." Victor beamed at me.

One Sunday, we explored the town on our bikes. Going through the main streets was a bit hazardous as they were busy and very narrow, but moving outwards we discovered the flea market. In a maze of paved streets, tables are piled with objects for sale, ranging from semi antiques like old flat irons and curious bottles, to faded, sad looking etchings, cartons of musty books, collections of old tools and quite a lot of junk. Many things are simply spread out across the pavement. Several of the sellers looked a little like the etchings, faded, but others seemed to spend more time talking to other stall-holders than taking care of their goods. I was happy wandering along, pushing my bike and looking, but Bill, impatient to move on, tried to drag me away. Then I darted forward eagerly.

"Bill! The same knife and fork rests that my grandmother had. We *must* get them."

Silver, or maybe only silver plate but what did it matter, bars with a cross at each end which you put by your plate to rest your knife and fork on between courses. Eight of them and a large pair for the servers. I was so excited.

Bill immediately went into his haggling routine. He handled them, casually, as though he was not terribly interested, but maybe could be persuaded to buy them if the price were right.

"*Monsieur*, how much?"

"Fifty."

"Fifty euros? You must be joking."

"Forty." The vendor realised this was going to be a game, and threw himself into it. He picked one up, breathed on it and polished it on his sleeve and held it out. "Good silver."

"Ah, come, *Monsieur*…" Bill threw all the range of doubt into that phrase.

Another polish. "Good silver plate."

"Twenty."

"Twenty?" Scandalised. "I won't make any profit!"

Bill put down his piece and made to move away.

"Twenty-five."

"That's your best price?"

"My last price." A little swagger. The vendor had caught his fish again. But he did not know Bill.

"Pity. I would have given you twenty. Come on, *chérie*, we're wasting our time."

"Twenty-three."

"Twenty-two."

"Done!" The vendor smiled at Bill and began to wrap the pieces. "Got a polish, *Monsieur*? They'll come up beautiful you know."

"I have, yes."

The exchange of notes and package took place and I was handed my treasure. It gave me a great thrill of pleasure to envisage these on our table, a link with my grandmother, in our new home – when eventually it would be finished.

La Rochelle had German submarine pens and a bunker in the centre of the town; now open to the public. But this didn't attract us. We were discovering you can't go anywhere in France – or at least our corner of south-west France, without seeing signs such as the one we'd seen in Périgeux about the execution of Resistance members, sometimes in towns, sometimes in the middle of the countryside. We were walking on a limestone plateau one day, not far from Riberac, when we saw a curious line of posts. An information panel explained this was the demarcation line between Occupied and Unoccupied France and each post would have been painted in the German colours. What it meant was that villagers living on the other side of the line from the *boulangerie* had to show their pass each time they crossed to buy their daily baguette.

As late as 2015, a commemorative column of another execution was erected on a cliff by a German bunker, outside La Rochelle, with a panel describing the change from peaceful countryside to fear of German marching boots.

They don't want to forget, or they feel they ought to remember?

We learnt the war is a subject avoided. "How could we celebrate the fiftieth anniversary of the end of the war, like you British, when that would open up the rifts between collaborationists and non-collaborationists, which we have been carefully trying to patch over these last years," explained one of my friends.

It surprises us that feelings are still strong.

The day Victor took us on his tour, there was a gusty wind, so as we walked along the wall walk, towards the *Tour de la Lanterne*, we clutched our macs around us, and my hair was whipped across my face. Victor, now talking in French, said this rampart was part of the old fortifications. We certainly had a perfect view over the top of the wall out to sea. Approaching, he pointed out the crenellations and machicolations, as well as an octagonal tower with a glass covered lantern. He said this had originally been used to guide ships into the harbour, but with the building of the two lighthouses, one in the estuary and one onshore, it had become obsolete and so the tower had been used as a prison for English, Spanish and Dutch sailors over the centuries. Inside he showed us the prisoners' carvings, their ship, or dates or other mementos, on the walls.

No-one could live long near La Rochelle without hearing about THE SIEGE. When Victor realised I knew a little and was interested to know more, he said, "You really must come to a lecture about the siege. It's on Wednesday evening."

"Really? Oh, I'd love to, thanks."

"But why are you so fascinated?"

"Well, it must be one of the major parts of La Rochelle's history and I want to find out all about that."

"Sounds to me as though you're a glutton for punishment. But do come."

The lecturer had white hair, tied back in a ponytail, and an exuberant white moustache. He talked with his hands as much as his voice, producing his slides almost as a conjuring trick. Henri IV had protected the Protestants, but after his death they began to worry and had gathered together in La Rochelle. They rose against the king, Louis XIII, who retaliated and demanded their submission. They refused.

At this time, 1627, the town was surrounded by fortified walls on the land side, beyond which were treacherous bogs, and two towers and the sea on the other. However Richelieu, who was in charge of the siege, cut off their access to the sea by building a huge wall right across the entrance to the estuary. The townsfolk's hearts must have sunk. From a slide of an engraving at that time, it looked a little like Hadrian's Wall, with forts at regular intervals and it was this that prevented the English army Charles I had sent from helping, leaving it frustrated on the Ile de Ré. With the sea entrance blocked and an army camped round the walls, the town couldn't get any supplies. The town was truly locked in on itself. When it finally capitulated a year later, only 5,000 of the 28,000 inhabitants remained. It seems Richelieu took no reprisals against the townsfolk, perhaps believing they had suffered enough, but he did order the major part of the ramparts to be destroyed, hence the isolated gateways to the town Victor had shown us.

I left the lecture full of knowledge and dying to impart it to Bill.

CHAPTER 23

Bill's Brilliant Idea and Grandmother's Recipes

When I left the language school, I had had many requests from the Language school students, either to give individual lessons, which I didn't want to do in case Barbara caused trouble, or at least to keep in touch. Up until now I hadn't really seen a way to do this, then we had a brainwave, we created The Dining Club. Bill is a *'bon vivant'*: he loves eating out, so we dreamed up this scheme. The idea was that the Club enabled all those who wanted, to meet together to have a meal in a restaurant of our choice, speaking English for the entire evening. We organised everything and led or encouraged conversation, the only 'fee' being the cost of our meal. The majority of people came every month and it became a real social occasion. It was not just the ex-language school students who came. I also invited people I met through the professional lunches at Sup de Co and even our insurance agent, who spoke good English but felt she was getting rusty. Of course it also gave us an excellent reason to try out restaurants in La Rochelle, just to see, of course, if they were suitable venues! Our social life was growing, with one set of friends in La Rochelle and one set in Chambon.

One month Bill and I had a row, a rare event in our lives. He had talked to Josiane throughout the Dining Club meal, totally ignoring the other guests. Not only was I angry, I was also embarrassed.

"How could you devote the whole evening to one person? And Josiane!"

"I didn't really, did I?"

"You know you did! You recited the Rubáiyat of Omar of Khayyám. Alright, you find her attractive, but did you have to demonstrate this to everyone?"

He gave a funny little smile.

"And Lucille and Guy had come for the first time today. I bet they won't come again. Promise me you won't do that again."

"D'accord."

He actually seemed subdued. But I was not only annoyed, but disturbed.

Bill had met Celia, a young English *assistante* in a local *lycée*, at a wedding. She'd told him she was finding it hard to make friends, so, naturally, he invited her to join the Dining Club. This wedding had been a revelation for us. It was for some friends who had given every appearance of being already married, with two teenage daughters, but it seems it's a perfectly ordinary situation in France to live together for years and then get married. When I'd said to Isabelle the English tended to marry even though this frequently led to divorce, she'd replied with a twinkle in her eye, "Ah, Gilly-Anne, but is such a long and complicated procedure to get divorce in France."

Some weeks afterwards, Celia turned up on our doorstep with a lemon tree. It had two lemons on it and stood nearly a metre high.

"This is for you two, because you have transformed my social life."

"But there was no need to buy us something," I protested. "Really you shouldn't have. But thank you, thank you very much indeed."

"I wanted to, and I wanted to find something that you wouldn't have in England."

"Bill," I called, "it's Celia. Come and see what she's brought us."

Bill arrived, rubbing his earthy hands on his dungarees. "Hey! That's terrific. I've always fancied the idea of a lemon tree." But he too protested she shouldn't have bought us a present.

"It's to go on that new terrace you were telling me about, Bill."

So we gained a lemon tree, which we put on a trolley with wheels and wheeled out onto our terrace for the sun and brought it in every evening during the winter. We felt very proud talking of our *citrons* to the family in Britain. We loved boasting of the sunny climate and all things French.

Doing our 'research' for restaurants for the Dining Club, we found too many of the restaurants, unfortunately we think, serve much the same menu regardless of the region. We began looking for restaurants that served regional dishes and I found myself picking up local recipe books in the bookshops.

"Why don't we get a local recipe book, Bill, then we could try them out ourselves?"

"We could, but I'm really into Middle Eastern cooking at the moment. Anyway, it might spoil our pleasure of trying out the dishes in restaurants."

"Well, I might get one, just the same."

"Hey, wait a minute, what's this? A takeover in my kitchen? I'm not too keen on that; cooking is my hobby. And you like what I produce, don't you?"

"Of course."

When I found a recipe book entitled, *Recipes of Charente Maritime*, I was quickly disappointed. Ninety percent of them were fish recipes, only to be expected of a coastal area, but not something that enticed me to try my hand. I returned it to the shelf and decided to continue to enjoy Bill's cooking.

Yvette, Martine's mother, rang to say a good friend of hers was opening a restaurant with a difference and that she was organising a group of friends to go for a trial evening. Of course we accepted and the eighteen of us filled the restaurant. The would-be restaurateur, Fabien, welcomed us. He was a large man, with an enormous chest and stomach, covered by a, straining, striped apron. In a very deep voice he explained he was in fact an artist, but had always been fascinated by cooking, in particular traditional recipes.

"*Mes amis,* those of you who know me, know I am an artist. For several years we've had friends here most weekends who sampled my cooking. Now I've decided to do this as a business and so I'm opening this restaurant, but still only at weekends, that way I can continue to paint during the week. I'm calling it *Le Bateau Lavoir,* after the Montmarte *Bateau Lavoir,* a centre for artists, such as

Picasso and Modigliani. That way I retain my link to the world of artists.

Nouvelle cuisine is all very well, but I think it's a great pity that in the whole of Charente- Maritime, there is no restaurant that serves the sort of food my grandmother used to put on the table. She was someone who liked to marry *la terre et la mer* (the land and the sea*)*. Tonight I have prepared sixteen dishes, all her recipes, for you to sample, so that I can judge what would be popular. I trust you'll enjoy them."

Bill was some way down the table, next to Yvette, and not listening, so missed the vital point that there were sixteen dishes, which even for French meals, was many more than usual. I took a small spoonful each time, as did the others, but I noticed Bill helping himself liberally to each dish, and even having second helpings. Several times I tried to send him a warning signal, but couldn't catch his eye. We moved from hot oysters to gizzard salad, fish soup to cod pie, eel stew to snails (not for me thank you) followed by a strange spinach-based dish heavily flavoured with pork, brains (again not for me), sautéed chicken with oysters and boeuf bourguignon, after which I couldn't consider anything further, but the others continued.

Finally Fabien reappeared and said, "I have prepared one more main course dish to taste, before the cheese and dessert, it's *tripes Saint Jean d'Angély.* But can anyone eat any more?"

I heard my gourmand husband say cheerfully, "Tripe, my favourite. Yes, I'll try some."

He and one other were the only ones to do so, and according to him, it was the best of the lot. But as we eventually staggered out to the car, Bill complained of having eaten too much.

"Why didn't you stop me, or at least warn me?"

"I did try to warn you, but you were too busy chatting with Yvette. Anyway, if you'd been listening when Fabien explained . . ." I didn't finish, because at this point Bill leant heavily against the wall and asked if I'd mind bringing the car to him. He was too ill to walk any further.

Five years later, Fabien has trebled the size of his restaurant, and become so well-known, that he has appeared on radio and television as a specialist in the gastronomy of his region. I wonder if he still has time for his painting.

You could say we had become food orientated. I wouldn't say we'd got to the point of dreaming about food, but we did become increasingly fascinated by things to eat and by the fact that to a greater extent than in England, vegetables and fruit are still seasonal.

That autumn half term we went to the Dordogne - in Evita, of course. Here, in the flat river valley, acres and acres are planted with walnut trees. As well as for cooking, they are crushed for oil or made into an absolutely delicious liqueur. Any that are on the road or footpath are free for passers-by, so we stuffed our pockets full.

A woman passing on her bicycle, stopped and shrieked at us, "You! You're pinching our nuts!"

"I can assure you, *Madame*, we're only picking up what has fallen on the road," I replied politely.

"No, you're not. I know you. You were in the fields. You people think you can come here and help yourselves to our walnuts, but they're our crop, our livelihood."

"I assure you, *Madame*..." I repeated firmly.

She got back on her bike and wobbled off, still shouting about these people who steal walnuts. This rather spoiled our pleasure, and we didn't pick up any more. But having discovered the delight of picking up our own nuts, we began to look for, and recognise, the walnut trees around Chambon, as many old houses have one in their garden. And so our walks or cycle rides took on a new orientation. We rarely went out without a plastic bag in the hopes of collecting something.

In late November we were in Cahors, and called in on the market where there was an area like no other part of a market I had ever been to. Here there was none of the usual cheerful badinage, none of the exhorting of customers to buy the best. There was only quiet. Tables were laid out with something that was obviously part of a bird, either a rich yellow, white or a pinkish colour, each marked with a ticket stating its weight. To me it looked disgusting, and yet it had a fascination. Women stood behind, stout in their winter coats, with an apron over the top, eyeing potential customers.

"What are those things?" I asked Bill.

"The *foie gras* livers, from the geese."

I could see he was as fascinated as I was. We watched as people came close, bent over and peered at the shiny things, before discussing the price. From the comments we overheard, we gathered that the white was the most succulent.

At the side of the table was a stack of necks, carcasses, giblets and feet. French butchers do not hide the fact that their produce is from an animal carcass, but nowhere was it more blatant than here.

"Are they selling those, Bill?"

"Of course. They'll be made into soup. Nothing's wasted. The meat has been preserved in fat - you know the *confit* we have sometimes in restaurants."

No, nothing is wasted in France.

CHAPTER 24

Mushroom Crazy! And What Is a Picnic?

Our firm intention when leaving Britain was to immerse ourselves in the French culture. We had heard too many stories of groups of English who had recreated a mini-England in both Spain and in the Dordogne: we wanted to integrate as much as possible. Our first initiation was in the cult of mushrooming. Our visit to our friends in Arcachon had started us off, but now we decided to consider it more seriously.

First we needed to buy a good identification book. Even if we thought we had correctly identified something, Pierre had warned us never to eat anything that had not been checked by an expert.

Imagine walking into Boots the chemist in any High Street in an English town .... 'Good, afternoon. Could you identify my mushrooms, please?' 'What did you say?' 'Could you identify these mushrooms I've found, please?' 'You what?' Repeat the request. 'What those?' with a wrinkling of nose. 'You must be joking.' However chemist shops in France, during the autumn months, display charts and information posters and one of their jobs is exactly that, to check your identification of your mushrooms.

The first time we took our basketful into a busy chemist we were a little apprehensive. As we approached the counter, the manager's eyes lit up and he disengaged himself from the queue and came across.

"What have we here?"

"We're not sure, we're new to this, but we think we've got …" And I proceeded to reel off the names of three I thought I had identified.

"*Eh bien*, you've got three sorts alright – those to throw away, those good to eat and those you *can* eat but have no taste."

By this time, the other customers, forgetting their ailments, gathered round to add in their advice. We stood back as an elderly woman explained how best to cook the parasols, cut off the stalks and throw them away, then cook the heads in oil, preferably walnut oil. She was contradicted by an old man who queried throwing away the stalks when they were tasty and insisted that cooking them in oil you lost the flavour, and it was far better cook them in just butter with a little salt. "No," she said, "you toss them in butter right at the end and serve it with chopped parsley." The exchange continued for about ten minutes. We stood there fascinated: we had become bystanders.

A few days later we were trying out a new restaurant – for our Dining Club, of course. We both chose *mignon du porc au sauce de cèpes.* "Because," Bill said, "then we'll really know what these *cèpes* taste like."

Tiny slivers of succulent mushroom that melted in the mouth, a sauce so wonderful we couldn't help wiping our plates with our bread, even though we were in a restaurant.

"Now we know, we'll have to go *cèpe* hunting." Bill sat back with a satisfied smile.

By the end of our second season we had three reference books, one we'd bought and two given to us by friends who were amused at our interest. We'd also bought another freezer, just for the mushrooms. We were, by now, well and truly initiated into this cult. And cult it is. Anyone with a basket in the autumn is a mushroom hunter, and any mushroom hunter is willing to share his identification skills – but not the mushrooms or where to find them – with others. There are too many reports of deaths from eating the wrong mushroom for people not to be careful.

Despite this and the constant warnings on the radio, for us the bug had bitten and we returned for another visit to Pierre and Juliette's, who had now moved to the Lozère, an isolated part of the Massif Central, enthusiastic to do some more mushroom hunting with someone knowledgeable. Pierre treated our enthusiasm rather as that of wayward children and developed an infallible technique of classification.

"*Alors,* good to eat, good for the Broomes, and good only for the bin."

"What's this 'good for the Broomes'?" Bill queried.

"Well, *we* wouldn't eat it, but you want to try everything that's edible. So, go ahead then you can decide for yourselves. Therefore, I say again, good for the Broomes."

In this area the mushrooms were totally different. Most common were the various *russules,* reddish purple coloured, only some of which are edible and these fell into the 'good for the Broomes' category. We also found the *cèpes,* we'd tasted in the restaurant, a little slimy in texture but with a tasty, nutty flavour, and two others which are rarer and quite delicious, the *tête du nègre*, easy to tell how it got its name as it did look just like a negro's head, and a *morille* (morel in English) looking a little like an inverted cauliflower.

We returned feeling we had found treasures.

While sitting savouring our delicacies, Pierre told us an unforgettable story.

"*Ecoutez bien*, listen carefully. There was a young man in despair. He was madly in love, but his girlfriend had left him for another. He decided to commit suicide, so ate a mushroom called *cortinaire de rocou*. He felt no adverse reaction, but knew it was marked as deadly in the book. Some days later his girl-friend returned. He rushed to the doctor. It was now the sixth day after eating this mushroom. Too late. The effects were irrevocably destroying his kidneys and there was nothing the medical profession could do to reverse the process. On the eighth day, he died." Pierre had watched my reaction as he told this story, and he added, "So, be very, very careful."

A sad story but one we haven't forgotten.

Every October a group from the commune, our collection of villages, sets off for the pine woods near Royan, an hour to the south of us, on the coast. Here we disperse to spend the morning mushrooming. We return at mid-day with our collections, when Jean-Marc, our local expert, identifies each and lays them out on a large table for everyone to see. Descriptions state clearly whether or not it is edible and a skull and crossbones indicates the really dangerous ones. All ages join in this activity, fused by their interest in mushrooms. It is a popular event and is taken seriously.

With an *apéritif* in the hand, everyone checks his finds and discusses the harvest. Then the true social side starts.

This is the second aspect of French culture that we have learnt to enjoy. Having a picnic in France is not the same as it is in Britain. Here each family brings their table and these are laid end to end to make a banqueting table. And this is indeed what it turns out to be because each family brings almost enough to feed the whole group. Most is home-made – pâtés, pies, quiches, salads of all types, home-cured ham, cheeses and tarts galore. Each is passed round the table at which there are approximately twenty-five or thirty people.

At our first picnic, we had made our usual sandwiches and we could see surprised looks as we pulled out our sandwich box and a drink of water.

"Is that what the *Anglais* call a picnic?"

"Well, yes," I mumbled.

"Ah well, never mind, you're in France now, the land of good cooking." A pitying look and tone. "Try some of my home-made pâté."

These poor British ... "Hey! *Les anglais* haven't anything to eat!" Quiches, pâtés and salads were heaped onto plates and passed to us with commiserating smiles and beakers filled with someone's home-made wine placed in front of us.

The meal itself is a real social occasion, a good two hours being normal. While the adults take their time, the children play hide and seek or chase amongst the trees. Part of the pleasure of the communal picnic is the chat that buzzes round the table. This is never concerning politics, rarely the weather as from May to August good weather is normally certain, but is usually about the commune and friends. Often it is simple conversation and humour that arises out of the people having known each other since childhood. For me, who left home when I was a student, it seems strange for people in their fifties or sixties to talk about when they were at primary school together.

Banter dances up and down the table. "Why is Didier still eating peanuts when we're all on our cheese course?"

Didier pauses, peanut half way to his mouth, but before he can answer, someone quips, "It's because he's a teacher – can't stop talking!"

"And isn't it good that I've lots to say? Don't I keep you all amused?" was Didier's response. "I shall continue at my own pace, thank you." He gave a half bow and continued with his peanuts.

CHAPTER 25

Teaching and Elections

It wasn't long after I'd started at Sup de Co, that my boss told me the local *lycéé* was looking for a teacher for their European class. I was intrigued, so went to see the headmaster. The school was a beautiful, eighteenth century building, long and symmetrical with two wings and a formally laid out garden with neatly clipped box hedges in between. The headmaster was keen to persuade me to take the post. Apparently, all academic *lycéés* offer an extra class where either history or geography is taught in English, in the last two years. If I took the job, I would have the top level students of these years twice a week and it was up to me to arrange my programme with the relevant teachers.

He spent more time trying to compare what being a head of a school was like in Britain with his own situation. He envied me the freedom I'd had to appoint my own staff. Apparently French heads do not choose their staff, they are allocated centrally and once in place are virtually impossible to remove. He told me about a music teacher he had who'd been there for twenty years and was hopeless, but there was nothing he could do about it.

"I'm a manager. I have no influence over the teaching in this establishment, that's the role of the inspectors. I'm here to organise and to administer."

And, I thought, that is the way the role of a head-teacher was heading when I left Britain, which was one reason why I was happy to resign. He then surprised me by saying that it was not part of my job to deal with any discipline problems. There was a teacher whose responsibility was just that.

Needless to say, I accepted. Since they were studying the revolution in French history, I suggested I taught the Civil War period in English history, particularly as it was a period I knew reasonably well from having taught it at Primary level in Britain. (Primary to the equivalent of 'A' level, in one jump!) What it took me some time to realise was that these pupils were being asked to fit my classes in over and above all their others, so that they were either at eight in the morning or at lunch-time or last thing in the afternoon, ending at six. Quite an extra load for already overloaded pupils.

I found it hard to merge the teaching of facts with the practice of English and quickly found the pupils had no experience of discussing a subject in pairs, typical of English language teaching. Their attitude was to arrive, open the exercise books and spread out a variety of pens – underlining headings in colours is taught early on in French schools – and then wait. Once I had started they would dutifully scribble furiously, much preferring it if I put notes on the board for them to copy.

When I marked the first essay I set for homework I was pleased with the majority, but there were six, all belonging to boys who had not shown much enthusiasm in class, which were appalling. Returning them, I commented on how bad they were and how they would have to work harder. One boy, leant back in his chair and said, rather insolently, that it didn't matter since I wasn't a real teacher, only an English *assistante*. I assured him I was a regular teacher. I noticed alarmed looks being passed around this group of boys, but was not prepared for the complete change of attitude, when, at the end of the class, they lined up at my desk and politely asked if they could please redo their essay.

Marks are extremely important in French schooling: poor marks can mean repeating a year. For example, Bernard's youngest son, who was not very bright, had in fact repeated two different years at *collège,* lower secondary school. I noticed when I visited his school for an English day (a day of English visitors, English word games and an English lunch) that he towered above his classmates and his was the only voice in his class that had broken. French schooling does not have the same concern for a child's social welfare that an English school does, instead schools here concentrate on learning. In fact teachers only come into the school for the hours they teach, and the pupils arrive in school for their first class at whatever time of the morning that might be; there is not the idea of the pupils being delivered into the care of the school for the day. Perhaps it is because teachers are not required to be present throughout the school day that they do not get involved with their pupils out of class, as so many committed English teachers do. There do not seem to be the after school clubs that are so typical of a successful, community minded, secondary school in England. On the other hand, the majority of teachers seem to be respected for their professionalism, which, I think, is missing now in England.

This got me thinking about other ways French schooling differs from English. Perhaps the most remarkable is that children start as early as two years (although I believe this is about to change to three) in the equivalent of a nursery school. When I said to one of my friends that I thought that was a bit young, she looked amazed.

"My daughter started *école maternelle* three days after her second birthday. The *école maternelle* is great. Kids learn to socialise, to develop all sorts of skills of arts and imagination, which is really important as unfortunately this is discontinued as they move on to the primary school and learning becomes more academic."

"But at two," I protested, "isn't it a bit of a long day?"

"8.45 to 11.30, with a break mid-morning? I don't think that's too long. And in the afternoon they finish at 4.30, but the youngest ones sleep after lunch and just have an hour's class afterwards."

I kept quiet. It obviously depended on what you were used to, and having campaigned for so many years in England for nursery schooling for all, could I really object to a system that was providing it?

School days in France are longer, eight till five or six. Until very recently there was no school on Wednesdays. At the *lycée,* Wednesday was a half day, and there was school on Saturday mornings. The government is currently revising school hours, with outcries from parents at possible changes. For the last three years of secondary schooling pupils choose between the type of *lycéé* that is appropriate for them and their future career, a little like the grammar and technical school situation that used to exist in England.

On my way to the language school one day, I'd drawn up at traffic lights, surprised to see a white rabbit with floppy pink ears, a Mickey Mouse and a belly dancer milling around accosting drivers. A youngster with a beard, but wearing a white tutu thrust his head through my window, greeting me with a cheerful smile. Since they were asking drivers for money I presumed it was some kind of rag event, so asked what the charity was, only to find the money was for themselves, to celebrate for the last time before giving themselves up to serious study during the one hundred days left before their exams. Were they serious? Apparently so. When I arrived, I told the secretary what I had just seen and asked if it was usual. She told me it was a custom in this area, but not everywhere in France. But, she said firmly, they really do have to work hard to get their *bac.* No going out, no discos, no lounging around in cafés, just slog. For *le bacalauréat,* pupils have to pass in all their subjects, there is no choosing individual subjects as in England, and so it does create a tremendous strain, which is reported regularly on television news.

One day, when chatting with Martine, I had casually referred to France as a Catholic country. After all, as a tourist, I'd seen panels announcing the times of mass outside each village and crucifixes everywhere in the country. She ticked me off tartly, retorting that France was not Catholic, it was lay. So when discussing French and English systems of education, I was reluctant to mention the role of religion. But one day, one of my colleagues, the one who'd spent a year in an English comprehensive at Rugby, spoke of this crazy custom of singing hymns and saying prayers first thing in the morning. Cries of 'no!' and 'it's not possible' greeted this information and I had to explain that not only are there some form of assemblies, but religion, albeit nowadays religions, plural, because of the varied cultures, is taught throughout all schools. In France, if parents wish their children to study religion, this is done either outside school, which is the original reason why there is no school on a Wednesday, or parents can choose a Catholic school.

Once my year at the *lycée* was finished, and having decided I preferred teaching university students, I took a job teaching English at the science faculty of the university. (All these jobs were a few hours per week.) The system functions differently from in England, in that all students who have passed their *'baccalauréat'* are guaranteed a place at university, usually their local one. There is none of the browsing through brochures and choosing a university for a particular course it offers, let alone choosing one away from home, as in England, unless choosing a private *école supérieure*. As we assembled for the pre-term staff meeting, I realised what a problem this system causes. When I asked how many classes there would be, I was told there was no way of knowing yet, since it depended on how many students turned up.

All students in France, regardless of what they are studying, have to not only study English, but to pass its end of year exam. I found that if they failed, they could have to repeat the academic year. This is all part of the recognition that English is the universal language for business.

After the almost aggressive reaction of the students at Sup de Co, I was disappointed to find the students at the science faculty were passive learners. They sat dutifully ready, pen in hand to write down the information the teacher wrote on the board, but, once again, interactive learning was something new to the majority of them. I emerged from my first session moaning, "It's just like school for them." My other English colleague was quick to agree, but our French colleague looked up in surprise.

"Well, what's the problem with the French schools then?"

Oops, I'd only just started and seemed to have put my foot in it without thinking. I had better go carefully here. "Well, the pupils seem overworked and, er, rather teacher dependant."

"What do you mean by that?"

"Erm, there doesn't seem an awful lot of encouragement to think for themselves. It's more a case of learning, or rather remembering, what they have been taught."

"I totally disagree with you. Teachers do encourage pupils to think for themselves, but most pupils find it easier to repeat what the teacher said. Just because you haven't seen good teaching, doesn't mean it doesn't exist. For example..."

For the next few minutes she elaborated on examples of creative teaching that had taken place in the *lycée* where she used to teach. I felt humbled. From my limited viewpoint, I had made judgements as though this was typical. How could I have done? And yet, this was definitely the impression I had got, not just from what I had seen, but from what I had heard both from students and from teachers themselves complaining about the system.

"Of course," she finished, "not every teacher is a good teacher. There are always the others."

And wouldn't I have risen to the defence of the English system, and cited the best examples too?

Later in the year, the head of department at Sup de Co phoned to ask if I would be interested in a course teaching the undergraduates for the following year. This involved the basics of government, education, welfare and the legal systems in Britain as a preparation for the students who spend at least one, if not two, years at an English university.

"Good heavens! I don't think I could do that!"

"Of course you can. You're English, so you already know it all. Just remember all that our students need to know is enough to understand the systems when they're in England – give them enough background to be able to follow the news."

Put like that it seemed simple enough, but I found it surprising how inexact my knowledge was. I would have to do some research. In fact the more I learned about the British systems, the more I wanted to know about the French.

Election time gave me the perfect opportunity to begin. What a complex process. We found it hard to absorb all the names of the different parties, all in acronyms, to make sense of the daily news we watched so assiduously on television. I asked Anne to write out a list so that I would understand which were to the right and which to the left, then we would sit there list in hand trying to fix the position of each party. Victor tried to explain the differences between the parties. As he was a socialist, I learnt more from him about the parties to the left. He struggled with his beginner's vocabulary, through all the political vocabulary, determined to complete what he wanted to say. He finished by saying, "In France we have a custom, we go from the left to the right, and then to the left, like the thing that moves in a big clock, what you call it? Ah, a pendulum. And that way we have balance."

As British citizens we were unable to vote, we could only follow the proceedings, although since our arrival the law has changed and now foreign residents can vote at the local elections, but only the local ones. I was surprised how strong the National Front was, the extreme right party, being particularly popular in the east of France.

The local elections are the first round of the national elections, and were of more personal interest to us. The position of mayor in France is an important one as he, with his council, wields considerable power. When talking politics, people tend to talk about local politics, not national, perhaps because the national government is reported less widely than in Britain.

To our surprise, in local elections of small communes, people do not vote for candidates individually, but for a team and we had two of these. There was the obvious one, the deputy mayor and a team of well-established, middle-aged councillors. To our surprise we discovered that our friend Stephane with the sparkling eyes, was someone of importance, being in fact the current deputy mayor. The opposition was a team of our friends from the *foyer*, a much younger, untried, group of idealists, led by the bombastic Didier, the teacher, and Martine. We had always known she was idealistic, dashing up to Paris to demonstrate for better educational facilities, and demonstrating in La Rochelle against a proposed motorway on behalf of an environmental group. We had not, however, envisaged her as becoming involved in local politics. We now had an interest in both camps and tried to view things objectively. As the date came nearer, so the political rivalry grew.

The slogan of Didier's group was *'Progressons Ensemble'*. Let's move forward together. The first 'progressive' thing they did was to deliver an information sheet of paper with the photos of each of the team and a statement of their aims. This type of manifesto might be common in England, but apparently is not, in this particular corner of France. Stephane's group, not to be outdone, managed to reciprocate, and delivered a similar one the morning before voting day, which is always a Sunday.

"Well, that puts them in the lead," summed up Bill. "People will remember the last one they read when they vote tomorrow. A pity Didier's lot didn't leave it till later because then the others wouldn't have had time to copy his idea."

Almost inevitably, Stephane's group, the known and tried, won the election. But the feelings brought to the surface in the last few days was an introduction to the schisms in our apparently peaceful village.

After the local elections came the rounds of national elections. Having tried so hard to follow the campaigns I wanted to see how the process actually worked. I offered to drive Jacques and Louisette to the voting station, which was the *mairie*, but to my surprise they said they weren't voting.

"Local, yes, of course we vote, it concerns us, but national. . ." Jacques shrugged, "*Bof,* how does that concern us?"

So I asked Bernard and Marie if I could go with them. On arriving the person has to show their identity card. Even though everyone knows everyone else in our village, this is a procedure which has to be applied. Then they are handed a small envelope. On a table are piles of leaflets from all the parties. To my surprise, Bernard hummed and hawed over which to pick up, picked up five or six and disappeared into the voting booth. To my surprise Marie did the same. I saw a pile of leaflets dropped into the waste paper bin and then they both emerged clutching their envelope, now sealed and containing the leaflet of their choice, which they dropped through the slot of a large Perspex box. They then signed to say they had voted and turned, ready to go home. When I asked them why they'd picked up so many leaflets, was it because they hadn't made up their mind, they replied not at all, it was so that their choice was private, no-one could work out who they had voted for. "It's always like that," Bernard said simply. I couldn't help thinking if everyone did the same, what an awful lot of waste paper it created, but at the same time I couldn't help admiring the simplicity of the system, there could be no spoiled voting papers here nor misunderstandings.

CHAPTER 26

Joining In

Now that we had moved into our house, and the first frenzy of renovation was easing, it was time to see what went on in Chambon. Martine, my ex-student who spoke English well, had talked a lot about all the activities of the *foyer*, a type of social club. Now she decided it was time for us to join in.

"There's gym on a Monday, computers for children on a Tuesday, Badminton on a Wednesday, computers for adults on a Thursday and then there's the car rally, the cycle rally, mushrooming and socials."

"When do you have time to be at home?" Bill joked.

"Sounds excellent, we'll join." I added.

That was her first step accomplished. For us it opened a new social life, through which we made many friends. Martine's next step was to persuade us to come to the AGM.

This was held in the village hall or *salle des fêtes*. (And that name sums up the French attitude, a 'room for celebrations', they seem to us to be a nation that loves finding any excuse to celebrate.) Approximately twenty-five people were sitting in a semi-circle with the president, treasurer and secretary, Martine, at a table facing them. That and the order of the agenda was the only thing in common with any AGM I had ever attended in Britain. Here everyone talked at once. Even the reading of the annual report was constantly interrupted.

"Do you remember that was when little Pierre fell in the river?" one said.

"And what a scream he looked wearing his Dad's sweater which came down to his ankles!"

This was only a business meeting in name: it was in fact a social occasion at which somehow or other they ambled through the agenda.

"And I've got an idea for next year's outing – *une vacance*. Clisson, in Brittany, for three days, staying at the *Maison Familiale*. It's right on the river, we'll organise canoeing, mountain biking and horse-riding, as well as visiting the town and castle," a fat, jolly lady announced.

A holiday. This was news indeed. I discovered that from time to time, the *foyer* organised a three-day weekend at the incredible price of roughly ten pounds per person. Subsidising meant that no-one in the commune would be left out.

Next was the election of the new committee members. Martine mouthed across to me, "What about you, Gilly-Anne?"

"No, no," I mouthed back hastily. "Perhaps another year."

The next thing I heard was, "And our new friend Gilly-Anne is willing to stand."

Before I could protest my name was on the board. Oh well, I thought. I'll give it a go.

I was elected along with two other new members. There was also one vote for Bill, even though his name wasn't on the board.

Afterwards was the traditional *coup d'honneur,* cider and cakes, which we've learnt, is the standard ending of all *foyer* meetings and events in our commune.

The following week an emergency committee meeting was called and I was plunged straight into the politics of the commune. I listened to the feelings expressed by the committee regarding Stephane, the newly elected mayor. It was clear that they considered him a devious, egocentric person, seeking power and acclaim. This was not simply a case of him having defeated Didier's group, all of whom were key *foyer* members, at the election, but stemmed from way back in the past when he'd done something 'terrible' as a teenager. (The problems of not moving away from your childhood area!) The meeting had been called over the opening of a library in the village.

Apparently, over the last two years, the *foyer* had been researching the idea of creating a public library and had been in touch with the main municipal library and county councillors. It only had not been set up for lack of a site. The election of Stephane coincided with the moving of the infant half of our village school to another village, so he had announced he was opening a library in the empty classrooms. The meeting had been called to write a letter to him accusing him of taking not only the idea and work of the *foyer* but also the credit.

I listened to the indignation for a long time and watched as the letter was drafted on the board. I turned to my neighbour and said quietly, "But the library's going ahead. Surely that's good, no?"

"But it's *our* idea and he's pinched it lock, stock and barrel. What's more, he's presenting it as *his* idea!"

Feelings were vehement and the letter vituperative and not very adult. Should I say something?

"Er, excuse me …" Suddenly there was quiet and everyone looked at me. "As the only person here who was not involved initially, perhaps I could add something objective."

I wasn't sure what reaction I would get, so I paused, but they all looked expectant, so I carried on. "Perhaps the letter would have more effect if we altered one or two of the words to make it sound more …" I hesitated again, I could hardly say *less puerile*. To my surprise they encouraged me and we went through the letter again, editing out some of the more emotive expressions. Perhaps having expressed them, they then felt ready to do so.

The meeting ended with everyone satisfied with what had been written, but I went home with a greater awareness of the dislike and distrust of the new mayor.

At one *foyer* committee meeting, the president read out a letter from an American who was looking for work and who wondered if there was a need for English classes in our commune. After discussing this for about ten minutes, Martine suddenly said, "This is crazy! Why are we considering employing a stranger when we have Gilly-Anne here, who is in fact looking for work?"

Amazed looks all around and everyone stared at me.

The president said, "That's true? You're looking for work?"

Feeling very self-conscious, I nodded. "Well, I could do with a few extra hours, really."

"Then there's nothing else to consider. Let's ask Gilly-Anne. Is everyone in favour?"

I ended up with two classes, one of primary school children and one of adults. When the list of people who had chosen to learn English was given to me, I saw an almost insurmountable problem.

"Look at this, Bill. They're all our friends, who don't speak English but also Martine, who's virtually fluent. How do I fit that lot together?"

"Perhaps they *do* speak English."

"Well, they never have so far."

"They don't need to with you around."

"Yes, but Bill, they know how you struggle and they've never helped by speaking English. Look Luc's on the list, he's one of your closest friends and he certainly doesn't speak English."

"Don't get het up about it. It'll sort itself out; you'll see."

At the first lesson, there they all sat, twelve of them, uneasy but expectant, round the enormous polished wood, oval table used for mayoral meetings. One of my first questions was to find out why they wanted to learn English, for business, or for holidaying … the answer was, right round the table, to have better conversations with Bill. He should be gratified!

It seemed that none of them had wanted to feel ridiculous speaking hesitant English and so had never tried, despite having a basis from their schooling. In a class, the situation was different: here they could all practise and develop the confidence they so badly needed.

Bill felt overcome. He decided he ought to reciprocate, so joined French classes in La Rochelle, two hours twice a week. He started with enthusiasm, returning with tales of silent Kurt, the German, who sat with his arms folded and his legs stretched out under the table. Of Farouk who was always asking question starting with 'Please, not understand ...' and of Islah, the beautiful Turkish girl who kept whispering to Bill 'Please explain me...' It was something new and he enjoyed it, particularly the role playing afternoon when he excelled himself in his creativity and sense of fun.

Then one day, after about two months, he came home and threw his books on the floor.

"That's it. I'm finished."

"Why? Whatever happened?

"We had to do some written exercises today and first Marie told me that I would have to improve my handwriting and then that my spelling was bad and my accents non-existent."

I could imagine Bill's reaction. "So, what did you say?"

"I told her I'd always had a secretary to type my correspondence, and now I have you and that as for spelling and accents it was totally irrelevant as you would do any writing that was necessary. And I told her that I was there, like most of the others, for conversation not written exercises. Anyway, I'm not going to be treated like a thirteen year old."

Nothing I could say changed his mind. He insisted he could cope very well and he had better things to do with his time. In fact I had to admit he understood extremely well and that with his repertoire of gestures and his 'franglais' he fared better than one would expect, so much so, that I was sometimes envious that he could so easily become the life and soul of a party.

CHAPTER 27

We'll Never Drink the Local Wine Again!

At every large market there are wine stands. Various wine bottles are arranged on the stand, often decorated with grapes and twists of vine, and glasses are laid out at the side. There is always a group of men standing around it, peering into their glass of wine, or swirling it thoughtfully, before passing their judgements. This is a fairly serious procedure, usually accompanied by wise nodding of heads, and is obviously not something to be hurried.

Wine is an all-engrossing subject: French people will settle happily to discussing it for hours, the types, the year, and where they get their stocks. Along the roads further south, in the Cognac and Bordeaux areas, are the *dégustation*, or tasting, signs, but Bill admitted he didn't know how to set about buying in wine. However Guy and Bernard settled that for him by inviting him to join them when they went to their favourite '*cave*' for their wine.

They set off, all three, at around eleven one Saturday morning. They reappeared around seven that evening. I looked through the window: they were reeling out of the car (whoever had been driving?) clasping each other by the hands and elbows and shouting joyfully at each other. I couldn't make out what they were saying, but there was a lot of stabbing each other in the chest with one finger and clutching on to each other's shoulders. Finally Bill separated himself from the other two and stood propping up the doorway.

"Had a good day, Bill?"

"Whassat?"

"Did you get any wine?"

"Wine? Yurs. Got su-wine, yurs."

"Where is it, then?" By now I was amused: I'd never seen Bill actually drunk before.

He gestured in the direction of the car, causing him to nearly fall over. Using both hands, he pulled himself up the door jamb. "Bernar's a goo' chap. Goo' chap 'Nard."

I thought perhaps it was time to move him from the door, so offered my help.

He looked at me as piercingly as he was able. "I'm orrl ri'." And he lurched the short space across to the sofa and collapsed on it. That was goodnight, Bill.

The following morning he said, "Never again." Bernard and Guy seemed to have had the aim of having a 'good day out', and all he'd ended up with, apart from a hangover, was a crate of mediocre wine, twelve bottles all the same. He'd decided it was better to buy what he liked when he saw it, after all, as we didn't have a *'cave'*, a cellar, we hadn't really got much storage and he wasn't knowledgeable enough to buy in wine for ten years later.

The process of grape growing and cultivation had fascinated us ever since we came to France. I had never realised the amount of work that goes into growing grapes: it is not simply picking them, there is the annual pruning and spraying of the vines in addition to the staking and caring for the ground. From February onward it seemed there was always someone doing something in the vineyard. What amazed me was that the vines grew in such stony ground, so long as it was an area that caught the sun, they did not seem to need rich soil. Nor did they need irrigation, yet somehow they ended up juicy. We found ourselves increasingly choosing walks that led past vines, vines that hung heavy with bunches of green grapes, or that glowed fiery reds and yellows in the autumn sun. We watched fascinated as one field of vines was pruned back in February to only one shoot but in another field to two. We presumed it was something to do with the variety of grape. To me it seemed a shame to cut back so rigorously all the year's growth except for about two inches, yet it grew so rapidly I decided vines must be the fastest growing plant I knew. (Except that wretched convolvulus that thrived on our vegetable plot.)

We'd often wondered if we couldn't somehow do some grape-picking. We'd watched Jacques and Louisette ride off cheerfully in tractor trailers to help various friends with their picking and return late in the afternoon rosy-faced and vocal. But we had not yet been invited to join in, even though the traditional pattern is that everyone turns out to help at their friend's *'vendanges'*, or grape picking. Then Albert invited us.

The second Saturday of October was the day. Albert is only a small vineyard owner, one third or half a hectare, but it is enough to make wine for his extended family for at least a year.

A line of cars along the grass verge marked the rendezvous at eight. Greetings all round. Laughter and chat. But we hardly knew anyone apart from Albert and his family. Grape picking scissors and buckets were handed out, then we started. Snip, one bunch of purple-black grapes into the bucket. Lift the leaves, snip again. We worked concentratedly, in lines, on either side of the vines, but chatting as we went along.

The ages ranged from teenager to seventy odd, with as many women as men. One young man spent the morning lifting the full buckets up to Albert on the tractor-trailer. I was glad, as the buckets were heavy.

Fascinating scraps of conversation drifted through the vines, Dadaesque, as you couldn't see the speaker. A pair of young legs in fur trimmed boots, "You'll never believe it, but he walked straight in, made for my bedroom and lay on the bed expectantly!" (It was only later I learnt she had been talking about her cat.)

Another woman's voice, "The aim of the course is to write a novel…"

A man's voice, "I went to one of Piaf's concerts in '52. She didn't have a big range of voice, but *the way* she sang struck you to the core…"

The recognisable voice of Bill answered, "Do you know how Piaf dressed her salad? *'Je ne vinaigrette rien'.*"

Laughter.

"Remember last year? All that mud, the drizzle and the cold?"

"What about the insects? Everything, mud, insects and all, into the press along with the grapes!"

"Not for the faint hearted."

At 9.30 Martine served coffee, drunk mainly by the women. At 10.30 Albert served wine, drunk mainly by the men and someone produced homemade cakes, eaten by all.

Conviviality was at the centre of the proceedings – picking was no chore.

I was reminded of the farmer Bill had been chatting to who spoke of the efficiency of his grape harvesting machine, but regretted the conviviality. "Now it's just another job, and all I have at the end of a day is a buzzing in my ears from the tractor," he'd said.

On the trailer, Albert turned the handle of the grape-crushing machine. To me, the uninitiated, it looked like an old fashioned mangle with a box fitted on top. The grapes were tipped into the box, the handle turned and the juice and crushed remains fell into one of the waiting bins. By the end of a couple of hours, all these were filled and Albert drove off with some strong young men to empty these into his *'cuve'*, an immense concrete tank. He then returned with the bins washed ready for the white grapes.

Here I was surprised. Whereas the red grapes had all seemed perfect, many of the white were beginning to rot in the bunch. I started trying to pick these out.

"No, no, put the whole bunch in. *Pas de problème*. It improves the taste."

Reluctantly, I dropped the whole bunch in my bucket, looking round furtively to see what the 'old hands' were doing. Indiscriminate picking. "Oh well, if that's how it is…"

There was more laughter as the wine that had been drunk released a greater camaraderie.

"We had some of Michel's 'first pressing' last week and didn't we regret it the following day," said one.

"Oh it does that. It cleans your insides out."

"Sure did!"

"Ow! I've cut myself," cried the woman with fur-trimmed boots.

"Call an ambulance!"

"Call the police! Get to a phone. Help! Help!"

Someone produced a plaster.

By midday the vines had been cleared in record time as so many friends had turned out to help. We stood around, bantering for a while before driving back to Albert's. Here we gathered in the building where he makes his wine. The white grapes were already being pressed in an upright press which looked rather like a large, wooden, slatted park bin, fitted with a cross ways press that screwed down. The juice streamed out of the slats at the bottom into a container.

Albert handed out glasses of this juice. "This year's pressing. *Santé* – your health!"

I sipped cautiously, remembering the rotten grapes. In fact it was beguilingly pleasant.

"Where are all the black grapes?" I asked.

He slapped the side of his *'cuve'*, twice as tall as him, and said, "In here, Gilly-Anne, to ferment. They'll double in size. Come back mid-week and you'll hear this lot bubbling."

"Like a lot of old women at a party," someone interrupted.

I climbed the ladder to look inside. A huge press was pushing down the bulk because unless the grapes were kept covered the wine would become bitter. Albert told me that the fermentation would start just two days after the picking, the fourth day would be the crescendo, then it would die down. The time it takes depends on the temperature, but since the weather was mild, it would start almost immediately.

He then showed us his row of barrels waiting to be filled by the red wine and the rosé, an impressive row of perhaps a dozen medium-sized ones.

"The white, I put straight in the barrel. It ferments there, unlike the red. To produce rosé wine, I treat the red grapes like white grapes, I press them immediately and put them into a barrel. Without the bulk, it becomes a more delicate wine, but the fermentation takes longer. After a month, I filter both rosé and white into another barrel."

We stared, impressed. I turned to Bill and asked quietly if all wine was made this way. He smiled and explained that though in large vineyards the winemaking process is basically the same, for a *grand cru*, the rotting grapes are picked out, and a professional will sometimes add sugar or certain chemicals to his fermenting juice.

Later Albert explained how he was allowed to make his own *pineau* (like a sweet sherry) because his parents were granted a licence to distil a spirit called *eau de vie* when they planted the vines. But like so many of his generation, this right ceases at the death of his parents, as the issue of these licences was stopped in the fifties.

All this time we had been standing in the wine-making building, where everyone was chatting volubly. But eventually we went into the house where Yvette, and some of the other wives, had been busy cooking all morning. A rich aroma of a wine sauce made our mouths water. Twenty of us sat at an enormous table, nothing extraordinary for a French family, all ages, all backgrounds, but united in having helped our friend harvest his grapes. More toasts, this time with last year's homemade *pineau*, which we decided tasted better than his wine, served with delicious, hot, pastry savouries. Tongues were loosened even further. Strangers became firmly bonded friends.

The celebratory meal lasted the usual three hours, six courses, and between each a pause for conversation, which flowed freely, helped by the many glasses of wine. Vegetable soup, home-made pâté, smoked salmon, a delicious, garlicky potato dish accompanying snails (three hundred or so cooked in a rich wine sauce), or stuffed tomatoes for those who, like me, only fancied the sauce but not the snails, then a variety of cheeses with salad, and last of all apple and pear tarts. The whole meal was followed by a cognac, *un digestif*, so called because, after all that, you need something to help you digest your meal.

We went home in a haze of goodwill, gratefully clutching our thank you bottles of gut-cleansing, first pressing, grape juice. That was *that* weekend, and we had been invited to help with Claude's *vendanges* the following week. What could be more French than grape picking?

CHAPTER 28

The Barn in the Pyrenees

Our friends Jean-Marc and Yvonne invited us to their retreat in the Pyrenees for the October half term. We knew their retreat was a converted barn, a high pasture *grange,* but we did not know what to expect.

When we had first met them, at a *foyer* dinner, Bill had immediately said what a beautiful woman Yvonne was. It was true, she was tall with classical features and soft brown eyes. It was on the same occasion that I felt I had put my foot in it, as, having been introduced to Jean-Marc, I said something about his wife, referring to Yvonne who was standing next to him.

"This is not my wife, this is the woman I've chosen to live with," he had said simply.

I had started to feel embarrassed, then realised that neither of them were, they were simply clarifying a point. This frank attitude to relationships is very French.

Jean-Marc is certainly someone who likes things to be clear, a fact is a fact, and at times this makes him seem unimaginative. He is big, with Bill beside him it looks like 'Little and Large', not only in size but also in the way he speaks. Often he is ponderous, you have the feeling that he rarely says anything lightly, and certainly he is used to being listened to. But as you get to know him, you discover a sense of humour and wit. It took me a while to realise this forceful personality was the father of the quiet, petite Lysiane.

He is a font of information about everything to do with the countryside, having started as an observant child, particularly during the occupied war years when he seems to have spent most of his time skulking in the marshlands. He used to be a geology lecturer and so knows well areas that other people barely know exist and has a knack of making a quarry, for example, seem the most exciting place ever to be visited. Since he had met Yvonne at about the same time as I had met Bill, we were all at the same stage of playfulness and romantic allusions.

"When I retired," he explained one day, "I decided to walk from here to my *grange* in the Pyrenees. I'd every intention of making it a marker between one stage of my life and the next, almost as a meditation. My wife had died some two years previously and I felt it would help clarify my mind."

"Go on," Yvonne joked. "Tell them about how your plans were ruined."

He looked at her, annoyed at her interruption, but she continued to gaze at him fondly, knowing what was coming next.

"Well, somehow, *someone* came with me. Neither of us is exactly clear how it occurred. We'd known each other for years. Yvonne happened to be retiring at the same time, declared my idea of 'the pilgrimage' was an excellent way to mark the transition, and the next thing I knew, we were doing it together. Mind you, I made it clear that there was no room for another woman in my life, this was to be just walking companionship."

"*Oh absolument*," agreed Yvonne.

"And then, standing on a bridge in the moonlight, with the Pyrenees looming large ahead of us, the water rustling below us – magic." They looked at each other lovingly. "And that was it," Jean-Marc concluded.

Bill looked at them thoughtfully and gave my hand a squeeze. "Know the feeling." For a moment, each couple was lost in their own reminiscences.

The idea of our October stay was that we would overlap for a day and then they would leave us to explore on our own.

Their barn was high in the central Pyrenees, way above the town of Arreau. We wound our way past clumps of tall green trees, back and forth across a raging torrent of a dark river, with, all the while, a stone wall curving alongside the road.

Following their directions, we drove slowly across the narrow bridge over that racing river and bumped up the track. There was Yvonne sitting outside, sorting through a great mound of mushrooms. The building itself was of the brown granite so typical of this area. It snuggled into the side of mountain, solid, dark and with a big chimney. Yvonne saw us and waved.

"Welcome to the barn."

Our first impression was of darkness, despite the wide glass panelled door. The floor and walls were rough dark stone slabs and the only windows were small squares set in such thick walls that they only let in pools of light. But there was a huge fire burning in the fireplace and this lit up one end. I blinked to adjust to the gloom.

"I told you it's a barn. Jean-Marc will tell you the story of its renovation."

He arrived at that moment with a wheelbarrow full of arm-sized logs.

"Great to see you. Help me unload these, will you?" He was not one to waste time and words on niceties.

The whole end wall next to the fireplace was one immense stack of logs to be kept dry. In fact the barn was very snug and we quickly adapted to gas lamps and the big stove which had to be fed regularly to provide hot water.

Supper that night was trout caught that morning, grilled on a rack placed over the open fire. I feared it might be charcoal in places and raw in others, but it was obvious they had perfected this way of cooking, for the fish was excellent.

"When I bought this barn, for virtually nothing, twenty years ago, I realised that I was on to a good thing. Many people have bought barns as a holiday place, but then can't get there for six months of the year because of the snow – after all they were built as summer pasture barns. But the road up past the bridge, the one you came up, leads to the hydro-electric station, so, *voilà,* it's always kept clear of snow, which means we can get here even when other roads in the mountains are impassable."

"Yes, but we often have to leave the car at the bridge and trudge up the track with our things."

Jean-Marc shrugged. "No problem. It's access that's important."

"What was it like when you bought it?" As usual my curiosity was aroused.

"If you want an honest answer, deep in shit. I dug fifty-six barrow loads of sheep droppings out of here."

We gaped.

"Well it was an old shepherd's summer barn. In spring he would set off with his flock and come up here. They slept in here, so he slept in here too, on that shelf over there."

'That shelf' was the stone slab on which the wood was stacked. I tried to envisage it.

"At least he'd be warm at night, with the fire."

"Oh no, no fireplace. I put that in. But the number of sheep in here would have kept him warm on chilly nights and the thickness of the walls would have kept him cool when it was hot."

"All down that side was the manger, made of boxwood, too bitter for the sheep or goats to chew. And that was all there was. The only access to the hayloft were stone steps outside, so we put in our staircase up to what are now the bedrooms. And we brought stones up from the river bed to make the floor."

"But how did he cook, wash, anything like that?" I continued questioning, still trying to imagine what it would have been like.

"Wash? He didn't. Life was basic. Cook? Well his womenfolk came up regularly from the village with food. But basically he ate his dried sausage, cheese and a hard bread. He had plenty of plenty of ewe's milk and of course he had his wine."

I couldn't imagine existing on such limited fare for so many months and pulled a face.

"And do you realise, this way of life only ended about thirty years ago. When I bought the barn the custom had only just fallen into disuse. There are some areas where it continues."

"Good excuse to get away from the wife," said Bill with an impish look at me.

Jean-Marc being our local mushroom expert, the choice of walks for the following day, was based around what we wanted to collect.

"If we cross the river and go east, we'll find *trompettes de mort*, those black ones drying over there." He pointed to two large boxes of shrivelled black mushrooms. "If we go south to the valley, there will only be a few mushrooms but good views. But if we go up above the lake, we'll find a great variety."

We settled for the variety.

The walk was incredible, for me, not because of the mushrooms, keen mushroomer though I am, but because of the carpet of autumn crocuses. There were areas of footpath where it was impossible not to tread on one they were so thick – and they were so beautiful, delicate mauve cups with bright orange stamens, but no leaves. I have never seen so many. It was like a splash of colour from an Impressionist painting.

We walked along the ridge looking down on the miniature lake with a toy castle on a tiny rock at one end. The sky was a brilliant blue and the sun hot. In late October we were walking in shirt sleeves. Our ears were full of the drowsy sound of bees buzzing and then the plaintive mew of a kite. High in the sky, we could see it circling above a clump of trees.

I stopped Bill in his tracks. "Look! How about doing that?"

Floating across the valley were three paragliders, their blue red and green sails showing up clearly against the sky.

We watched. It was dreamlike: they hovered, before slowly descending, lifting, then descending again.

"I've fancied doing that, ever since my parachute jump," Bill said.

"You've done a para drop, Beel? When you were in the air force?" Jean-Marc asked.

"No, a few years ago. I had to lie about my age as I didn't have a medical certificate and forty-five was the limit and I was fifty eight. It was the most amazing experience: I was hunched up by the exit door, not so sure I wanted to jump and I was shoved. Instinctively I curled up in a foetal position with my eyes shut, then, I said to myself 'Hey, you're paying for this experience' So I opened my eyes. Magic. I felt like a king, up there surveying everything down below. When I landed I was so excited I jumped up shouting 'Again! I must do it again!'"

"And did you?" asked Yvonne.

"Not immediately, but a year later I did a tandem jump and that was even better – higher of course, but you're attached to an expert, so you've no worries. It was such an intense physical sensation it gave me as good a high as sex. Ever tried it, Jean-Marc?"

"Him!" laughed Yvonne. "He'd drop like a lead balloon with his weight."

Jean-Marc lunged at her playfully and they scuffled like puppies, despite the said weight. It was not that he was fat, because he was not, but he was solid.

Then it was the more serious business of searching for mushrooms. It was very useful having an expert on hand to immediately classify our finds and we returned that evening with eight different species of edible mushroom which we prepared and cooked for supper.

After Jean-Marc and Yvonne left to return to Chambon, and Bill and I stayed on, we decided to make the most of our four days' walking. The first three days went well. We stuck to the routes marked in the guide book Jean-Marc had left and saw a variety of scenery, following the river thrashing along the valley, up through sombre pine forests to the wild, bareness of the lower mountains. The weather was beguiling and the valley lay dreaming, soaked in the pinks and apricots of the early evening sun. Smoke rising straight from chimneys, caught the colours, sometimes wheat yellow, sometimes a soft rose. And then, on the last day, we chose our most challenging walk.

We set off before nine, slightly bothered that the mountain we had decided to climb was completely shrouded in cloud.

"Do you think we should change our plan, Bill?" I felt anxious.

"No, you'll see, it will lift later this morning."

In fact it created a marvellous experience. Having climbed up through the cloud, we were on a grassy ridge with a few trees and a stone hut, but below us was a wreath of white cloud through which floated distorted sounds from the unseen village, voices, church chimes and the horn of a baker's van. It was surreal.

"Come on, no time to marvel. Look up there, that's where we're going. Look on the map." Bill tried to shake me out of my dream.

High up we could see the empty ski station and the peaks of higher grimmer mountains, one already dusted with snow.

We saved our breath for the hard climb and plodded up in silence. Our reward was the sight of a stag with huge antlers rising up, a few metres beyond Bill, who was in front as usual. Without undue hurry, it loped diagonally beyond us giving us an excellent view of his white striped rear. It paused, silhouetted on the skyline, as though considering, then strolled on over the ridge.

We reached the deserted ski lifts, looking as though they were a leftover of a previous age, and saw large fan-like objects planted at intervals on what would be the ski slope.

"What are those, Bill?"

He looked at me oddly. "They're the snow-making machines. They have to make sure there is enough snow."

I suddenly saw the snowy mountains as business ventures, rather than picturesque scenery.

Before going on, I looked back. Scarves of mist floated round islands of hills. A shepherd's shelter, built low and of solid stone was the only object to stand out in a sea of grey-green grass. I turned back to the path ahead, zigzagging up the mountain.

As we topped the top of the ridge we saw an inverted bowl created by the surrounding ridges of mountains, in the centre of which was a small pool, a perfect place for lunch. The grass here was soft and long, luxurious to laze in, so I was reluctant to move on again, but I knew we should if we were to complete the circuit before dark.

Marching as briskly as my tiring legs would allow, along the muddy track following the rim of the ridge, we were passed by two Land Rovers packed with young people.

"I don't know. We spend all morning climbing and these youngsters come up in a Jeep in ten minutes," I felt disgruntled.

But as we topped the next ridge we saw why. They were not walkers but paragliders. They were busy laying out their sails on the grass with much excited chatter and laughter. Suddenly a signal was given, they lifted their cords and ran leaping into the air which billowed out their sails. It was amazing. One minute the mountainside was full of noise and activity and the next moment, silence and the sky full of floating colours.

Having watched for a few moments, we continued. It was now around half past two and we were a good three quarters of the way round our walk. Very satisfactory.

"Sorry, *chérie*, a bit of rock climbing here."

"Bill, you know I hate that. Isn't there another way?"

"Well, this is the path, look here we are on the map. Let's see… Ah, here are the markers, on the rock … and I don't see an alternative route. Follow me and do as I do. Lean into the rock."

Ahead was a pinnacle of rock, craggy, but blocking the path completely. On one side was the steep slope of the paragliders, on the other, a sheer drop, nothing between me and three sheep the size of golf balls.

"DON'T LOOK DOWN!"

Too late.

'Self-control. Swallow and take a deep breath. Right foot forward. Edge along. Hold tight. Yes, there's the ledge - one foot, now another. Nearly there…Keep going... PHEW. I've done it.'

"Well done, darling. See, it wasn't so bad."

'Huh. Little does he know,' I thought. I looked ahead and was glad to see no more crags. I stood still, trying to control the after-the-event shiver.

Bill encouraged me. "Just a little further on, the path goes down and we're back in the gully with the cart-track where we started. In an hour we'll be home with a cup of tea in front of the fire."

Half an hour later we had to admit there was no evidence of our path, or indeed any path. Up until then, it had been clear and distinctive, even the rock pinnacle had been waymarked. Now we were faced with a multitude of goat tracks meandering along the contour where our path ought to be going. But which was the right one?

"I'm going to sit here while you investigate," I said feeling very tired all of a sudden.

Twenty minutes later a despondent Bill reappeared. I knew something was wrong because instead of pulling me to my feet to move on, he sat down, looking at me apprehensively.

"I'm sorry, *chérie*, we have to go back. There's no sign of our path, just scree going straight down, and it's pretty sheer."

I looked at him. It was obvious he was not joking. Go back? But we'd spent all day getting this far, it was now three o'clock and it would be dark by six. Despite a feeling of despair, I reacted quickly.

"If that's so, we've got to move. We'll never do it in daylight, but we must at least get through the village and onto the big track before dark, or we might never find it." I forced myself onto my feet, trying to feel positive.

"Great stuff. Come on then."

"BUT, I'm *not* going back over that rock scrambling."

"Okay. Now we know where it is, we'll find another way."

Of course there was no other way and I had to retrace it. But this time I kept repeating, like a mantra, 'I've done it once; I can do it again.'

It's amazing what you can push yourself into doing when it is essential. Although I was tired, I was so determined not to be on the mountainside in the dark that I marched down at speed. By cutting out our lunch-time ridge, we reached the village at dusk and found our final track before it was totally dark.

"Hold my hand, *chérie*, and don't let go."

I needed that contact. But I need not have worried. Fortunately for us, it was full moon, so comparatively light. There we were, walking hand in hand, along an old donkey track, half way down a mountain in the moonlight. If we had not been so tired, it would have been romantic. The worst part was the rough stone track which followed, with high banks and hedges on either side blocking the moon light. Unable to see the path, we stumbled, one foot after the other, clutching at one another, over the stones.

Finally, our feet touched the smooth surface of tarmac. Hooray. So much easier, even though we were still walking in the dark.

"Only half a kilometre to go now, then over the bridge and home," Bill said cheerfully and began to sing 'Home Sweet Home'.

"To a nice hot shower," I added.

But no, we were foiled. We'd left the stove for too long and it had gone out. Bill had to relight it and we had to wait for our showers.

I slumped in front of the fire. Bill brought me a cup of tea.

"Thanks, *chéri*. But could you add some whisky? I need pepping up a bit."

His eyebrows rose. Good whisky in a cup of tea? But he said nothing. He understood.

As the warmth of the fire and our drinks spread through us, we began to feel euphoric, despite our exhaustion. We'd done it – what a day.

CHAPTER 29

Markets and a New Experience

I adore markets. Just a hint of market stalls and we have to turn off our route. As I remarked one day, even the potatoes look clean and inviting. As for the mounds of shiny tomatoes, all smelling that particular green smell, my mouth starts watering at the thought of tomato and basil salad. And then there are the glowing stalls of peaches and apricots piled high, a reminder that these are ordinary fruits here, not specialities. There is always a queue at the cheese stall, where we find difficulty in making our choice, usually opting for whatever is the local cheese. I usually pass the meat stall quickly, but I can't fail to notice the appropriate herbs laid out by the relevant meat. Somewhere is the appetising *rotisserie*, with chicken sizzling that makes even my mouth water.

La Rochelle is perfect for wandering in the rain —and yes, it does rain in sunny south-west France, but usually a very fine misty rain. The two main streets going to the market square are colonnaded, so the pavements are wide and sheltered. The shops here are small (all the big stores are outside the town) so you can pass dress shops, hardware, bookshops, gift shops, opticians and even garden shops, all squeezed tightly together in these narrow streets. Our favourite shops were the *chocolatiers*, shops devoted to selling chocolates. The chocolates are artistically arranged in the windows on dishes or on stands, and the smell of chocolate seeps mouth-wateringly out of the door every time someone goes in or out. At Easter time the displays show rabbits, as they might in England, but also fish as the April fish is the sign of an April Fool's joke. When I went in to choose something for Bill, finally settling for a clown with big feet and a bright collar as well as the traditional Easter Bunny, the assistant broke the ears when wrapping it. As she automatically replaced it, I asked what happened to broken models and she said they were melted down and recast. So, each chocolate maker was making his own chocolate models. No wonder they were so expensive.

On market days the market spreads through, not just the square, but up two of the adjacent streets and traffic is blocked from the town centre. Everyone has their market basket and spends as much time chatting to friends as buying. The weekly markets are those devoted to food, bread, meat, fish and cheese, indoors and vegetables and flowers outdoors. It's surprising the number of stalls, all competing with each other, and each therefore, trying to lay out its goods in the most tempting manner possible, shiny fruit piled in pyramids or displayed in attractive baskets, and fish arranged in fan shapes, heads together, tails spread outwards.

I tried to persuade Bill to shop with me on a Saturday at the market.

"You pay more for the pleasure of greeting people in the street. They're not cheaper than the supermarket," he said.

"But maybe it's fresher, and it's definitely more fun."

"Fresher, I doubt it. More fun, possibly, certainly if you know people you'll be likely to meet."

"But it's the French way of life," I protested.

The deciding factor, of course, was that we spent Saturdays renovating our house in Chambon, and so, reluctantly on my part, I gave in about going regularly to the market.

Anne phoned. (We'd stayed in contact, even though she'd left the school) "Have you done all your Christmas shopping yet?"

"No, I've hardly begun."

"What about doing it together on Saturday?"

This sounded a pleasant idea to me, although Bill thought I was mad to choose to shop on the last but one Saturday before Christmas.

"It'll be murderous, you mark my words."

But it wasn't. There was none of the frenetic buying that occurs in England. Let alone Christmas shopping forays that start in early November, with Christmas decorations going up in mid-October, such as had happened in Bromley. We were able to amble comfortably along the pedestrian streets, admiring the Christmas trees hung with presents outside each shop – and not chained to the wall, as there was no risk of them being stolen – and linger in front of the gaily painted cabins selling Christmas gifts. We collected the presents she wanted for her parents and a typically French, navy beret for me to give to Bill. If we were living and working in France, he might as well dress the part. We ended, of course, in my favourite bar, sipping hot chocolate and exchanging jokes about our classes.

The bar was my favourite because it seems to me to epitomise things French. It was decorated in the period of *belle époque* (early 1900s) with huge mirrors doubling the size of it, gilt decorations and small round tables at which you perch while watching the people around you, both in reality and as reflected in the mirrors. In warmer weather the tables spilled out onto the pavement and square, under the colonnade. One of the nice things about it was that it was a meeting place for all ages.

Through the window we could see another cluster of Christmas cabins, painted in russets and blues and beyond that - but I wasn't sure what I was seeing, people seemed to be gliding round in circles.

"That's the new ice rink, put up for *les fêtes.* Do you want to have a go?"

"I couldn't, Anne. I can't skate."

"Nor can I. But does that matter? Come on, let's have a go."

We left our shopping at the café, and I walked towards the rink with images of me gliding round like a professional, mixed with humiliating images of me flat on my face on the ice. It was in the middle of the square, surrounded by a waist height fence. It wasn't particularly large, but at that time there were only about a dozen youngsters on the ice, some holding onto the fence and stepping cautiously, others more adventurous and gliding across the centre. I had a horrid feeling I would spend the next half hour either clutching the fence or falling over.

We paid and were quickly fitted with skates. I spent the first five minutes clutching at security, as I had predicted, trying to glide round the edge. Holding on, it wasn't too bad, but I knew I ought to let go and venture in the middle. Anne let go sooner than me and called from the centre for me to give it a go. I slid forward with my hands in front of me ready to grab at her. I didn't fall. Amazement. Slowly I got something of a rhythm and found it pleasurable. Whoops! I was down, sitting firmly on my bottom with my legs spread out in front of me. A young lad was gliding past, spun round and came to help me to my feet. Solicitously he asked if I was all right and insisted on holding my hand until I moved tentatively forward. With a smile he murmured, "*Courage, Madame*", before gliding gracefully off, his hands behind his back. Anne and I slid slowly round, holding hands. I can't say we were gliding effortlessly, but at least we were skating. I loved the sensation, it was a little like ballet. At the end of our half hour, we were both doing quite well and felt pleased with ourselves, until, that is a youngster in a black leather jacket entered the rink and started gliding backwards and spinning. Oh, well, we hadn't reached that stage.

CHAPTER 30

Our Second Christmas

Our second Christmas in France. In some ways I was more excited about this than our first, because then I had been caught up in a hectic, non-stop merry-go-round of new impressions. Our children all had different plans for Christmas, so Bill and I were looking forward to having our first in our new home, alone together, in fact the first since we had met. We planned to have an intimate, romantic few days, followed by entertaining our various friends.

I got an absurd thrill of pleasure in buying and decorating a tree, with decorations some of which I had had as a child, and some bought when mine were small, all in one of those boxes that had arrived from England six months before. An evocative time. Bill organised the traditional decorations of holly, which he cut from a wood nearby, and mistletoe from Bernard's apple tree.

First it was the pre-Christmas village dinner dance, organised by Chambon's band and held in the *salle de fêtes*, or village hall. Yvette and Albert had invited us to join their party and we were looking forward to it as yet another marker of our participation in village life.

I agonised over what to wear – a typical female dilemma. Was it really informal? How informal? I decided on a turquoise silk blouse with a full skirt, black with discreet swirls of peacock colours, hoping it would be appropriate. As soon as I saw some other ladies taking off their coats in the vestibule, I realised I had chosen exactly right, a blouse and skirt was a popular choice. At least I need not worry any more about that.

Stephane was at the door to greet the guests.

"Welcome, both of you. By the way, I'm not here in my capacity as deputy mayor, but as bandleader, in case you were wondering."

"I didn't know you were the bandleader," I exclaimed, without thinking.

"Ah, you don't know everything, Gilly-Anne." His eyes twinkled with amusement. "But you must come to our next concert. I'll let you know the date – you will come, won't you?"

"We'd love to; wouldn't we Bill?"

Then Yvette swept us off to meet all those people she thought we ought to meet. As she is a socialite in our commune, this seemed practically everyone and our heads were reeling with names.

"Yvette, I think these two have met enough for the moment. Let me take them to our table." This was the stable Albert. We gratefully accepted.

At the table we met the two other couples in our party, who greeted us in the typical French manner with kisses and handshakes all round. After answering questions about why we had chosen to settle in Chambon and they having explained where they lived and how they had known

Yvette and Albert since primary school, we were free to look around.

"Albert," I caught his attention by touching him on the arm, "Isn't that the baker?"

"André? Yes, and there's his wife over there, in black and gold."

I had never seen the baker divested of his voluminous white apron before and thought to myself he must eat what he bakes, since he was enormous.

The little man with a limp, who walks past our house every morning came across and shook us by the hand before moving on. We still did not know his name.

Bill was busy studying the menu card propped up on the table, but I kept looking round. There was a farmer in a smart tweed jacket that I knew by sight who lived past the windmill. On the next table I saw the three old ladies who lived on the main road, all three dressed in white blouses and black skirts. Coming through the door now was the jolly mason with the beard and wild hair. He was obviously a popular person as his arrival caused a stir and people regrouped round him. On the table opposite was the post lady, who caught my eye and waved.

"Ah Anne-Marie, our village postie," said Albert, waving back. "And that's her husband there." He pointed out a tall distinguished man from Martinique.

The village hall was packed. Balloons hung from the ceiling, swaying and bobbing with the heat. We had arrived at eight-thirty, it was now nine-thirty and still most people were standing in the centre chatting or moving from table to table greeting those who had chosen to sit down. The sound of excited voices filled the hall, and there was a lot of kissing and handshaking or arms draped casually around someone's shoulder. The servers were struggling to get through the crowd to bring baskets of bread to the tables, but there was no direct route and they had to backtrack and re-route. Gradually people began drifting towards their tables.

"So what are you doing for Christmas this year? Is your family coming over," Yvette asked.

"No, not this year." I explained what they were all doing and how we were looking forward to an intimate Christmas at home with just the two of us.

"Oh, but you must spend it with us. You're more than welcome to join us." Yvette looked concerned. "Martine and Luc are joining us with their two boys, so you'll feel quite at home."

I thanked her profusely and explained we really were looking forward to our first Christmas alone together. For a moment she looked at me doubtfully, then placing her hand on mine she said, "I understand. But if you *do* change your mind, don't hesitate to let me know."

"I will," I said warmly, pleased she understood.

Suddenly the babble was broken by the compère with his microphone:

"Welcome, *Mesdames et Messieurs*. I hope you have an enjoyable evening, in fact I shall do my best to ensure you *do* have a happy evening!" Laughter. "So let's start with a waltz."

Yvette, who adores dancing immediately leapt to her feet and took the arm of the man she had been talking to earlier and led the way. Within minutes the floor was crowded with couples, including Bill and I, circling round and round.

The dancing was ballroom with a little bit of rock and roll. Bill and I threw ourselves into the rock and roll with gusto and tried most of the others, but were unsure of the polka and the tango. We danced with our new friends at the table and I found myself remembering dances which I had not danced since I was at school, pushing round a partner to a gramophone in the gym.

A pause in the dancing brought the soup. The wine flowed and so did the courses of this, then a taste of that. In fact the meal was well spread out through the evening lasting, until two or three in the morning, as the dancing carries on, mainly between courses, but the enthusiasts barely stop to eat.

When we were not dancing we watched the others. Stout farmers firmly holding their partners ten centimetres away – is this a regulation ten centimetres? Their equally stout wives their feet squeezed into tight high heel shoes tripping neatly round the floor, many with a fixed expression on their faces. Elegant couples moving supply to the rhythm. Women dancing together, full skirts billowing out to the polka. A couple who obviously were experienced dancers, tangoing, with showy turns and leanings over.

I danced twice with Stephane, a good dancer who certainly did not believe in the ten centimetre gap before Bill seized me for a smoochy waltz.

I was dancing a cha cha cha with Alain, from our table when the music changed to that of a Viennese waltz. He whirled me round the floor, circling in and out of the other couples expertly. I began to feel a little dizzy and tried shutting my eyes for a moment. The music continued and so did we. It stopped.

"*Merci,*" he was saying just as I saw the floorboards rise up towards me.

The next thing I knew there were agitated voices all around me and a cup of water at my lips. I looked up and saw a moon of faces above me. I shut my eyes again, then pulled myself together, remembering where I was.

"I'm fine, thank you, it's only that the floor seems… not very flat," I said inadequately, trying to explain.

Finally I was helped to my feet and Bill led me into the vestibule for some fresh air.

"Fainted, did she?" someone asked sympathetically.

At the next dance we went to I cautiously tried another Viennese waltz, keeping my eyes firmly fixed on Bill's chest as I had seen others do. Quick. Another retreat to the fresh air needed.

I do not dance Viennese waltzes any more.

CHAPTER 31

Are They Our Friends? Problems and Pleasures

The first summer we let it be known that our house was in reasonable condition, we were inundated with visitors, our friends from Britain who wanted to see how we were getting on.

Before we left for France a good friend of ours who had moved to France three years previously, gave us some sound advice. She lived near Tours, en route for the Châteaux of the Loire, Dordogne and all those tourist areas down the south-west coast as far as the Pyrenees and on into Spain. She said she often felt as though she was running a bed and breakfast place, but without pay, as everyone used her home as an overnight stop. She had advised us to make a list of all the friends we *really* wished to keep up with, because others would be bound to ring up to ask if they could come to stay. And this was true.

One day the phone rang.

"Hello. This is Graham. How are you?"

Graham? Who was Graham? While I made cautiously polite noises, my mind was working furiously, but the name meant nothing to me.

The long and the short of it was he and his girlfriend were going to Spain and thought they would love to come and see how we were getting on, catch up with good old Bill and, in fact, would like to stay the night on their way down.

Without thinking I said we'd be delighted, wrote down the dates and said I'd send them a sketch map of the route.

"*Chéri*, we're going to have visitors on April fourteenth," I said cheerfully when he came stomping back from Jacques' in his muddy boots.

"Who?"

"Graham and his girlfriend."

"Graham?" Bill frowned, puzzled. "I don't know a Graham."

"He knows you."

He thought and then said puzzled, "You surely don't mean that chap from work? I hardly know him. You did say no?"

"Well, no. I thought he was a friend of yours. I said yes and that we would send him a map."

"Then make sure you forget to send the map. I hardly know the chap. We were never friends, only colleagues. We only overlapped for six months or so and our paths very rarely crossed. And," he said triumphantly, "he's definitely not on our list."

As he disappeared into the garden I heard him muttering against opportunists who wanted free lodging.

Certainly, with only the friends on our list of specials, we had visitors non-stop, from the beginning of May until mid-September, with only two days to ourselves in the middle.

At the end of that time, we felt we could easily work for the tourist office, so well did we know the tourist attractions. It was lovely seeing family and friends, but that year we were over-saturated.

With each set of visitors we showed the sequence of photographs of the house. Each time we did so, we felt amazed at what we had accomplished. We got adept in explaining what we had done and how we had done it, while at the same time our brains ran through a series of cameo images of unforgettable moments.

Bill's son, Henry, sleeping with a mosquito net over his bed, not against the mosquitoes but in case any insect dropped from the roof, and with buckets all round the bed to catch the drips because it was raining. He had turned up unexpectedly shortly after we had moved in and before the second half of the roof had been renewed.

Guy and Bernard looking polite but puzzled, at the way Bill had done something. They kept saying, "*C'est rustique, Beel*", to such an extent that we decided to call the house *La Maison Rustique*. Their perfectionism was often at odds with Bill's discovery methods of working. For example, when the electrics had been finally approved and the domestic line installed, they had come across to give Bill a hand with siting the lights. Guy spent ages measuring.

"*Alors,* half a centimetre to the left, Bernard, no, check it, a quarter more…'

"Why bother? No wall's straight, nothing's regular or at right angles in the whole house. Half a centimetre here or there won't be noticed" was Bill's response.

Then there were the unexpected kindnesses. We arrived one morning to find Bernard had popped over the evening before to cement the hearth tiles for us. Another time, we were leaving for a week in Britain so he suggested he tiled the dining room and kitchen while the house was empty. We returned to find our flattened cardboard floor covering a thing of the past and golden tiles giving a new vision of spaciousness.

And Luc, with his unexpected gift of an oil-burning heater. When we had first started renovating the house both Luc and Bernard had asked Bill what type of heating he was going to put in. In his airy fashion he had answered, "Heating? We don't need heating. I've come from Scotland and it's a darned side colder there than here. We've come to France because it's warm so we won't need heating." Not knowing Bill too well at this stage, he was believed.

The September that I started work at the *Ecole Supérieure*, I was sent to England for a week's conference on business ethics. While I was away Luc arrived one morning and said, "Listen Beel, I've brought a stove – it's not for you. It's a present for Gilly-Anne and I'm going to install it right now. I've just put in new heating in a house and this was being thrown out. It's in excellent condition." Little did he realise that Bill would have eventually installed some form of heating.

We couldn't forget the negative things, two in particular. The day after Bill had taken off the roof tiles it rained and we arrived to find the floor covered in a white sludge formed from the chalk dust and the rain. It looked awful and our hearts had sunk. They would have sunk even further, had we realised how long it would take to clear. The second was the cold, unexpected after such a prolonged warm autumn. Even Luc's stove was not enough to heat our '*séjour*', in fact our dining room, when the front door was simply the original doors of the barn, ill-fitting and draughty. Bill had delayed fitting a front door because he had not worked out a way to do it. I sat at the table marking exam papers, with my jacket over a thick sweater, and a rug round my legs, and complained I had not come to southern France to sit wrapped up in a rug like an old lady. Bill stuck his hands in his pockets, rocked back on his heels and mumbled, "I know, I'm sorry. The trouble is, I just don't know how to fit the door as the height is so low. No ready-made doors will fit."

It was a red-letter day when Bill finally said he had worked out how he could fit a French window in place of a door and we went to buy it. We were so proud of our new a double glass-paned front door, we kept finding excuses to go out and come back in again. The rug was folded up and put away.

My son Gareth came to stay for a few days towards the end of January. He was amazed and full of praise for what we had achieved.

"Give me a paint brush and I'll give you a hand."

Bill took him at his word and detailed him off to paint the window frame on the landing. He came down later, rubbing his hands and saying how cold it was. We banked up the fire in the *salon* and sat there snugly, sipping hot spiced wine and catching up on news. When we said goodnight, we joked about how he could lie in bed and watch the flames of the fire. (We had by then moved upstairs, which involved getting changed downstairs, running up the ladder and jumping into bed as quickly as possible.)

The following morning the sky was forbiddingly grey. As I wasn't working that morning, we went into Surgères, our local town, to the supermarket. When we came out, I looked round surprised, the ground was covered in snow.

"I thought you didn't have snow here," Gareth said.

"We don't, normally. It must be one of the 'once in every ten years'."

I cautiously eased the car out and onto the main road. I crawled along. No sign yet of the gritting lorries, even though this was a main road. Ahead I could see a line of cars, stationary and presumed someone had had an accident. When we got close, we saw that five or six cars had stopped, blocking the road in both directions, and the owners, all youngish, were making the most of the unaccustomed snow, sliding, throwing snowballs and shouting joyfully. I eased my car onto the grass verge and ventured round them, anxious to get home before Bill started worrying. Gareth thought it a hoot that drivers would simply abandon their cars on a main road to play in the snow like schoolboys.

I walked into the house, stamping the snow off my shoes, and told Bill there was no way I could go to work that afternoon, to drive twenty-six kilometres in the snow was insane, so I'd better phone to inform them.

"Why don't you wait a bit," Bill said calmly.

"But they haven't even got the gritting lorries out yet!"

"What gritting lorries? They probably don't have them. After all if it's a rare event, why would they have gritting lorries? You're not in England now, you know. Tell you what, why don't we go for a walk and enjoy the snow."

So we did, enjoying the crunch beneath our feet, the sight of ledges of snow precariously balanced on branches, and the fun of the snowball fight we inevitably ended up having.

On our return, I was still concerned to phone to say I wouldn't be able to get in, but again Bill suggested I wait. He was right to do so. By midday, the snow had melted.

"You needn't have worried, Mum, it's obviously too warm here for the snow to settle.

It may have been warm enough to melt the snow, but the following day the temperature plummeted. No more snow, just a penetrating icy cold. By five o'clock that afternoon, we all three ended up in front of the fire, huddled on the sofa, with our duvet spread over us. Gareth joked about how he should have brought his arctic clothing. We replied with jokes about once every ten years, draughty old houses, and, eventually, the luxury of modern central heating. We couldn't deny we were cold.

When Gareth left the following morning, he said, "Well, you two, you've done wonders with your house, but that's the last visit I make in winter. It's too jolly cold. How do you cope?"

It was useless saying it was never normally that cold, it had been uncomfortably so. Obviously we would have to do something. For a while we would not be boasting of our warmer climate.

As the weather turned to spring sunshine, we had our first serious disagreement.

I was at Louisette's getting some eggs. Jacques was mending the gate.

"A few clouds this morning. Rain's forecasted, you know – the garden could do with a drop of rain." This was a usual greeting, the state of the weather, particularly in relation to the garden. But Jacques continued, "Beel says you're cutting down the tree."

"What tree?"

"Your big ash tree."

"You must be mistaken," I said, not taking him seriously.

"That's what Beel said," added Louisette, arriving with the eggs. "He and *le chef* were discussing it yesterday."

I saw Jacques give her a look, as if to hush her up, but once started this was hard.

"Yes, they were measuring and walking up and down, discussing the best way to cut it and for it to fall."

I did not wait to hear any more, but raced back, forgetting about the eggs.

"Bill! Bill! Where are you?"

He emerged from the *salon* where he was working on the accounts.

"What's up?"

"What's all this about chopping down my tree?"

"*Our* tree, to be exact."

"Don't split hairs! Answer my question."

"Calm down, *chérie*; I was only discussing with Jacques the possibility –"

"*No* possibility. That tree stays. I *love* that tree."

"Alright, alright. Let's have a coffee and talk about it."

Taking our coffee we went outside and gazed at the offending tree. It was one of the biggest in the neighbourhood and right now was covered in feathery shoots of spring. I had had visions of hanging a swing from a branch for our eventual grandchildren

"You have to understand, its roots go right under our vegetable patch. We'll never get the best vegetables while that tree stands."

"So? We don't have the best vegetables. That's all."

Bill looked at me and must have realised how strongly I felt, because all of a sudden he said, "Okay, you win. The tree stays."

All through that summer I made sure we placed our table under its branches so that we could enjoy the half shade while eating, even though it meant carrying everything to the bottom of the garden. I made no comment, but Bill understood my tactics. He even admitted how pleasant it was to sit under the tree.

When the family came to stay, they inadvertently sealed the fate of the tree.

"Aren't you lucky to have a big tree like this. It's lovely to sit here in the shade and look up the garden at your house."

It was true, it was one of the best views. From there, we could see through the red hot pokers and purple dahlias, across our lawn to the house. It was hard now to remember the ramshackle building, grey-black with neglect, that we had bought nearly two years ago. In its place was a cream stone-fronted cottage with blue-grey shutters and small-paned windows giving onto a honey-coloured terrace edged with African marigolds. Cherry-coloured hollyhocks lined the east wall and a deep-red rambling rose the west. In the shelter of the hedge, was our prize plant, a pink oleander.

"You've made an incredible transformation, you know. When we came out that Christmas, we thought you were mad – well you must have guessed. But now. . . "

Gareth's voice tailed off. "I wouldn't mind that sense of achievement myself."

"I just wish we could have been around more to give a hand." Rachel seemed sincerely regretful. "Well, at least you can get to the beaches and travel around more now."

It was true, now the house was comfortable and since we were in no rush to finish renovating, we had started exploring in Evita.

CHAPTER 32

La Pèche a Pied

No-one can live near the coast in France for very long without becoming aware of the passion for shellfish hunting. Every low-tide you can see several wellie-shod male and female hunters bent double peering and collecting from the low water rocks. In La Rochelle there are over three hundred restaurants and virtually all of them specialise in seafood. The seafood platter is for a leisurely lunch, and arrives with whelks, mussels, shrimps, prawns, crab claws and winkles piled high on a bed of sea-weed. Usually they are decoratively arranged and crowned by a langoustine, a large prawn with tiny claws which are bent up and over making that inimitable artistic feature. These platters come with a set of implements that look similar to those you would find in a dentist's surgery. Every last morsel of pincer or crab leg is poked with a fine steel lance, and enormous nutcracker like tools crack the large claws. It can easily take an hour to work your way through one of these platters.

At work, I often took my sandwiches to a park set along the low cliffs on the further side of La Rochelle entrance to the harbour. Even in winter I could eat here in the sun and it was always quiet, often deserted. However, one lunchtime I was surprised to find the car park full and the rocks below covered with people all busy collecting things. I watched fascinated. So many people, perhaps fifty, searching so assiduously, some returning to their cars, shoulders lopsided with the weight of the finds in their bucket. On my return to work I mentioned what I had seen.

"It's the highest co-efficient, the equinox tide and the best time for the *pèche à pied*."

When I got home I asked Bill if he had heard the term. "It's literally fishing on foot, but it looked more like on all fours, or knees, to me."

I persuaded Bill to try it ourselves the next day, since this was Saturday, while the tides were still low, and we decided to go to the Ile d'Oléron. We went to a beach we had already discovered, that we knew had good rock pools.

On leaving the anonymity of the car, we felt very self-conscious carrying our wire basket, a bucket and a hand-

rake. After half an hour we had only found a few mussels.

"I don't think this is the best area," I said despondently.

"Don't give up too soon, come on, keep trying."

But I was watching a woman raking the sand not far from the water's edge. She obviously was not looking for mussels, but she was filling her bucket with something. Curiosity drove me across.

"Excuse me, *Madame*, could you tell me what you're looking for?"

"*Palourdes*," she said, hardly looking up.

The name meant nothing to me and she sensed it.

"You don't know what *palourdes* are?" Evidently I should have done.

"No, you see I'm English and all this is new to me."

"Ah." There was a wealth of meaning in that word, these poor English who not only don't know what a *palourde* is but also don't understand the satisfaction of looking for shellfish, let alone, probably, the pleasures of eating them.

"Well look, these are *palourdes* and they're delicious if you boil them for a few minutes and serve them with cream, a delicate flavour. You can also eat them raw."

I would not contemplate that, but I was intrigued by her bucket full of shiny surfaced small bivalves, just a little bigger than a fifty pence piece.

"Thank you. And you find them in the sand?"

"Only at very low tide, on the edge of the sea. Look, here's one" And she raked it out and held it up for me to see.

Thanking her, I raced back to Bill.

"Forget the mussels. Come and help me find *palourdes*. They're those things you had in the restaurant last week."

"Those tiny clams? They were delicious."

"So you said." I had a vision of Bill digging his fork into a pile of spaghetti covered with small shellfish, twirling up the strands and lifting his forkful to his nose gently sniffing. His face had changed from cautious to ecstatic and conversation had ceased until his plate was empty and he'd said "that was…" he kissed his finger to his lips. No, I didn't think he would hesitate to find his own.

We chose our spot well because by the end of an hour we had enough for lunch. There is nothing more satisfying than food you've found for yourself. Oh yes, I was becoming very French.

At the next high co-efficient we returned to the Ile d'Oléron in Evita. We had parked for the night in an isolated spot, overlooking a beach on the western side. With the associations of Rachel and Brian's engagement and our visit here, we were feeling very romantic. We sat arm in arm watching the sunset, with first apricot linings to the clouds, then the sky lit in a mixture of oranges and pinks. Finally the red ball of a sun sank below the horizon and we turned to go in.

In what seemed like the early hours, we were woken by a car pulling up, doors slamming and voices. By the time we had roused ourselves enough to peer through the window, we saw two men trudging off across the rocks with what looked like a crowbar, rake and bucket. One was elderly, but despite needing the aid of a stick, was obviously determined to keep up with the younger, who was jumping from ledge to ledge, bending low and peering. Suddenly he was satisfied, and beckoned the other over. The old man directed with his stick while the younger poked and trawled the gully with his crowbar and rake. They were certainly finding plenty of something, as we could see them throwing whatever it was into the bucket which was obviously growing heavy. Every now and again they would stop and peer before continuing.

"It's only six o'clock, Bill!"

But he had already leapt out of bed and was dressing quickly. "Come on, lazybones. I want to know what they are finding."

Mussels.

As soon as they had gone we were out like a shot to carry on where they had left off before the tide came in. Bill improvised and used a tyre lever instead of a crowbar, while I remembered the small handrake we'd bought for *palourdes,* now stored in the cupboard with our walking boots. With no bucket we felt rather silly walking down to the water's edge carrying a saucepan, but as there was no-one around it did not matter.

"Nothing but mussels," Bill directed as I stopped to see if I could catch a prawn.

Even so, it was hard not to be diverted by the sideways scuttling crabs and the beauty of the green and purple sea anemones. But Bill was single-minded.

When the saucepan was full of shiny blue-black mussels, I straightened up, easing a back-ache from all this bending over.

"I'm ravenous," I said. "It's ten o'clock and we haven't had breakfast yet."

"No, but look what we've got for lunch. And anyway, if we'd stopped for breakfast this gully would have been covered. You can see how fast the tide is coming in."

There are two mussel specialities of our area, *mouclade* and *éclade*. The first is when the mussels are cooked with a creamy saffron sauce and this had become a favourite when we ate in restaurants. The second remained a mystery, but a mystery that everyone spoke of with the typical finger to the lips kissing gesture that meant it was absolutely delicious.

On one of our *fondue* group get-togethers, Isabelle, with the brown eyes, arranged a mussel-farming trip, after which we would return to her flat for an *éclade*. Her brother was a mussel farmer and was willing to take a group of us out on his boat to his mussel farm at Charron, north of La Rochelle. Apparently Charron is ideal because it is a wide curved bay, with very muddy shores, so that there are no tourist beaches or pleasure craft which might interfere with the 'farming'. In addition these mussels, we were told are particularly fat and tasty.

Pierre was late and Isabelle was worried. "If we're not there on time Jean-Luc will start without us because if we're even ten minutes late the boat will be stuck on the mud. Oh, I *do* wish Jean-Luc would hurry."

She phoned and there was no reply. Obviously he was on his way. She fussed and fretted and finally announced we would have to leave and what was more would have to drive fast if we were to reach the boat before it set off for its day's work. We drove off with many backward glances to see if Pierre was following, but he wasn't. We arrived with only seconds to spare: the engine was already running, the fore ropes already cast off and Jean-Luc scanning the road for his sister and her friends.

The boat was flat bottomed with a steering cabin at one end. The six of us settled against this, using our haversacks containing our picnics as cushions, and watched the coast recede. We could understand Jean-Luc's panic as already there was a strip of mud along where the boat had been moored.

We chugged out to sea and after about half an hour we saw the bright yellow buoys marking the farm, bobbing on the brilliant blue water. Jean-Luc steered the boat alongside a pole. I saw thick ropes, the size of my wrist, stretched between it and the next. While one of the crew held the boat steady, Jean-Luc lifted the ropes, inspected them and returned them to the water. Isabelle explained these were the young ones. Then the boat turned towards the coast, but not the river estuary we had left from. The next set of poles, had ropes coiled round them, bulging with big, fat, bluey-black mussels. Now all four of the crew sprang into action. A machine I hadn't really noticed before was a pair of claws which were lowered to the base of the pole, closed and then drawn upwards, pulling off the rope with its mussels. This was dropped onto the floor of the boat, and the next pole stripped, until the boat was piled high with these garlands. Finally the crew used another machine to pull all the mussels off the ropes, dropping them onto a tray which juddered and vibrated while seawater was pumped over it, to clean off any pieces of seaweed or debris. This was a noisy process, making conversation impossible, so it was a choice of watching or sun-bathing. Bill pulled out his newspaper. But I noticed he seemed to be using it as a cover for observing the beautifully tanned Isabelle in her bikini! Eventually the noise stopped and the cleaned mussels were packed into sacks. While this process was going on, we ate our sandwiches and dared each other to go for a swim. This was all talk and no action, despite the sunshine, as the water here was muddy-brown and totally uninviting.

The day, as usual with this group was fun and we returned sun-burned and salt-sprayed, clutching a large sack of mussels for our *éclade*. Just as we were stepping off the boat, Jean-Luc turned to Bill and asked if he liked mussels, and when he found he did, pressed anther sack into his hand.

Back at Isabelle's flat it was everyone to work. The girls prepared the salad, while the men discussed which wine we would drink. Bill and Isabelle cleaned the mussels while I rubbed in after-sun cream seeing how red my nose was. Then it was everyone to work, fitting the mussels into the grid of upright nails.

"No, Gilly-Anne, turn the mussel upside down, so the ash doesn't go inside."

I watched and copied the others, wondering all the while how this eclade was going to work. In typical French fashion, as we worked, my friends discussed other recipes for mussels. The boards were then put on her balcony and completely covered with pine-needles. These would be lit, the heat being enough to cook the mussels, which open. Now I understood about the ash falling in if incorrectly placed.

It seemed to me an elaborate way to cook good mussels.

We settled at the table, ready for our tasty dish. Bill used his hands to play a trumpet fanfare as Isabelle lit the needles. But, being dry, they flared up and burnt out virtually immediately.

The mussels were disgusting! Having only recently learnt to appreciate them, these were everything I had imagined I would dislike, slimy and tasting mainly of salt. I used gallons of water and plenty of bread to gulp down my helping. What a disappointment.

Bill, being gallant, accepted a second helping. He told me afterwards these were much tastier - perhaps because a new set of needles had been lit over them, so they were better cooked. I'm convinced that those I ate were largely raw.

We learnt later that the art of cooking an *éclade* is to use green needles which burn slowly, releasing their oil as they do so, not dry ones like ours. A good *éclade*, we discovered when trying again in a restaurant, is delicious.

Our real induction into the art of *pèche à pied* was with the *foyer*. Every year a spot is chosen and about eighteen families set off together from the village. Dressed in shorts and pumps or old tracksuits and wellies, according to the weather, the identifying features are the knife, the hand-rake and the bucket.

We set off towards the rocks armed with our implements. Mothers call anxiously to their fast disappearing children, giving last minute safety instructions and the rest of us amble along catching up with the latest news. Someone starts the typical joking.

"Who's for oysters?"

"Who needs the aphrodisiac?"

"What about you, Beel?"

Comic gesturing from Bill and laughter all around.

"That way for the mussels and oysters, and over there for the *palourdes*."

It's usually the women who go for the *palourdes* as it is a fiddly job compared with cutting an oyster off a rock. The children splash excitedly between the groups and try to catch a crab to wave in the faces of those most likely to shriek.

Some see the morning as a job and work without talking. For others it's a social occasion and there's more talking than working. Martine is a talker and will pick a serious subject to discuss. Scraping the sand desultorily while discussing the role of women in French society or the latest educational changes, is an interesting way to spend the morning. But it causes snorts from Bill when he finds my bucket virtually empty.

Mid-day is a clarion call for a return to base for the *apéritifs* and the big picnic, about twenty-five people sit typically at a row of tables with food passed round and shared. For a long time after our first picnic, it was believed that these poor *Anglais* needed feeding and our plates were always heaped with food.

"Where's Sylvain?"

"Still gorging oysters."

"Oysters! Watch out then Suzanne!"

Good humour and jokes are often bawdy but part of the day.

The Third Year

CHAPTER 33

Village Concerns and Revolution

I was first made aware of the snail cult when we were travelling after just having emigrated. It had been late August and we had stopped in a campsite in the Lot valley, surrounded by hedges with a little copse in one corner. The hedgerow was laden with fat juicy blackberries so I could not resist picking some for our supper. Returning to the site carrying my colanderful, another camper sitting outside his caravan in the sun, greeted me with, "*Bonjour, Madame.* How many have you got, then?"

"All this, full. Big fat ones."

"Really? I collected this morning. Wouldn't have thought there'd be so many at this time of day. They tend to hide when the sun comes out."

I was bewildered. Hide? Blackberries? He got up and came to inspect my haul.

"*Bof*! It's only blackberries," he said as though I had collected something truly worthless. "I thought you'd got snails!"

"Snails?" I repeated stupidly, thinking but what would I want snails for?

He stared at me thoughtfully. "I guess from your accent you're English, yes?"

I nodded.

"And you don't eat snails." This was uttered as though it was the most abnormal thing he had ever considered. "But are you interested? Come and look."

Underneath his caravan he had some large containers and a big saucepan with a lid. I looked even more perplexed.

"That's for cleaning them. Can't just eat them the way you find them. Since you don't know what they've been eating, you've got to clean them first."

Having captured my attention, he proceeded to explain further. For two days snails should be put in flour, after this it is one day in vinegar, next two days in water. At the end of that, they are clean enough to eat. I could not help thinking, if they have not died of the process first. I certainly could not imagine wanting to eat them after all that. Nonetheless, I had a certain admiration for the lengths people would go to, to make their snails edible.

In Chambon, after rain, snail hunting becomes a serious activity. Our neighbours go out in Wellington boots with their buckets to collect perhaps a hundred or so. In summer when it is light, this can be as early as six a.m.

It intrigued Bill. He would watch and comment.

"There goes Louisette with her bucket to get her snails. Too late – Marie was out half an hour ago."

People from other areas drive to our part of the commune because we have hedges with ditches and the two together make the damp areas loved by snails.

Our neighbours quickly understood that though I will not touch them, Bill loves snails. So Bernard and Marie invited us to a snail lunch. I had watched Bill eat snails in restaurants, either served in a rich Bourguignonne sauce, or on a special dish with hollows for the snails cooked in garlic and parsley butter. Nothing prepared me for Bernard's 'special'.

Being a sunny summer's day, we were eating outside. Having heated the barbecue, he simply placed the snails on a grid and put it over the glowing coals. I did not like the sizzling sound and even less the froth emerging from the cooking snails.

We sat round the table normal fashion, men one end discussing cars and 'masculine' topics, and women the other, discussing 'feminine' ones. Marie had made stuffed cabbage for both of us, as she admitted she did not like the frothing either. Julie, their six year old daughter, was watching the men intently as they twisted the soft body out of the shell and munched it appreciatively. After a while she asked for some too and sat persevering at this manner of eating.

At length she looked up and said in surprise, "Why, I've eaten more than any of you. I've eaten twelve."

Sure enough there were twelve shells on her plate and considerably less on anyone else's. There was silence for a moment before her Dad said, "So you have."

No one mentioned the buckets under the table filled with the empty shells discarded from time to time by the others as their plates became too encumbered.

It was not long before Bill decided to try this storing and cleaning process for himself. The secret, so Bernard told him was to find a big enough container to store them until you had several hundred, enough for a meal, and *then* to start the cleaning process. Since it was only for himself,

Bill was not prepared to wait to for the large numbers and started with his first collection of around twenty.

He duly left them in flour for two days and had his vinegar mixture ready for day three.

As he lifted the lid I heard him exclaim in disgust.

A short while later he came in and said quietly, "I let them all go. The stench was terrible. I couldn't stomach eating that. Then they were all contorted ... I couldn't cope with another three days."

However in another fit of enthusiasm he decided to try again, putting in less flour at the beginning.

Again on the third day he went to the shed to change the flour to the vinegar mixture. I heard him calling me to come and look and I could tell from his tone that it was not to observe the changeover.

Going into the shed, I saw him staring at the ceiling. Snails. Up the walls, across the ceiling and along the floor, silvery snail trails everywhere. Somehow they had chewed their way through the plastic container and escaped.

I quietly helped him collect them and without thinking asked if he was going to give them to Bernard.

"Nope. I reckon this lot *deserve* their liberty."

He must have been the only man in France to be liberating a batch of snails back into the hedgerows.

Occasionally he mutters about finding a washing machine drum, which we have been told, is an excellent storage place for snails. But on the whole he prefers to eat them in other people's houses.

One subject of conversation is of all engrossing interest - which crops are being planted and then how well they are doing. The fields around us are planted with mauve opium poppies, rape, which makes a splash of acrylic yellow in the spring, sunflowers with their golden yellow in the summer, and the stiff rows of head-high maize. But the talk is of what we are all planting.

"I see Bernard's putting in his beans," (little man with the limp).

"Already? The soil's not 15 degrees yet." (Monsieur Lavergne)

"He reckons it's time."

"Well we'll see. I'm leaving mine for another few days."

Or another annual conversation around April:

"I've sown one hundred tomato plants." Jacques enthused.

"For two of you?" The farmer by the mill scoffed.

"So that I can give some to my neighbours."

One day the man with a limp asked curiously "What's that you're putting in then?"

"Asparagus, just a few plants," Bill said.

"They like a sandy soil…" the little man said dubiously.

"I've added some. Anyway, we'll see. I like trying things out."

The little man walked away, muttering something about *'ces anglais'*. And he was right, the asparagus did not thrive in our heavy soil.

One day Jacques came to lean on the gate. After the customary salutations, he said, "Busy?"

"Just preparing my bed for my sweetcorn." Bill stopped his raking.

"I was wondering if you'd have a moment –"

"Of course."

"Ah, that's good of you. It's just some blocks I want moving. Can't do it on my own."

"No problem. Now?"

Jacques grinned. "In a moment. Go and check your insurance is up to date first. These blocks are heavy."

Later he said to me, "I was saying to *la patronne* this morning, Monsieur Beel is a good neighbour, and *costaud*, a strong one."

We were simply glad to be able to repay in some way all the help we had been given when we arrived.

Another concern was the quality of bread. The village positively came alive over this subject.

In France people buy their baguette daily, in fact in towns, often twice a day. It is eaten as a matter of course with a main meal, but in our area, never with soup as it is in Britain. In the country a piece is either broken off or, if it is a loaf, it is held up to the chest and cut in, towards the body. One slip of the knife – but this never happens. Baguettes are the standard fare, or *pain*, a larger version, and people put out their long bread bag on the gate if they are not at home and the baker drops in the usual baguette. Neither of these breads last well, and they need to be eaten the same day, but *pain levain*, being a much heavier texture, does. In some country areas, these loaves are huge, so chunks are cut off and sold according to weight.

Our village had its own baker and his wife drove her van round both ours and the neighbouring villages every morning. This not only provides a means of buying bread but a meeting point and time for a chat.

One day Louisette knocked at our door.

"Look at this, Gilly-Anne. Just look at this!" she held up the baguette she had just bought. It began to bend in the middle, as though it were taking a bow, slow motion. I stared fascinated.

"Where did you get it?"

She carried on, ignoring such a stupid question. "Just look at it. Who wants to eat bread like that? I don't know what's come over André – his bread's getting worse and worse."

"We've given up buying his bread."

"Well the time has come to ask another baker to do the rounds of Chambon. Yes, another baker. Perhaps the baker at Le Thou, he's not too far away." Brandishing her rubber bread she marched off to enlist the help of our neighbours in her project.

A switch of loyalty to a baker in a small community is a major event. Many of our neighbours had been at school, both primary and secondary, with André. Their parents and grandparents had always bought their bread from the village baker, and his livelihood depended on the custom of the villagers. For a couple of weeks there were heated discussions in the road, and as our house was at a junction, this often meant outside our garden. There were reminiscences of the previous village baker, and of 'young' André when he took over fifteen years earlier. The words 'baker', 'quality of bread', 'loyalty' and 'misplaced loyalty' resounded in my ears. Then it stopped.

The following week a new horn was heard, a two toned one. The new baker. Everyone flocked out to buy bread, standing around congratulating themselves on the manoeuvre. Suddenly it was as though a school playground bell had been rung: the road was empty. Five minutes later the usual baker's horn was heard. The baker's wife sat at the wheel and waited, and waited.

Closed doors. Silence. She tooted her horn again. Still no movement. Slowly the van moved away.

Loyalty to André was partially restored after another innovative idea of Stephane's, boycotted by one half of the village, praised by the other.

"Gilly-Anne, now the library has been open nearly a year," (oh yes, I thought, the controversial library) "we're planning an anniversary celebration. I'm organising an exhibition of people's talents in Chambon."

I thought of the faith healer. Did he have 'a talent'?

"In fact it's anything that people do, paintings and pottery – well anything." His eyes sparkled mischievously, "Come on Gilly-Anne, what can *you* offer?"

"Nothing. I don't have that sort of talent."

"Don't believe you. You've got plenty of talent – there must be *something.*"

"Only stories," I mumbled.

"Excellent. I knew you'd have something artistic."

"But they're in English."

"Pity…Never mind, you do translations, you can translate them."

"Yes, I do translations, but they're factual. Literary style is another thing altogether, and I can't do that."

"Oh, I'm sure you could."

As far as he was concerned, he'd solved the problem. But I knew the intricacies of translating into a literary French style were beyond me.

In fact the exhibition was a fascinating mixture of villagers' interests, talent in pottery, crocheting, lace-making, patch-work, woodcarving and paintings, ranging from rather crude acrylics to soft water colours, from one of a boat on a palm tree beach that I couldn't believe had been done by a twelve year old, to some that could easily have been on exhibition in La Rochelle. Who would have thought we had so much talent hidden away in our village? There were also people's collection of old farm implements, a hand plough, a butter churn and an early haymaker, on display in the yard, as well as a collection of photos of people in the commune working collectively in the fields. Dominating one side of the room was a fascinating display on the history of bread-making, texts, photos and samples of the different breads. Why is a croissant crescent-shaped? Because it was originally made to commemorate a victory over the Turks, so imitated the symbol on their flag.

Automatically people were drawn to something connected with their daily lives. It prompted questions and reminiscences, and requests were made for André to start making some of these 'historic' breads again. His popularity soared – in my opinion, higher than the quality of this bread. Eventually a compromise was reached and the two bakers now call on alternate days.

CHAPTER 34

Witness at a Wedding

One thing I had introduced into the *foyer*'s activities was an annual ramble. The person who is the keenest walker was Jean-Marc, so we planned them together.

On one of our rambles, Jean-Marc suddenly took my arm and increased his speed, to move away from the group.

"Gilly-Anne, I've something significant to tell you, but it's a secret and you mustn't tell anyone."

"Of course not."

"Well, Yvonne and I are getting married."

For a moment his whole face softened.

"That's great!"

"It's only to legalise things of course," he added quickly. "It won't change anything. It'll be just the civil ceremony, with you and Beel and two other close friends. And I want you to be a witness."

"We'd love to come and I'd feel honoured to be a witness."

"That's settled then. By the way, we haven't told our families yet, so Lysiane doesn't know – please don't mention it."

"Of course not. When will it be?"

"As soon as Yvonne's divorce comes through."

I remembered what I had been told about divorces being difficult and lengthy processes and hoped it would not be so for Yvonne. But it was a whole year later that the ceremony took place. In the meantime we set our minds to thinking what we could possibly buy them that would be appropriate.

"They won't want anything for the house. Remember what happened to us, we had two housefuls of everything," Bill said.

"Yes and look what happened – our children did well out of that. I gave masses of my stuff to Gareth not realising you had done the same thing and given loads of your stuff to Henry, then we arrived out here with no china and no kitchen stuff. It was just as well Rachel was abroad or we would have had no linen either."

"But we had fun going round the antique shops and stalls restocking, didn't we?"

"Of course, and now we've got our own stuff. But what about Jean-Marc and Yvonne?"

"Something for the barn? After all, it's pretty basic."

"But perhaps they like it that way." I said doubtfully.

"It could certainly do with more lighting –"

"Brilliant idea."

"We could get a Campinggaz lamp. They're pretty efficient."

"That's hardly suitable for a wedding present, Bill. What about an oil lamp?"

"That's even better. That's settled then."

But we found nothing locally and could not think where we would be likely to find one. An image of an intriguing shop with everything from saddlery to kitchenware in Elizondo, in the Spanish Pyrenees, kept coming to mind. If only it were nearer.

"Wait a minute, Bill, I've got it. Ascension Thursday is coming up so that will give us a four-day weekend. We can go to Elizondo to that *ferreteria (Spanish for hardware store)*. You remember the one, where you nearly bought that hollow stick for blowing the fire like a bellows? They had masses of oil lamps there."

"Are you sure?"

"Absolutely certain."

"Well, it makes an excellent excuse for another trip to Spain."

Elizondo is just over the Pyrenees, high on the Spanish side. It is a dark town, built of the brown granite, solid buildings which march down the hillside. Half way down the main street is the *ferretaria*. As soon as we approached and saw the stack of pots and farm tools stacked on the pavement outside, it reminded us of the delights within. We had spent a whole hour browsing there on our last visit. This shop sells everything from horse saddles on one side of the room to vases on the other. In between is a range of mountain walking sticks, earthenware, ironmongery and the fire blowing-sticks that had fascinated Bill.

I led the way confidently to the oil lamps. Sure enough there were seven to choose from, solid looking rectangular ones to flowered curves. We spent a long time considering which would be both attractive and efficient.

When the shop owner learned we had come all the way from La Rochelle to buy a lamp at his shop, we found ourselves the centre of attention. Not only was he and his wife extremely helpful, but as we continued to browse, I could hear him bringing it into the conversation with every customer that came into his shop.

Having selected the lamp, we wandered, Bill veering towards the ironmongery and me towards the pretty things. One of the first to catch my eye was a china chamberpot with bright flowers painted on it. I fetched Bill and pointed it out.

"For us?" He looked a little puzzled.

"No, silly, for them. You know their loo's downstairs in the barn and it's one of those ladder type staircases, not much fun to go down in the middle of the night."

"Well done. We'll have it."

For some reason I decided to buy a very large wooden spoon which I would decorate by scorching their initials in dots. I had in mind a Welsh love spoon but when Bill saw it he immediately thought I was thinking of 'the stirrer'.

"Bit near the mark, isn't it? I mean, which of them is supposed to be the one who stirs things up? Or does one award it to the other as appropriate?"

Perhaps it was not such a good idea, after all. I hesitated, but finally decided to buy one and decorate it anyway.

When I next saw Yvonne, I asked her what she would be wearing, whether she wanted confetti, white ribbons on the car, or what.

"*Mais, non*! Good heavens no. We're only legalising things. We don't want all the trappings that go with a normal wedding. Keep it light-hearted."

Keep it light-hearted … We thought about that when we were discussing with the other couple, Pierrette and Claude, what we should do to make it memorable.

Pierrette looked at us. "I know, since Bill's Scottish, he'll go in his kilt. In fact both men can wear kilts, that's even better."

"I would if I could, but I haven't got one anymore," Bill said with regret.

"Don't worry. I know where we can get kilts, and I'm game if you are," Claude said. "Just leave it to us."

Apparently some years earlier, the entire commune had created a Scottish float for the La Rochelle carnival and sixty men from the village had all worn kilts.

On the day, Claude and Bill looked true romantic figures in red tartan kilts, black waistcoats and a forage cap perched jauntily on their heads. Pierrette and I looked very ordinary by comparison. We stood by the entrance of the *mairie* waiting for the couple. The look on Jean-Marc's face when he turned into the courtyard was a mixture of incredulity and amusement.

"*Ce n'est pas vrai!* I might have known you two would get up to something. I should have kept you under lock and key." But as he was chuckling we knew he was not objecting.

"Just look at those two gorgeous men," was Yvonne's reaction.

We were both curious about the procedure. Me, being incurable romantic, ridiculously sentimental. However, almost as soon as the ceremony had started, it ended. Five minutes to state the names, the mutual responsibility for a marriage, and to conclude. I could not believe how short it was. But then followed a surprise because it is the custom for the mayor, on behalf of the commune to give presents, in this case a bottle of *pineau,* for the groom and flowers for the bride.

We went back to their house for champagne. Now we learnt that our presents had a significance we knew nothing about, so the comments as they unwrapped our gifts were at first incomprehensible. The lamp was received as expected, with appreciation, the chamberpot, with giggles.

"So you're planning onion soup are you?" laughed Yvonne.

"Onion soup?" we said, mystified.

"You mean you didn't know?" she saw our bewildered faces. "No, obviously not. Jean-Marc! They didn't know!"

When the four of them had finished laughing, Jen-Marc explained. "It used to be the custom that around three in the morning following a wedding, the married couple were ceremoniously brought onion soup, served in a chamberpot."

It began to be clearer, but I was still puzzled.

"To revive the flagging energies of the groom. And look, you've even provided the spoon." Yvonne brandished this at Jean-Marc who made to grab it from her, seizing her at the same time for a kiss.

"Fancy choosing all the appropriate things, yet not knowing they were so," added Pierrette.

"So who's bringing the soup?" finished Yvonne.

"Where will you be? Or is that a secret?" Bill asked.

"No secret, we're looking after our grandchildren and their friends while their parents consort with you two Broomes at a party."

"On your wedding night? You're babysitting?" I said, incredulous.

"We kept telling you it was only a legality…"

We four witnesses passed amused glances as the couple was once more locked in an embrace.

Walking into the restaurant later caused a romantic fluttering from ladies at other tables, not because of the bride and groom, but because of the swirling kilts.

Bill had asked me to translate a short speech, because he felt it was an honour to have been asked to be a witness and therefore his *Franglais* was not suitable for the feelings he wanted to express. I had written it out phonetically so that it should sound correct and he had spent time that morning practising it. So the group was surprised when he stood up, asked for silence and made his speech in perfect French.

"I feel honoured to have been asked to such a special occasion. Jean-Marc and Yvonne have become very good friends since we have settled in Chambon and I am delighted to attend their wedding. I wish them long life and happiness together."

It was not a long speech, but only I know how much effort Bill had put into it to make it sound right.

Claude rose to toast the couple with Bill, and the people at the tables nearby, suddenly realising the nature of the occasion, toasted them as well. Jean-Marc and Yvonne, looking very self-conscious, hands interlaced, thanked Bill formally. Then Jean-Marc joked, "But Beel, if you speak French so well, I don't need to learn English anymore."

Since the restaurant was at the Venise Verte, with its magical network of canals, Jean-Marc had arranged for us to take a barque for the afternoon.

"Sit back and enjoy yourselves while we do the work," we said.

As Jean-Marc sat down in the stern, the bows shot up into the air. When we had successfully adjusted the balance between us, we set off and they were able to sit arms round each other, supposedly peacefully in the stern.

Either a hired punter punts the boat for you, or you are given paddles to do it yourself. We chose the latter. Not being used to each other's stroke, we first swung from one bank to another, crashing our lovers into bushes and nearly sweeping them into the water with overhanging branches.

"Very romantic," muttered Jean-Marc, brushing leaves out of his hair.

"Wait till we get our rhythm," Claude said.

"Have confidence," Bill added.

"That's what we haven't got at the moment," Yvonne laughed.

A group of girls in a passing punt called out, "Are you really Scotsmen?"

"*Bien sûr*! Of course we are," called back Claude, very much in the spirit of things.

Since there were many boats on the canal where we were, I suggested we went off the marked route and explored some of the smaller, quieter ones. This was much better. Here we were able to enjoy the mauve and cream comfrey growing on the bank and we even watched a coypu swimming ahead of us. At last our couple felt they could relax.

Being a hot day, the only way to cool off was to return to their house and dive into the pool.

That evening the anomaly of our situation was brought home to us – having spent the day as close friends of Jean-Marc and Yvonne, we were now going to a party with his daughter, the delectable Lysiane, and her age group. Here we danced until three in the morning. A full day.

CHAPTER 35

Grumbles and Fairyland

I was now working, not only at Sup de Co, but also at the engineering school that tried its best to make their students bi-lingual. Here more than anywhere I enjoyed the camaraderie of a staffroom as well as the lively interaction with the students. I was also teaching in two international companies whose meetings and reports were all in English, and therefore their managers were required to be proficient in business English. This was demanding, but very well paid. Unfortunately many of my classes in the companies were at eight in the morning, before the phone lines became busy, and the last sessions with the students did not finish until six thirty. So I found the days long.

A Friday was 'Bill's Day', the day I kept free of work so that we could go away at weekends in Evita and explore our area. In effect this meant the rest of the week was crammed and I began to realise I was virtually working full-time, but in only four days. Gone was the leisurely routine of part-time work and no homework of the language school.

Periodically I would grumble, but as I was now bringing in a good salary and still had long holidays, this was intermittent. Also, now my reputation was established, I was in a position of being able to choose only the work I enjoyed. And one of the things I enjoyed most was the variety of people I met, from company directors to earnest young students, who would be the company directors of the future.

I learnt how reluctant many French managers were to adapt to the fact of English being the international language of commerce and to the changes in the way of conducting work that seemed to be inevitably following. The lunch-hour had been sacrosanct, a time when the buildings were deserted and the local restaurants were filled, many people going home for lunch. Twelve midday was a time of traffic jams in La Rochelle as everyone rushed off punctually. Now, for the first time, the hour and a half, or even two hours break, was being eroded. One of the two companies I worked in, that sold mainly through catalogues, was taken over by an American company who quickly introduced a working lunch hour. However, it was fascinating to see how a French employee interpreted this. First, she organised to arrive at ten instead of eight; second, she obviously needed a microwave. At ten o'clock she duly arrived carrying a wicker basket with her lunch covered by her tablecloth. A lunch hour for her, sitting at a table duly laid with her pretty tablecloth, was a far cry from the sandwich snack working lunch hour that her American boss had envisaged!

However much I enjoyed the variety of my work, there seemed to be an increasing amount of extra work that was being expected. As soon as I had a course organised, there were new ideas or modifications to be incorporated and the need for reports and meetings dramatically increased. It was not that I did not enjoy my teaching, but I began to want to use my time in a different way. I was developing a fascination for writing. An anecdote or even a phrase heard would spark off an idea for a short story. At first I crept away to write while Bill thought I was marking students' essays. When I became more confident, I gave him one to read.

"But this is good. Why don't you do more?"

"Because I don't have the time."

He thought about this and said, "Perhaps we should make sure you *have* the time."

But what with my work and our time exploring, there was little left over for writing.

Going away in Evita, gave Bill a chance to evaluate his renovation work. He decided not to continue with the spare bedrooms upstairs, as we didn't really need them, and he preferred to devote his time to the garden and our weekends and holiday times to exploring. But he did decide to fit a staircase.

We had been camping out in our house for virtually two years and climbing a well-worn hay loft ladder to go upstairs had become perfectly normal, even though it meant coming down backwards. Therefore to fit a staircase was not only a big step, but one that would make our house more conventional. Countless measurings were taken before we went to choose one because our limited space meant we needed a turn, but at an appropriate place, and the nature of our rustic house meant we wanted something simple. In addition Bill wanted it in kit form, as a good wood staircase is expensive.

Having got our kit home and having struggled to fit it over two days, Bill had to admit defeat. His frustration was trying to fit the turn of the staircase where there wasn't a beam immediately overhead. He rang the shop for help.

The expert arrived (everyone is an 'expert' in France), took his measurements and assured us the computer would solve the problem instantly. In fact he would take it away and assemble it for us and bring it back in two days.

"Excellent," said Bill, "but the main problem is not the turn itself, but the height of that beam there. All our beams are unusually low" (I had a quick vision of Alan cradling his stone crusher under the offending beam.). "Look, the beam here is very low. Unless it's the correct distance from the beam, we'll hit our heads going up the stairs."

Despite Bill declaring the height was the important factor, the expert did not measure it. In exasperation Bill did so and insisted it be written down with the other details. We now have a beautiful staircase of polished Beechwood – ideal for dwarfs. Everyone else needs to duck as the turning step is exactly below the beam. What an 'expert'!

However, the installation of the staircase immediately lifted the status of our house into a 'real' house. A significant step had been made. Our bedroom is open plan to the ground floor, very practical as the heat from Luc's stove now heats that as well as the downstairs. We bought a carpet and I made new curtains to create a proper bedroom, rather than the camping out version we had had before, and we felt we were living in luxury.

"All I need to do now, is turn this next room into an ensuite bathroom. I think I'll tackle that next winter. What do you think, *chérie*?"

"That would be perfect."

I hugged him.

It was shortly after this that we invited Stephane and his wife for a meal, in the course of which he was surprised to hear how much we had paid for our building permit.

"But you didn't need one!" he exclaimed. "You haven't altered the exterior or extended the building."

We looked at each other. I knew exactly what was going through Bill's mind: the book said….

"We understood it was necessary," I faltered.

"And you've paid it?"

"We have another tranche to pay, twelve hundred francs."

Stephane whistled then thought for a moment. "Look, leave it with me and I'll see what I can do."

The following day he rang. "I can't get you back what you have already paid, but you can forget that twelve hundred. They are prepared to call it quits if you pay forty. And the rest will be accepted as a misunderstanding."

"Stephane, that's marvellous! How can we thank you?"

"Oh, you'll find a way, Gilly-Anne!"

Bill was amazed and greatly relieved when I told him. "That's what comes of being friends with the *maire!*"

One evening I had a staff meeting at Sup de Co. These didn't happen very often, but when they did, they were long. At least they were followed by a buffet.

When I got home around nine o'clock I sank onto the sofa, exhausted, expecting Bill to sit beside me for our usual exchange of news. Instead he disappeared upstairs.

Coming halfway down again he beckoned. He had one of those smiles on his face that meant he was up to something. Curious, I went towards him. He took me by the hand and we went upstairs.

Fairyland.

The room was ablaze with dozens and dozens of birthday cake candles. All around the wooden bed-head, the chest of drawers, and the bookcase, were little flames of gold.

"Bill, it's beautiful."

"Like you, my darling. I did it for you because I love you so much." He seized my hand and kissed the palm.

CHAPTER 36

The Fascination of Skiing

In early February Bill suddenly looked up from watching the weather reports on the state of snow there was in the various ski reports, and said, "*Chérie*, how about us trying skiing?"

"Oh, but I never have."

"That doesn't stop us from trying. Imagine vast areas of pure white snow and us whizzing down gracefully. Anyway, it would be a challenge!"

Not one I was enthusiastic to try, but seeing the eager look on Bill's face I agreed. "What about *ski de fond?*" I temporised. I didn't see myself zooming down steep mountainsides alongside competent skiers, but cross-country skiing might be better.

"Right then. I'll do a bit of research and plan where we'll go."

Skiing is so much a part of French culture that school spring half terms are staggered region by region to avoid overcrowding at ski resorts, and every evening during the season there are reports on snow conditions. The season starts in mid-December and continues into April in the Alps, although the Pyrenean seasons finishes earlier. Our friends were very surprised when we'd said we had never skied,

We'd been watching professionals, figures in skin-tight, brightly coloured ski suits, bent virtually double, speeding down snow-covered slopes, zigzagging past markers and gliding to a standstill amongst cheers. In the World Cup events held in the Vallée de Chamonix, incredible speeds are achieved in the slaloms and, in a moment of enthusiasm, Bill looked up the facts: the best skiers did the vertical descent of 870metres over 3343metres in length in two minutes flat. He was impressed, but figures mean little to me, however the angle of the body and the way the markers flashed past, showed me that the speed was phenomenal. We were surprised to find that many of the skiers were very young, some even under twenty. But it is not only the professionals that are shown, the evening news shows shots of holidaymakers, including young children, gliding, bending and jumping.

One evening we were eating our supper and watching the news. All of a sudden our forks were suspended in amazement. We were watching the same acrobatic leaps and turns as we had seen the skateboarders do so many times in the park in La Rochelle, but this time in the snow. Snowboarding. To see youngsters leap acrobatically in the air to the background of snowy peaks was breathtaking. This we could never hope to achieve, but skiing itself was made to look so graceful and easy. Perhaps we could learn how to do it.

The day came and we set off for a small ski station specifically for *ski de fond*, the west end of the Pyrenees, not far from Bayonne, on a direct route south from us. I had overcome my initial fear and was excited. Bill was singing cheerfully as he drove, one of the Scottish folk songs of his youth. The day we arrived was gloriously sunny, spring-like although it was only February with yellow hazel catkins dangling, so we did not think of problems such as snowy roads or the need for snow chains. Our friends had told us all the ski station roads were kept clear. It was not until we were three quarters of the way to the top that we realised this was not necessarily true. There was no snow at all in the valley, and we were just saying that maybe there would not be enough snow at the top for skiing, when we turned the corner and met a different landscape, a blanket of white. Unfortunately, we realised, it was only for the big ski stations that the roads were kept clear.

Evita lurched to a stop.

"Bother," said Bill. "It'll be difficult to start her again here."

"Don't worry," I said cheerfully, "I can dig her out."

I got out and stamped around in the snow to see how deep it was – five or six centimetres. Hmm. Deep.

"What are you going to dig it out *with*?" Bill asked, rummaging in the boot cupboard where we kept our outdoor things. "We've got nothing suitable. Obviously, we'll have to get some chains."

"I'll try with a spoon. It'll take longer, but it will work." What optimism.

We set to work with two tablespoons digging out an area in front of the back wheels so that they could grip. The snow was new fallen, so easy to clear. If anyone had passed they would have thought we were two lunatics, digging out a camping car with tablespoons. But we cleared down to the tarmac.

It was now that I began to panic. Suppose Evita slid? After all, the road was steep here. On one side was a hedge and presumably a ditch, under the snow, on the other a slope with a copse disappearing down to the valley. When we got back in, I sat on the floor at the back, telling Bill I did not want to see the road ahead. He made no comment.

He put her in gear and edged forward. She held and began to move forward easily. I could hear the wheels crunching through the soft snow. I sat there, holding on to the two sides, my stomach churning, trying not to imagine us slipping.

"It's alright, darling. The snow's soft," Bill called back to me. "The wheels are gripping."

But I stayed where I was.

In fact we were not far from the station. He pulled in and parked. Feeling shaky with nerves, I went to make a coffee, but Bill leapt out to investigate the ski centre. When he got back, I said I'd get lunch.

"No time for lunch. It's best to go skiing now, there's more snow forecast."

"But I'm hungry. It's almost twelve o'clock."

"Exactly. They'll be closing for lunch soon. Grab a biscuit or something. But come on."

His eyes were shining with excitement and he was hopping from one foot to another, impatiently. I grabbed a handful of nuts to nibble, put on warm clothes, a scarf, a bobble hat and over the top, my kagoule and waterproof trousers. Feeling ready for the Arctic, I stepped out and plodded through the snow to the centre to catch up with Bill.

We were kitted out fairly quickly. I stood up in the snow uncertainly. I had felt sure someone would help with the first steps, give us some guidance, but no. The young man waved cheerily in the direction of the first waymarked post.

"The snow's ideal, just follow the posts, they mark out your route round the mountain. It's a maximum of two and a half hours, less according to your speed. Enjoy yourselves. See you after lunch."

I slid one foot forward tentatively. Then the other. It was fine. Again…gradually I worked out a rhythm.

"Bill, this is great."

"Wait till you get to some slopes," he cried gleefully.

I was not so sure about the slopes, but this part was most enjoyable.

As we slid smoothly over the soft snow I had time to look around. We were on a relatively small mountain and the track appeared to be following a contour below the peak. The snow was a brilliant white and sparkling in the sun. We were passing through dark conifers laden with snow. Every now and again snow lumps would dislodge, start to slide, pick up speed and splosh in the soft snow under the tree. This was the only sound apart from the swish of our skis. No one except for us was around. We skied silently, not wanting to break the atmosphere.

As we came out of the trees, we could see the valley below and the slopes of other mountains. Small spirals of blue wood smoke twisted up from miniature chimneys and I could see a yellow postvan cautiously making its way up a lane.

"Beautiful," I breathed.

Bill nodded and continued. I felt a sense of being suspended in space and time. I thought to myself, if this is skiing, no wonder it is so popular.

Bill began trying out a few turns, speeding ahead, twisting round and flying back towards me. But I was happy to keep swishing on evenly, saying to myself that I was taking the opportunity to look around.

The very last few metres were down what seemed to me a steep slope. Bill was zooming down at speed, looking proficient – until he landed in a sprawling heap in a drift of snow at the bottom

He picked himself up, laughing.

"So who thought he was ready for the Olympics then?" I called down.

By now I was tired from the unaccustomed exercise and very hungry. I decided to play safe and go down cautiously. As I reached the bottom, Bill said quietly, "Hello, Granny Kay." My mother. He was likening me, after my new-found skill, to my disabled mother who hobbled with two sticks.

"You beast," I muttered, but he was already speeding away towards the centre to return the skis.

As predicted it began to snow. It snowed all the way through our lunch and I suddenly realised we had to get back down this mountain. Would it be safe? Then I saw a snow plough emerge, turn round in the car park and start to make its way down again.

"Quick! Follow it. While the road's clear – come on, Bill."

I dumped the lunch things in the washing up bowl and got into my seat, strapping myself in. I held on to the handgrip firmly. As we crept out of the car park, we could see the newly cleared road already filling with snow. Bill concentrated on his driving, going down in second gear and feeling the way carefully.

At last we reached the open road of the valley, green grass and no snow. I could relax.

"That was a brilliant idea, *chérie*," Bill said easing the tension out of his body.

The following day, fired by the success of our first ski attempt, we decided to try another ski station and headed for a bigger one at Somport. This was much higher and it took all morning to wind our way slowly up the mountain, but being a main road, there was no problem with snow on the road. This time we had lunch first; we would ski in the afternoon.

This was so different from the day before. The car parks were full and we could see people wearing brightly coloured ski-wear surrounding the centre and school parties gathering in groups. At the centre there was not only the ski boot rental area, but a gift shop, restaurant and bar.

Full of confidence, we got ourselves kitted out and set off. The way was marked out with double tracks for the skis, like inverted railway lines, which you were supposed to keep to. Because it was a popular station, there was a queue of people behind, wanting to push us forward. This turned it into a form of physical exercise and there was no opportunity to stop and admire the beauty of the scenery.

"This is no fun, Bill. I'm going back to change to *raquettes*."

"Do so if you want, but I'm carrying on."

Raquettes are like tennis rackets, but with tails behind them. They are light and make it easy to walk on the top of the snow. With these I had freedom. It was only afterwards that I learnt I had been supposed to keep to a waymarked track, well away from the skiers. Since no one had told me, I thought I could go where I wanted, admire the slopes and snowy trees, and watch the antics of the skiers. From time to time I went back to the track to greet my more energetic husband.

"How are you doing?"

"Great! But I'll stop for a moment, I'm too hot."

We stopped together in a glade surrounded by tall snow-dropping pines. Bill stripped to the waist and rubbed snow into his chest.

"Isn't this incredible?" His eyes glowed with enthusiasm. "Here I am in deep snow, with the sun shining – bare-chested."

It was true. I had abandoned my Arctic clothing. I realised 'snow' does not always mean the biting cold, tingling fingers and numb noses of England.

I set off again, swinging away from the track, up towards the summit. My greatest pleasure was to find virgin snow, somewhere no one else had gone. A vast sparkling white expanse billowing across dips and up slopes. I broke the cleanness with my giant fish tracks up to the very top. All around was the relentless white of the snow topped by the brilliant blue of the sky. Far below was another ski station with tiny dark figures and I realised I was looking down into Spain. It wasn't until some time later that I discovered walking across virgin snow can be dangerous, not just for yourself, but for others if you inadvertently set off a chute of snow, or worse still, an avalanche.

That night we camped in the ski station car park. Once the skiers had gone, the place was deserted. Silence descended. We were alone in a white world, an eerie feeling.

Before breakfast we walked to the crest of the pass, where I stopped, fascinated by a trail of footprints.

"Just look at those tracks in the snow. They're enormous."

Bill stared closely. "Whatever are they?"

"I can't imagine." There seemed to be a large pad print, roughly the size of my hand, with four smaller ones around it. Could it be a bear?

"I don't think there are bears in this part of the Pyrenees," Bill said.

"Well, I'm going to draw it and send it to Pierre. Maybe he can tell us."

I measured it approximately with a pencil from my pocket and later sent it off with a letter explaining the details. (Two weeks later I had an amused phone call from Pierre: instead of looking at it as one footprint, I should have seen it as a set, two front feet with the two rear feet brought up close as the hare ran across the snow).

That morning we repeated the pattern of the day before, me on *raquettes* and Bill doing cross-country skiing. I watched him becoming more and more expert. I was impressed. I caught a glimpse of him flying down a long fairly steep slope, knees bent with the skis tucked under his arm, then I realised he had not reappeared along the track. I plodded off on my much slower *raquettes* to find out how he was doing.

A muffled '*Au secours!* Help'. There, in a drift were two skis, vertical and a couple of legs, also vertical.

"Bill?"

"Gillian?" a voice from the snow. "I can't get up. I'm all tangled up."

The only way I could disentangle him was to take off his skis. Once on his feet, he looked a bit sheepish.

"I went a bit too far, too fast," he admitted. "I watched a group doing a down slope with a jump and reckoned I could do it too. But I ended up as you saw. Maybe I'll change to *raquettes* now."

But after the speed of skiing, he found *raquettes* boring, so he suggested we went for lunch in the restaurant. We sat on the terrace, in shirtsleeves, enjoying the sun, surrounding by majestic snowy peaks. Arctic gear was definitely not necessary. Everyone around us seemed to be a committed skier. At the next table the parents were encouraging their three year old to take his first steps, or perhaps the word is slide, on a wide children's board. He slid a little, looked to his parents for approval, and slid again, his parents encouraging him. But those at nearby tables also smiled approvingly, for that is how it should be, to start young. I was beginning to understand the fascination. However, Bill and I were a long way from the speeds of those who have skied all their life.

CHAPTER 37

The Village Holiday

We, the commune, left for our holiday at Clisson at seven in the morning, a coach load of mixed ages, plus a few carloads, all eager to get started. The ages ranged from sixty-four, Bill, to a toddler, with a fairly large group of teenagers. (This is something else we find typical of life in France, families are much closer and frequently do things together in a way you do not find easily in Britain.) Excited chatter filled the coach. "Did you remember…", "Can't wait to get on a horse…", "I want to canoe." The lad mimed the movement of paddling, until another, ducking, yelled "Watch out, Yves!"

Clisson is on the border of Brittany and therefore has a strong castle dating back to the times when Brittany was frequently at war with France. It overlooks a wide, fast-flowing river and our *Maison Familiale* was just outside the town, on the river bank at one of the prettiest spots, with huge boulders causing swirling pools. The dormitories, with bunk beds, were for six, so we were with Martine and Luc, Didier and Lysiane.

"And no hanky-panky, Beel," admonished Didier.

"As if I would."

"Huh! We know you, Beel!"

For us the most amazing thing was sitting down to a meal, all ages, children at one end, adults at the other, about seventy people altogether. Conversations flowed up and down the table. The children looked after themselves, even the small ones, the older ones helping them if necessary, there was no clinging to parents in a strange place, and no demanding of attention.

The highlight for me was the day of canoeing. Twenty-five canoes and kayaks set off from Clisson with one instructor.

"Follow me and do as I say. Do NOT go ahead. Queue up sensibly to take your turn at going down the chutes. I will give you exact instructions for these when we get there."

Within minutes, the first kayak had overturned. It was Martine's younger son of eleven. Cheers and hand-clapping from those safe and dry. Martine, who was in our canoe, seemed unconcerned, being far more concerned about trying to control Bill, who was not following the instructions.

"*You* paddle, Martine. *I* steer."

"But, Beel, you're steering the wrong way!"

"Just exploring. Don't worry you're quite safe."

"Gilly-Anne, explain to him that we have to keep together."

But Bill had other ideas, and, being skilled at canoeing, was able to disappear up backwaters, reappear and still keep up with the group. Finally Martine gave in.

For me it was a real pleasure. I had plenty of time to look at the birds, flowers and dragonflies, while sitting there lazily, being paddled. I day-dreamed. When it was my turn to paddle, I found I really enjoyed this too although I'd never canoed before.

We lined up at the first chute. This was in fact a mini weir stretching right across the river giving a drop of around a metre and a half – and we had to drop over that! I watched the others. You had to paddle hard, straight for the area where there was most water, where for one moment, the bows hung in the air, before tipping down and racing on into the next part of the water. I shivered in apprehension.

"Okay, now it's us. Go for it, Martine!"

They both paddled furiously and I held on to the bows, waiting to be suspended. The canoe shot forward but then stuck, me in the front sticking out as though on a diving board with the swirling waters below.

Cheers went up again.

"Trust Beel!'

"He's too heavy," roared somebody. Hoots of laughter.

"Wriggle it," the instructor yelled.

We wriggled it, but nothing happened. I felt odd suspended in mid-air like that and not too sure about what would happen when the canoe finally shot forward – a nose-dive with me at the front. But obviously we couldn't stay where we were.

I looked round at the other two. "It's true, Bill you're too heavy at the stern. Move forward - but slowly."

Cautiously, Bill inched forward. The canoe began to sway then swooped forward and we were down, spinning in the waters below, with hardly a splash.

"Next chute we change places," laughed Martine.

It must have been a question of weight, because we sailed over the other chutes without a problem, becoming more and more expert.

As we arrived back and started to pull up the canoes, Martine took her revenge on Bill. He was standing up to his knees in water, holding the stern of the canoe when she launched herself at him and they both went down with great splashings and waves of water swamping everyone else.

"Hey! What's up?" someone called out.

"It's Beel again!"

"Martine, what're you doing?"

Laughing, she tried to explain, all the while splashing him, how Bill had refused to listen to reason. He lost his footing and was now floundering around in the water. When she realised Bill had found his feet, she shot out of the river before he could do the same to her. He chased her up the bank, the group cheering on the chase. As she disappeared into the changing rooms he called, "You wait! My revenge will come!"

Unfortunately he could think of nothing better than putting prickly pine cones in her bed, but as he fell asleep early, he missed her outrage and even her indignant pelting of him with the cones.

For Bill it was the day of mountain biking that was the highlight. The area was rocky and hilly on one side of the river and rolling agricultural land on the other. There were two groups who opted for mountain biking, the teenagers and the others. Naturally Bill set off with the latter, but was no longer with them when they returned.

"Where's Bill?" I asked.

"Oh, he left us and went off with the young ones. We didn't go fast enough for him."

An hour later, hearing a noise, I looked out of the window. There were the teenagers, real mountain bikers, careering down a rocky slope the opposite side of the river, Bill amongst them. He waved, his bike wobbled and he raced off again.

When they eventually returned, two young shaven-headed lads thumped Bill heartily on the back.

"Great stuff! Do it again, yes?"

For the rest of the weekend, whenever one of the teenagers met Bill, he would be greeted with the equivalent of "Wotcha, Beel!"

On horseback Bill excelled himself again. It brought back the years of ranching in Kenya when most of his work was done on horseback. He leapt onto the horse and kicked her off as though he was still twenty-five years old. Because of his experience he was able to canter off over the hills on his own. Gratifying for him, but for once unnoticed by others.

My performance on the other hand was very noticeable, unfortunately. I had a vision of one day cantering along the beach beside Bill, so looked forward to my lesson, but with some apprehension about the size and perhaps unexpected movements of my mount. As the horses were brought out, I noticed one, a mare, slightly smaller and definitely quieter than the others. I made a beeline for it. The instructor urged me to take a larger horse, but it was friskier, so I explained I was a bit anxious and sat firmly where I was. I watched the others sitting laughing and chatting in their saddles, leaning forward to pack their horse's necks. I did the same, without the laughter. My stomach seemed very light and repositioned in my chest and I found I was clutching the reins so tightly that my knuckles were white. We were given our basic instructions and moved off around the paddock. This was okay. I could manage this, a nice quiet plod. I began to relax my grip on the reins. I even managed a trot although there was no graceful rhythm in my movements.

Disaster struck as our instructor called out to us to follow her and led us out towards the river. To do so we had to file down what seemed to me a steep bank. My placid horse tossed her head and began to increase her pace precisely at the moment when the angle of her body meant there was a void in front of me instead of her reassuring head and neck.

Panic.

"I've got to get off!" I yelled, convinced I was falling. I was shaking with fear. I somehow scrambled off my horse and sank against a tree. Such ignominy. I sat at the side of the path and watched the others disappear, my horse dutifully plodding after them. Slowly I took myself back to the centre. Diplomatically, no-one mentioned my failure. But my romantic vision of riding beside Bill in the early morning sun along the beach vanished.

At the last meal, as I looked round the table with all these new friends, I remembered the evening of the village's annual dinner. That also had been around a hundred people eating, all together.

"Remember that town in the Dordogne, Bill? And their annual meal?"

"Course I do. And I remember saying that when we were part of a gathering like that, we'd have arrived.

"And here we are," I finished.

"Maybe we've arrived."

The Following Year

CHAPTER 38

Bill's Sixty-Fifth Birthday

As Bill's sixty-fifth birthday approached, he planned how he was going to celebrate – and he was determined to celebrate with style.

"I think I'll have a big party. We'll invite all our friends."

"Fine. I'll ring round."

"No, I want to send out invitations. Anyway there'll be too many to ring. I want to invite everyone."

He began listing all our friends both from La Rochelle and Chambon, including Stephane, the mayor. Now I was surprised.

"You know you can't invite him if we've got our usual friends here. You know they have vowed never to speak to him."

"I *can* and I *will.*"

'Têtu' was one of the first French words Bill had learnt from me, 'stubborn'. I had used it about him often. Nothing I could say would budge him, but I saw this mixture as a possible cause for disaster.

"And I want to invite the little man with a limp."

"But you don't even know his name."

"Does that matter? We're friends and I want to invite him."

In the end, I managed to persuade Bill to leave him off the list. But Stephane remained.

Even though Bill's birthday was in March, we were hoping for enough sunshine to have *apéritifs* in the garden. At this time of year the jasmine along the front wall was just finishing, but the forsythia flanking the drive was a triumphant yellow and the clumps of daffodils, narcissi and tulips made bright splashes of colour. The terrace was edged with mauve and purple aubrietia and red and blue anemones. Considering the time of year, it was colourful and the green of the new lawn set it off well. (Well, I say 'lawn' but it was a mixture of grass and weeds, but once mown, at least it was green!)

I was proud of what we had created. What was more, every corner was a reminder of friends or places we had visited, the herbaceous border from my students at the language school, a buddleia from Martine's garden, a small pine, uprooted by a landfall, from the cliffs near Hondarribia in Spain, a cotoneaster along one wall given to us by Pierre and Juliette, Marion's lemon tree and old-fashioned English pinks brought from Bill's mother's garden in England. At the far end, the vegetable garden looked well-cared for and had produced so much that we had nearly bought an extra freezer, which would have been our third, for our produce, and along the side was the fruit area that resulted in both bottles of fruit and pots of jam, enough to distribute liberally to the family whenever we visited. Jacques called it a little paradise.

We decided to put out some small tables and chairs dotted around in the hoped-for patches of sunshine, so that people could disperse to chat, and so avoid any possible difficulties from the groups. About forty people, plus of course children had said they were coming and our terrace was small and would only take ten comfortably.

All Bill's catering skills came to the fore and he planned a wonderful buffet.

"We can't possibly do a sit-down meal with that number of people, so we'll do a finger buffet."

"They won't like it," I warned. "The French like to sit down round a table to eat. We could borrow Louisette's again."

"But it filled the room last time and this time we would have to add ours to it to get everyone seated. No, it's *my* birthday and we're doing it *my* way."

This was to be a phrase I was to hear a lot of over the next few weeks. I looked around. Obviously fitting in a large enough table was an impossibility, so I gave in and helped him plan his buffet.

"And it's not going to be the usual talking session either. I'll only fall asleep if it's all in French. We're going to play games."

"What sort of games?"

"That's your field, *chérie*. I'll leave that to you."

I wondered how I was going to find games that would suit all our different friends. In the end I settled for a variation of the 'Who am I?' guessing game and the drawing game, with two teams who have to draw, without speaking, a film title I would give them from a list, racing each other to finish first. We also decided on dancing, even though the space would be extremely limited.

On the day, the spread looked fantastic, the room was cleared and the very English Pimms ready near the door.

Most important of all, the sun was shining. As people arrived they were to be given a drink and directed into the garden. In fact it did not work that way as everyone brought presents. Martine, Luc, Didier and Lysiane arrived first – without children as specified – with an enormous carton gaily wrapped.

"Happy birthday, Beel! Open it quick."

In carefully enunciated tones, Didier asked in English, "How are you, Beel. I trust you are well?"

"Not now, Didi," Lysiane said impatiently. "Come on, Beel. Open your present."

Mystified, Bill started peeling off the wrappers. He pulled out a true jester's hat, with points and bells. Apparently these were popular on the ski slopes this year, but we believed it was the true Medieval Fool's symbol, a harlequin of colours. He put it on and that set the tone for the day.

"Search again," Martine said.

A big Pyrenean cheese, a dried sausage and some *foie gras*.

"We think you like your food," Martine laughed.

"We think? We *know!*" That was Didier.

"One more, Beel," Luc said.

"More? Surely that's enough." Bill thrust his hand in again and drew out a small rectangular package. "What's this? Not more food!"

"No, but you do put it in your mouth." Luc was beating time on the table, a complicated drum rhythm and singing, 'Hello, Dolly'.

It was a mouth organ. Bill looked perplexed for a moment and then his face cleared. He remembered the time he had admired Luc's.

"Fancy remembering I said I used to have one when I was in Kenya."

"*Tiens!*" Luc said beating an even faster rhythm. "Now we can play together."

"If I can remember how to play." Bill put it to his lips, but before he could try it out, Anne arrived.

A book on exploring Charente-Maritime, books on identifying mushrooms, plants for the house and a bush for the garden, the presents flowed in reflecting people's knowledge of their friend.

One of the most interesting moments for me was catching sight of Didier deep in conversation with Stephane. For a second I froze, remembering Didier stating adamantly not so long ago that he would never ever speak to 'that rogue' again. Yet here he was, out of courtesy to his host, politely listening and discussing the proposed motorway that might pass close to our commune. What a surprise.

Being busy greeting people we had not actually gone into the garden. When there was a lull, I walked round the corner and there, all huddled together, on the tiny terrace, were our guests. Our careful placing of chairs in convivial groups round the garden had failed. The chairs had been moved onto the terrace and edging lawn so that everyone was packed together like sardines. Those that could not sit, leant against the wall, but together – typically French, who all sit together at one table.

Finger buffets are not very familiar in Chambon and we found our neighbours looking for a table or at least a flat surface the equivalent of a table in both the kitchen and the *salon*. Guy was propping himself on one side of the kitchen table, Jacques the other, the chairs being in the garden.

However the food was greatly enjoyed and our only problem was that we had prepared far too much.

Later there was a surprise. Stephane said he had to leave as he had a meeting. Whether this was true or whether he was being diplomatic, I do not know. Just before he left, he made a very short speech that was very touching.

"Beel and Gilly-Anne have been here for three years now. I haven't really got to know any British before, but if all British are like these two, what a race they must be. In the short time they have been in our commune they have contributed to the life of the village. I am proud to count Beel as one of my friends."

We were so surprised because this was totally unexpected. But what came next was even more so. As soon as Stephane and his wife had left, Yvette asked for hush.

"Beel, come here."

She was standing in the centre, surrounded by our friends. Everybody watched as Bill went over to her.

"Beel, I just want to say – *je t'aime*. I love you." She put her hands up to his face and kissed him. Everyone cheered.

"Me too, Beel," said her husband Albert without the kiss, but with a warm embrace.

Bill was still standing there feeling slightly embarrassed when Lysiane jumped up.

"Me too, Beel."

More clapping and cheers.

Then Martine stood up. "And for you, Beel, I have made up a poem *in English."*

She proceeded to read out her poem.

Bill was feeling more and more overcome, but the poem let loose a torrent of 'My best neighbour', 'Our good friend', until Bill's arm was sore with being pumped up and down

Finally he said, "*Mes amis, j'aime tous de vous*" which is Bill's Franglais for 'I love you all'.

Quickly I put on some music for dancing. We danced together closely, giving him time to recover. Then we danced with all our friends. As Bill danced the lambada with Lysiane, the floor was cleared to give them the space as he bent her backwards and she swayed provocatively. Cheers rose. Those that did not dance wandered into the still sunny garden to chat.

Next it was time for games and we saw new sides of our friends as they stood up to take their role of Who am I? Some simply answered the questions until their identity was guessed, but others strutted and preened as the character they had chosen. Luc caused hoots of laughter as he capered about doing a dance while very obviously eyeing the girls. No questions were asked: "BEEL" everyone shouted.

Yet another surprise from a group of male friends led by Luc and Didier. They called for quiet and started singing Breton folk songs. As they had consumed a fair amount of wine, these were wild and full of pathos. There was silence at the end before everyone applauded.

The drawing game caused a lot of laughter as the silence reduced everyone to the same level of frustration – we obviously had no artist friends. The competitive element was taken as seriously as if it was the tour de France. Although I had laid out the drawing paper on a table in each room, the contestants ended on the floor and I, as the only non-participant, had a vision of heads down and bottoms in the air.

Around seven in the evening, everyone went home except for Martine, Luc, Didier and Lysiane. As we shut the door, they leapt to their feet and said they were the clearing up brigade.

"Sit down, Beel, have a drink and direct."

"What, another one? Do you think I should?"

Within half an hour the place was tidy. What friends.

"Have another gl-glass of champ-agne," Bill said, with a hiccup.

"A good idea."

And they settled back into the armchairs.

"So you really like living in France, Beel?" asked Lysiane.

"Ab-so-lute-ly."

"Give us your reasons," prompted Martine.

But before he could answer, Didier answered for him, waving his champagne glass to emphasise his point. "Us. His friends. A place is nothing without good friends."

"True," Bill agreed. "To friends. Hic."

When we were finally alone, Bill put his arm round me and said, "They like us, *chérie*. We're accepted. We've definitely arrived."